MÉTIS MUSIC

McGill-Queen's Indigenous and Northern Studies
(In memory of Bruce G. Trigger)
John Borrows, Sarah Carter, and Arthur J. Ray, Editors

The McGill-Queen's Indigenous and Northern Studies series publishes books about Indigenous peoples in all parts of the northern world. It includes original scholarship on their histories, archaeology, laws, cultures, governance, and traditions. Works in the series also explore the history and geography of the North, where travel, the natural environment, and the relationship to land continue to shape life in particular and important ways. Its mandate is to advance understanding of the political, legal, and social relations between Indigenous and non-Indigenous peoples, of the contemporary issues that Indigenous peoples face as a result of environmental and economic change, and of social justice, including the work of reconciliation in Canada. To provide a global perspective, the series welcomes books on regions and communities from across the Arctic and Subarctic circumpolar zones.

97 Fighting for a Hand to Hold
Confronting Medical Colonialism against Indigenous Children in Canada
Samir Shaheen-Hussain

98 Forty Narratives in the Wyandot Language
John L. Steckley

99 Uumajursiutik unaatuinnamut / Hunter with Harpoon / Chasseur au harpon
Markoosie Patsauq
Edited and translated by Valerie Henitiuk and Marc-Antoine Mahieu

100 Language, Citizenship, and Sámi Education in the Nordic North, 1900–1940
Otso Kortekangas

101 Daughters of Aataentsic
Life Stories from Seven Generations
Kathryn Magee Labelle in collaboration with the Wendat/Wandat Women's Advisory Council

102 Aki-wayn-zih
A Person as Worthy as the Earth
Eli Baxter

103 Atiqput
Inuit Oral History and Project Naming
Edited by Carol Payne, Beth Greenhorn, Deborah Kigjugalik Webster, and Christina Williamson

104 Ǫ da gaho dę:s
Reflecting on Our Journeys
Gae Ho Hwako (Norma Jacobs) and the Circles of Ǫ da gaho dę:s
Edited by Timothy B. Leduc

105 Called Upstairs
Moravian Inuit Music in Labrador
Tom Gordon

106 Otter Skins, Boston Ships, and China Goods
Voices of the Maritime Fur Trade of the Northwest Coast, 1785–1841, Revised Edition
James R. Gibson

107 Cultural Change among the Algonquin in the Nineteenth Century
Leila Inksetter

108 Métis Music
Stories of Recognition and Resurgence
Monique Giroux

MÉTIS MUSIC

Stories of Recognition and Resurgence

MONIQUE GIROUX

McGill-Queen's University Press
Montreal & Kingston • London • Chicago

ISBN 978-0-2280-2225-1 (cloth)
ISBN 978-0-2280-2226-8 (paper)
ISBN 978-0-2280-2227-5 (ePDF)
ISBN 978-0-2280-2228-2 (ePUB)

Legal deposit fourth quarter 2024
Bibliothèque nationale du Québec

Printed in Canada on acid-free paper that is 100% ancient forest free (100% post-consumer recycled), processed chlorine free

This book has been published with the help of a grant from the Federation for the Humanities and Social Sciences, through the Awards to Scholarly Publications Program, using funds provided by the Social Sciences and Humanities Research Council of Canada.

Funded by the Government of Canada | Financé par le gouvernement du Canada | Canada | Canada Council for the Arts | Conseil des arts du Canada

We acknowledge the support of the Canada Council for the Arts.
Nous remercions le Conseil des arts du Canada de son soutien.

McGill-Queen's University Press in Montreal is on land which long served as a site of meeting and exchange amongst Indigenous Peoples, including the Haudenosaunee and Anishinabeg nations. In Kingston it is situated on the territory of the Haudenosaunee and Anishinaabek. We acknowledge and thank the diverse Indigenous Peoples whose footsteps have marked these territories on which peoples of the world now gather.

Library and Archives Canada Cataloguing in Publication

Title: Métis music : stories of recognition and resurgence / Monique Giroux.
Names: Giroux, Monique (Ph. D.), author.
Series: McGill-Queen's indigenous and northern series ; 108.
Description: Series statement: McGill-Queen's Indigenous and northern studies ; 108 | Includes bibliographical references and index.
Identifiers: Canadiana (print) 20240363833 | Canadiana (ebook) 20240364406 | ISBN 9780228022251 (hardcover) | ISBN 9780228022268 (softcover) | ISBN 9780228022275 (PDF) | ISBN 9780228022282 (EPUB)
Subjects: LCSH: Métis—Music—History and criticism. | LCSH: Music—Canada—History and criticism.
Classification: LCC ML3563.9 G528 2024 | DDC 781.62/97071—dc23

This book was designed and typeset by studio oneonone in Minion 11/14.
Copyediting by Alicia Hibbert.

This book is for Manitoba – *manitou-wapow, manidoobaa*, the narrows of the Great Spirit – where I was raised and learned to fiddle.
A place I grew to love.

This book is for my children (Isobel, Georgia, and Alice) and my children's children, so they understand the relationships past and present that have shaped Canada, that they might find musical pathways to a better tomorrow.

And this book is for Métis peoples, whose music and music making continues to fill my life, and the lives of so many, with beauty and joy.

Contents

Figures and Tables ix

Preface: Acknowledging Indigenous Presence, Tracing Ancestral Lines xi

1 Recognition, Resurgence, and Ethical Responsiveness 3

2 Fiddle Dance in the Fur Trade and across the Métis Homeland 34

3 Writing Métis Music in Manitoba Newspapers 60

4 Exchange, Multicultural Compartmentalization, and the New Old-Time Style 86

5 Métis Music at Manitoba's Old-Time Fiddle Competitions 110

6 Cultural Festivals as Recognition and Resurgence 134

7 On Moving from *Louis Riel* to *Li Keur* 169

Postlude: Métis Music 203

Notes 209

References 231

Index 255

Figures and Tables

FIGURES

6.1 Three buildings in Duck Lake. Photo by author. 139
6.2 Duck Lake Hotel. Photo by author. 140
6.3 MacDonald, Riel, and Dumont, Duck Lake mural. Photo by author. 141
6.4 Cemetery. Photo by author. 141
6.5 Back to Batoche procession. Photo by author. 148
6.6 Item from Al Wiseman's display. Photo by author. 153
6.7 Youth dancers. Photo by author. 162
6.8 Jam session. Photo by author. 162
6.9 Métis Heritage Celebration signs. Photo by author. 164

TABLES

5.1 Manitoba Open's categories and prize money 115
5.2 Brandon Winter Fair categories and prize money 119
5.3 Manitoba Open Métis-style rules 122

PREFACE

Acknowledging Indigenous Presence, Tracing Ancestral Lines

> Relationality requires that you know a lot more about me before you can begin to understand my work.
> – Shawn Wilson (2008, 12)[1]

This book was completed from the territory of the Siksikaitsitapi peoples, more widely known as the Blackfoot confederacy, and the (contested) Homeland of the Métis Nation (Lethbridge, Alberta). Sections were written, or conceived of, while living in the territories of the Haudenosaunee, Anishinaabe, Cree, Oji-Cree, and Dakota peoples (in Toronto and Kingston, Ontario, and Winnipeg, Manitoba). I begin with reference to the peoples on whose lands I write out of respect for territorial protocols that Indigenous nations have followed for millennia (Hill 2019, 23; Snelgrove, Dharmoon, and Corntassel 2014, 4–5). Although it is in no way intended to stand in for Indigenous protocols, acknowledging the place from which I write serves as a reminder of the relationships of visitor and host on the land that many now call Canada and is a small step to redress the continued erasure of Indigenous presence, past and present – a theme that I take up repeatedly in this book. Furthermore, by beginning with an acknowledgment of the land that grounded me as I wrote this book, I hope to remind myself and my readers of the importance of always returning – bringing our minds, bodies, spirits back – to the places that we inhabit, to the relationships with place that created and continue to create us.

Borrowing from poet and scholar Clint Burnham (2010), with whom I became familiar through the work of Stó:lō musicologist Dylan Robinson

(2019, 20), I wish to fill in this acknowledgment of Indigenous territory with an acknowledgment of my own positionality as an "intergenerational perpetrator of colonialism" (Robinson 2016, 63). As such,

> I'd like to acknowledge that my ancestors were part of the Carignan-Salières Regiment that came to New France to destroy Haudenosaunee resistance.
> I'd like to acknowledge that my ancestors were Loyalists, and that Loyalists took part in a violent assault on Nishnaabeg lands and people (see Simpson 2011, 15).
> I'd like to acknowledge that my paternal grandparents settled on Métis, Assiniboine, Očhéthi Šakówiŋ territory in southern Saskatchewan in the early 1900s as part of Canadian expansionism westward.
> I'd like to acknowledge that I didn't know whose land I grew up on.
> I'd like to acknowledge that I owe my career to Métis musicians, and to the fickle desire among settlers[2] to indigenize the academy.
> "and I'd like to acknowledge the acknowledging that we are on stolen, ripped off, colonized, unceded, conquered, begged, borrowed, stolen native land doesn't make a damn bit of … difference and I'd just like to acknowledge that" (Burnham 2010).

Clint Burnham's poem is a call to critically consider what we are acknowledging when we make land acknowledgments.[3] It resonates with a growing number of critiques by Indigenous scholars who point to the failures of the settler ritual of land acknowledgment – failures that are significant enough for some to call for a pause in the practice. These scholars note that land acknowledgments address whose land we are on, but rarely ever name the specific processes of colonization, including violence and erasure, that have dispossessed Indigenous peoples of their lands, nor do they name the benefits accrued by settlers, both *past and present*. Just as significantly, they rarely ever articulate plans to return the land to Indigenous peoples (Daigle 2019; Sobo, Lambert, and Lambert 2021). For these reasons, territorial acknowledgments are often viewed as performative expressions of allyship (perhaps "non-performative speech acts" [Ahmed 2006]) rather than as a starting point for foundational and lasting change (see Couture 2019, 28).

As a corrective strategy, Robinson reminds us that acknowledgments need to be site- and context-specific, respecting the relational nature of Indigenous protocol (2019, 21). In the context of my scholarship, I hope that acknowledging the land on which this book was written and my own personal and familial connection to the stories within make it clear, from the opening pages, that this book is an expression of relationship: it is a relationship between me and processes of seeking knowledge; between me and the Métis peoples, music, musicians, and communities that are at the heart of this book; between me and my settler ancestors and contemporaries, who I am part of and who are part of me, and whose actions and lack of action have made this book necessary; between me and Canada, a country that I love, but that is also deeply flawed; and between me and my readers, who I hope are challenged and moved to act by my words. I further hope that by starting with the personal, I uproot the expectation that research can (and should) be a neutral presentation of facts. Rather, I understand my knowledge of Métis music as embedded in a network of relationships and pathways that are unique to me (see Perea 2021, x). This book, then, is one perspective on Métis music – one among many. My understanding of knowledge and relationality is indebted to Shawn Wilson, whose book *Research Is Ceremony* taught me to embrace our changing relationship with knowledge, and that "reality is not an object but a process of relationships" (2008, 73).

Emerging from a perspective of relationality, this book is at times personal. And so, I begin with a personal story about my family tree.[4]

✦✦✦

One story that my family tells from time to time is a story about our Métisness. Having come from a French Canadian family that first immigrated to what is now known as Canada a long time ago, it is only logical (or so the story goes) to conclude that we are indeed Métis. The assumption, it seems, is that living side by side for so long, we must have, at some point, become intimates. One of our ancestors must have been Indigenous.

Of course, this story overlooks the fact that one Indigenous ancestor does not make a person Métis, or otherwise Indigenous. But disregard that for just a moment.

On my paternal side, the ancestors that I have been able to trace began arriving in what was then referred to as New France in the mid-1600s. New France at the time was struggling: the settler population was small (about 3,200 French immigrants), and they were spread out among several settlements. These settlements furthermore faced attacks from the Haudenosaunee, who were trying to protect their lands and their trade interests.

In 1664, the French king's minister of finance proclaimed that "His Majesty has resolved to send a good regiment of infantry to Canada at the end of this year, or in the month of February next, in order to destroy these barbarians [i.e., the Haudenosaunee] completely" (quoted in Verney 1991, 3). Perhaps it was out of a hatred for the so-called barbarians that the French king agreed to send help to the colonies, although it is more likely that the king was hoping to better line the royal coffers (122). Whatever the case, the first few companies that made up the Carignan-Salières Regiment left La Rochelle for New France a little more than a year later. Eventually, nearly 1,300 soldiers and officers were sent to the French colony, with about 450 staying in the colony after the troops were withdrawn in 1668 (Marley 2008, 245).

The stories told about this regiment emphasize heroism, bravery, and the protection of the Catholic faith. As Marie de l'Incarnation (an Ursuline nun who had been sent to New France to establish an Ursuline Order) wrote: "Our French soldiers are so fervent they fear nothing, and there is nothing they do not do and undertake … It seems to all these soldiers that they are going to besiege paradise, and they hope to capture and enter it, because it is for the good of the Faith and religion that they are going to battle" (quoted in Verney 1991, 127). This, of course, is a story told from the perspective of French nationalism and Catholic universalism. Another story, recounted by historian Jack Verney, is that "they were rough men, who in their off-duty hours caroused, womanized, gambled, grumbled, and dreamed of making their fortunes" (1991, 127–8). Ordinary men.

Two of the men who stayed in New France were André Mignier and Rene Dumas. All that I know about Dumas is that he arrived in 1665 and married Marie Lelong (Verney 1991, 159). A little more is known about André Mignier. Mignier was also known by the name Lagassé. This nickname was derived from the term *La Gachette*, which refers to the trigger on a gun. The term was thus used to denote men who were sharpshooters. I don't know if he got this nickname in New France or before arriving, but it seems likely that his skills would have been used against the Haudenosaunee. Lagassé stayed in New France after the Carignan-Salières Regiment was withdrawn, and he married Jacquette Michel (Verney 1991, 152).

These men, sent to New France to secure the colony and destroy the Haudenosaunee, are my paternal ancestors.

In the mid- to late 1600s, there was a striking imbalance between the number of men and women in New France (Greer 1997, 16). For the colony to grow, this had to change. Between 1663 and 1673, the French king sought to ensure population growth by subsidizing the immigration of women. Because the king supported these women, they came to be known as *les filles du roi*, or the king's daughters. Marie Lelong (Dumas's wife), Catherine Ducharme, Jacquette Michel (Mignier's wife), Marguerite Raisin, and Catherine DeBaillon were among the eight hundred *filles du roi* who immigrated to New France.

These five women, sent to ensure the fruitfulness of the French settlement, are my paternal ancestors.

I know considerably less about my mother's relatives, although I do know that they emigrated from the United Kingdom to Turtle Island (i.e., what is now most often known as North America), and that they landed in what is now Michigan – or at least some of them did.

My mother likes to tell stories about her family, usually in little snippets that leave me wanting to know more and dig deeper. One of these snippets that I heard growing up is that some of my maternal ancestors were Loyalists who moved north into what is now Canada because they supported the British Crown. I always felt proud of this story. Loyalist. Such a strong word that suggests trust, virtue, and strength.

One day, shortly after I received a much-anticipated copy of Leanne Simpson's book *Dancing on Our Turtle's Back*, I learned another part of my maternal family's story, one that connects my family to Simpson's family. Here is an excerpt of Simpson's narrative:

> For my ancestors, the Michi Saagiig Nishnaabeg, our self-determination and sovereignty as part of the Nishnaabeg nation was relatively intact between 1700–1783. Over the next forty years we were forced to survive an intense, violent assault on our lands and our peoples. By 1763, the British Crown no longer needed us as allies; soon loyalists streamed into our territory and began occupying Michi Saagiig Nishnaabeg lands. Over the next fifty years, our people survived pandemics, violence and assault, unjust treaty negotiations, occupation of our lands, and a forced relocation. (Simpson 2011, 15)

I do not know if there ever was an encounter between my ancestors and Simpson's, but knowing Simpson's story complicates stories that I told myself about my maternal ancestors.

These are some of the family stories that I know.

Another story that I came to better understand as I dug into my family tree was the deep divide between my ancestors and Indigenous peoples of this land: despite a long history of living in New France/Canada, there is no evidence of substantial personal or community relationships between my ancestors and Indigenous peoples. I have not found a single Indigenous ancestor in my family tree. I grew up with this legacy, only knowing the land that I was living on as Manitoba – not knowing the Indigenous etymology of the word. Not knowing my neighbours.

And so, despite the story that is sometimes told in my family, I am proof that we can live alongside our neighbours for centuries without knowing their names or traditions and without acknowledging the harms caused as our ancestral lines became embedded in Canada, in Indigenous territories.

Sharing this story is not meant to cast judgment upon these ancestors. In fact, I have to admit that I feel pride when I think of *les filles du roi*, who must have faced untold hardship in a land that they did not know. I feel pride in being the granddaughter of hardworking farmers who survived in the dirty thirties in Saskatchewan, the granddaughter of progressive thinkers, including the first woman in one area of the continent to wear pants (or so I have been told).

Like many immigrants, many of my ancestors came to Turtle Island to build a better life, some to escape crushing oppression. And they did build a better life. I am grateful for what they have given me. Yet, in fleeing their past life, they became implicated in a colonial system that harmed Indigenous nations and, in some cases, brought with them mindsets that emerged from the persecution that they had faced (see Campbell 2012, xx).

This is the story that I carry with me as I write this book, a story that I can only claim as my own. (My family might tell a very different story – and indeed, this is a story "situated in a time, place, and context" [Kovach 2009, 21].) It is at the core of this book, which centres the meeting places between Métis and settler peoples and the ways that those meeting places have been erased or, alternatively, acknowledged.

But, even as it is my own story, it is part of a web of stories, a broader narrative that settler Canadians – especially those whose ancestors have lived in Canada or the United States for many years – tell themselves. And that is a narrative for which, I believe, all people who have benefitted must take responsibility.

✦✦✦

This book is about (some of) the stories told about Métis music. It is written with the hope that, by considering and acknowledging these stories, we will have a more nuanced understanding of the relationships embedded in and through Métis music past, present, and future, toward building new and more equal relationships in and beyond music. I furthermore hope that it can serve to give back to Métis communities and people (Kovach 2009, 11) from whom I have learned so much, and spark a surge in Métis-led research with Métis music.[5]

MÉTIS MUSIC

1

Recognition, Resurgence, and Ethical Responsiveness

> Wagner opera with eminent soloists, superb orchestra and chorus, elaborate costuming and sumptuous stage mountings! Well, well, how this young town of ours away out here in the wild and woolly west does take on metropolitan airs to be sure. Why there are good people still with us who recall the days when the only music was the weird beating of the Indian's tom-tom and it seems but yesterday that our most classic melodies were those scraped by the Metis fiddler for a Red River Jig.
> – C.W. Handscomb (1906, 8)[1]

> As a Canadian fiddler, I really want to be able to claim [Indigenous/Métis fiddling] for all of us, to be able to stand up and say, "Look what was created here – look what we did – look at our beautiful new baby." To some extent I have done this, in articles, on recordings, in performances and on the theatrical stage.
> – Anne Lederman (2009, 368)

The early twentieth century was a time of optimism and prosperity for (white) settlers living in Winnipeg, Manitoba. As historian Jim Blanchard notes, by the start of the second decade, the "dreams of the founders – people who arrived in the area in the 1860s and 1870s, such as John Christian Schultz and his wife Agnes, James Ashdown, C.V. Alloway, the Drewry brothers – seemed to have become reality" (2005, 5). The growth of the city at the heart of the continent was spectacular enough to attract far-ranging attention, with a *Chicago Tribune* article suggesting in 1911 that "All roads lead to Winnipeg," and that Winnipeg was "destined to become one of the greatest distributing and commercial centres of the continent" (cited in Blanchard 2005, 5).[2] Of course, this depiction of Winnipeg fails to address the complexity of this growth, most significantly, its impact on Indigenous peoples in a region that, until 1870, had been a hub of Indigenous life and trade.[3] Indeed, the massive influx of white settlers at the turn of the twentieth century overwhelmed the relatively small Métis population, while harassment and land theft – which were at the core of the "settling" of Winnipeg and are discussed later in this chapter – forced some Métis people to move westward. Others began hiding in plain sight if they were able.[4]

The desire to clear the land of Indigenous peoples – or to believe that so-called progress had already cleared it, or would inevitably clear it, of Indigenous peoples – is evident in many representations of life in Manitoba at the turn of the century, including historical and literary accounts. It is also evident in the ways in which non-Indigenous people were thinking about music performance and practice. As *Manitoba Free Press* critic C.W. Handscomb expresses in his review of a concert held in Winnipeg in 1906, the sound of Wagner wafting through a Winnipeg concert hall was audible proof of the change that was taking place in the "wild and woolly west" (1906, 8). Wagner, according to Handscomb, was replacing both "the Indian's tom-tom" and the melodies "scraped" by Métis fiddlers. Music, for that critic at least, was understood and imagined through what we now understand as a European Canadian lens of progress, erasure, and replacement.[5]

One hundred years later, Indigenous/non-Indigenous relations were being reimagined in the region. This was particularly striking on a frigid evening in February, a century after the great (white) boom described by Blanchard. It was the opening ceremony of the Festival du Voyageur, an annual winter festival held in St Boniface, Manitoba, in Winnipeg's French and Métis quarter. After a procession from The Forks to the site of the festival (Fort Gibraltar), attendees willing to brave the thirty below Celsius weather gathered around a deep-voiced speaker who stated – as a representative of each of Manitoba's founding nations (First Nations, French, Métis, and Scottish) stepped forward in era-appropriate regalia – that *at the heart of every Manitoban, lay the spirit of the Métis.*[6]

In light of more than one hundred years of denial and distortion of Métis history in and beyond Manitoba, this public and emphatic statement was remarkable, expressing a sentiment that was beginning to captivate public consciousness. Notably, in 2008, Manitobans created a civic holiday, Louis Riel Day, named for the (in)famous Métis leader, executed in 1885 by the Canadian government.[7] That same year, popular philosopher John Ralston Saul published a book titled *A Fair Country: Telling Truths About Canada*, arguing that Canada is a métis nation (in this case, appropriating the term métis, with lower case *m* to point to Indigenous influence and, to a lesser degree, racial mixing). Just one year later, ethnomusicologist Anne Lederman boldly expressed her desire to claim Prairie Indigenous fiddling – what is often thought of more narrowly as Métis fiddling – as *our* (Canadian) music (2009, 368). Settlers were reimagining Métis-ness (both in the sense of Métis as an Indigenous nation and Métis as mixed Indigenous/European) in the present and were even claiming it for themselves. As outlined in Darryl Leroux's book *Distorted Descent*, the appropriation of Métis identity has picked up pace over the last decade (2019).

This book examines 150 years of Métis/settler relations through music. It focuses especially, though not exclusively, on fiddling, the most popular expression of Métis musicality from the nineteenth to twenty-first century.[8] I argue that music offers a valuable means to consider the complexity of Métis life within Canada and to understand how power moves through and across spaces so often viewed as benign, apolitical, uncontentious, or even celebratory. It is perhaps no coincidence that, in English, we have the expression "fiddling around," referring to activities that have no real purpose. Yet fiddling and other forms of Métis musicking,[9] as I suggest in this book, are far from benign, even though they are rarely positioned as so-called "high art" and are often heard at "good timing" events (Dueck 2007, 36), which to some may make them appear not serious. I show that Métis music (both the act of Métis people making music and the subsequent representations of this music making) has long been a site of intercultural encounter – albeit a shifting site of encounter; and that it has been used to imagine relationships. By "imagine," I mean both the imaginary – that is, the creation of relationships and representations that are *not real* (cf. Francis 1992) – but also the generative – that is, the (re)creation of new, traditional, alternative, resurgent, or sometimes even unequal ways of coming and being together (cf. Luong 2022); imagining what could be.

The Métis Peoples in and beyond the Canadian Context

The Métis, or Michif, peoples[10] at the heart of this book are an Indigenous nation that emerged in the early nineteenth century – or possibly earlier (see Maraldo 2023) – in the Northern Plains, the boreal forests, and the subarctic regions of what is now known as North America (St-Onge, Podruchny, and Macdougall 2012, 3). This "Homeland" is a vast border-crossing (though somewhat contested) area that is most commonly understood as including the three Canadian Prairie provinces, as well as parts of Ontario, British Columbia, Montana, North Dakota, and the Northwest Territories. Born during and of the fur trade initially as the children of European men and Indigenous women, the Métis peoples have often been misunderstood as simply mixed-race, that is, a "hybrid off-shoot of two races" (Andersen 2014, 6; see also Adese and Andersen 2021, 3– 8). This focus on mixed-ness has been refuted by numerous Métis scholars who point to the dangers of racialized definitions of Métis identity. These dangers include the positioning of Métis as not fully Indigenous (which amounts to a racist, blood quantum argument) and the denial of Métis peoples' common history, sense of political consciousness, traditions, culture, and more (Andersen 2014, 11–12). Though I cannot ignore the racialized definition of Métis identity because it informs many representations of Métis peoples (and indeed, I have already referred to a racialized understanding of Métis identity via Ralston Saul's work), this book emphatically centres Métis as a peoples, specifically an Indigenous peoples of the Plains, not a racial category.

Métis identity is, nonetheless, complex, and it certainly is not monolithic. Though nineteenth-century Métis understood themselves as a distinct peoples (as they do today), many maintained close and ongoing connections with their Nehiyaw, Anishinaabe, and Assiniboine kin; intermarriage was common, and practices of belonging among these groups is fluid. As historian Robert Innes (Cowessess) notes, in the pre-reserve era, many Métis lived within multicultural bands on both sides of the Medicine Line (i.e., the Canada/United States border) with their Nehiyaw, Anishinaabe, and Assiniboine kin (2013, 43–69; see also Hogue 2015 for discussion of the Medicine Line's impact on Métis). Furthermore, though Métis are often described as having French Canadian ancestors – and certainly many did – others had Orcadian, Scottish, or English ancestry. Finally, Métis people engaged in a variety of work, with some families identifying as buffalo hunters and trappers and others with more agrarian or bourgeoisie ways of life – including clerics, teachers, merchants, and employees for the Hudson's Bay Company (HBC). These factors, among others, impacted connections with land and kin, language(s) spoken, spiritual practices, and world views. As a result, there were significant differences among and within Métis communities in the Northwest – there were diverse Métis histories and stories – even as Métis peoples developed a common sense of "groupness" (St-Onge, Podruchny, Macdougall 2012, 14).

Though it is far beyond the scope of this book to provide a detailed over view of Métis identity, history, and culture, the Métis Resistances and their aftermath are important in providing context for Métis/Canadian relations. The first Resistance began just two years after Canadian Confederation (1867), as the newly formed Dominion of Canada began moving westward, led by a Protestant, Scottish-born prime minister who viewed both Indigenous peoples and French Catholics as an impediment to creating the Canadian nation. Concerned about what it would mean for their land rights and cultural survival, Métis in Red River mounted the first of two major resistances (previously referred to by many Canadian historians as rebellions). Known as the Red River Resistance, this first resistance began in 1869, when Métis leaders in Red River established a provisional government to negotiate the terms in which Manitoba would enter Confederation. With Louis Riel as their leader, they were able to secure language rights and title to land, including 1.4 million acres set aside for their children, all guaranteed in the *Manitoba Act (1870)*. To address the land issue, Métis were to be provided with scrip, a document that was redeemable for land or cash. Unfortunately, the sense of victory was short-lived as the process for receiving and redeeming scrip was complex, disorganized, and delayed – likely intentionally so – making it difficult for many to claim. This failure in the process also opened opportunities for fraud and theft of scrip.

Just as significantly, the arrival of more than 1,000 British troops and militia in 1870, ostensibly to maintain peace, made life in Red River unbearable for many Indigenous people (Métis and First Nations alike) and ensured that Indigenous people would have little power within the new government. As Historian Fred Shore explained, "Since the militia was stationed in Fort Garry along with the Dominion Lands Office, the first Provincial Legislature and other government offices, Métis attempts at being part of the new power system were fraught with danger. Assaults, 'outrages' [i.e., sexual assaults or extremely violent assaults], murder, arson and assorted acts of mayhem were practiced on the Métis anytime they came near Fort Garry, while the situation in the rest of the Settlement Belt was not much better" (2001, 1). The violence during this period led reporters from Red River to Toronto to New York to refer to the events as a "reign of terror" (Shore 1991, 230). Faced with this violence and loss of land, many Métis people who had previously made Red River their home, at least for parts of the year, migrated westward into what is now Saskatchewan and Alberta, or south into North Dakota and Montana, places that were connected to Red River through long-established hunting and trading routes; all places that they had kin.

Fifteen years later, in 1885, Métis (including many who had been pushed out of Red River in the 1870s) once again resisted Canada's desire to settle the West without due regard for their land and lifeways, this time in what later became Saskatchewan. Known as the Northwest Resistance, Canada sent more than 5,000 men, ultimately defeating the Métis at the Battle of Batoche. Once again, communities were broken up, and many families resorted to living on road allowances, land set aside for future roads and ditches (Thistle 2016). Others, viewed as traitors, tried – if they were able – to blend into white communities, in some cases claiming a French identity (Ouvrard 2016; Vizina 2008, 178). Within a very short period, between 1870 and 1885, Métis peoples experienced a deep and long-lasting loss of social and economic capital;[11] they went from being a free and flourishing peoples to a peoples dispersed, landless, and poor – cut off from their livelihoods and means of sustenance. The impact, of course, varied from family to family. Some were able to sustain greater connections to the land and kin networks, even if it became much more difficult after 1885, while other families truly were pulled apart, scattered across and beyond the Prairies. Furthermore, as the border between Canada and the United States became more tightly enforced, it became increasingly difficult for families who had traditionally lived on both sides to maintain cross-border kinship ties.

The period after 1885 is sometimes referred to as the "dark period" in Métis history, or by some as *le grand silence* (Teillet 2017). During this time, Métis people – like other Indigenous peoples in Canada – were subjected to government-created and -enforced genocidal policies that aimed to eradicate Indigenous nations, whether by means of physical extermination or assimilation.[12] Canadian policies and attitudes during this period are neatly summed up in a remark made by deputy superintendent general of Indian Affairs, Duncan Campbell Scott, in 1920. Commenting on a proposal to amend sections of the Indian Act (enacted in 1876 as a consolidation of various regulations put in place by the British and then Canadian governments) that dealt with enfranchisement, Campbell Scott stated,

> I want to get rid of the Indian problem. I do not think as a matter of fact, that the country ought to continuously protect a class of people who are able to stand alone. That is my whole point. Our objective is to continue until there is not a single Indian in Canada that has not been absorbed into the body politic and there is no Indian question, and no Indian Department, that is the whole object of this Bill. (cited in Titley 1986, 50)

In Canada, Métis generally did not, and do not, fall under the *Indian Act*, although aspects of the Act, such as residential schooling, did impact Métis albeit often in different ways than First Nations and Inuit peoples, as outlined in volume three of the Truth and Reconciliation Commission's Final Report, titled "The Métis Experience" (2015a). Yet, as already noted, the same goal of eradication was applied to Métis people; in their case, the tools used included denial of Métis Indigeneity, the failed scrip system, violence, forced dispersal, and rampant racism, including forcing the population into a racialized binary of either "white" or "Indian." Many of these same policies and attitudes impacted Métis people south of the border, though the American government has never acknowledged the Métis as distinct peoples (e.g., there was never a scrip process and, to this day, there is no policy that distinguishes Métis from American Indians). Many Métis people south of the border, such as the Turtle Mountain Michif, have become part of Indian Tribes (something that certainly happened in Canada, though it is perhaps less acknowledged, though see Innes 2013). In contrast, the Little Shell Tribe of Chippewa Indians (many of whom have ancestors who lived in Red River) had to fight for over a century to gain recognition through the American federal acknowledgment process (see Vrooman 2012).[13]

In 1969, Canada's extermination- and assimilation-centred approach reached a turning point when then Indian Affairs minister, Jean Chrétien, wrote a white paper (often referred to as *the* White Paper) that proposed to solve the "Indian problem" (Government of Canada 1969).[14] Key aspects of the proposal included eliminating Indian status, abolishing the *Indian Act*, and turning reserves into private property. The White Paper became a key part of then–Prime Minister Pierre Trudeau's "Just Society" policy. While centred on the concept of equality among all – a concept that on the face of it seemed a lot better than the "discrimination, isolation and separation" that the Paper was (supposedly) intended to eradicate – it was widely condemned by Indigenous people. Activist Harold Cardinal (Cree) was instrumental in writing a formal response in a book titled *The Unjust Society*. In his opening statement, he referred to the policy as "a thinly disguised programme of extermination" (1969, 1). Due to the hard work and resistance of Indigenous peoples, the White Paper was abandoned. In the years that followed, numerous court cases in Canada affirmed Indigenous peoples' inherent rights (Bone 2002, 61–4). It had become clear that Indigenous peoples were mobilized and ready to address assimilationist policies.

The response to the White Paper, coupled with growing nationalism in Quebec, opened a new era in Canada's approach to underrepresented communities. Marked by the implementation of a policy titled "Multiculturalism within a Bilingual Framework" (1971), this new era centred the promotion and institutionalization of multiculturalism, and was viewed by many as a positive renunciation of the (overt) racism of the past (see Mackey 2002, 50–70). Emerging from recommendations of the 1963 Commission on Bilingualism and Biculturalism, as well as pushback on the Commission from Canadians whose origins were neither French nor English, the 1971 policy affirmed that Canada has two official languages, but no official culture, and that no ethnic group should "take precedence over any other" (quoted in Mackey 2002, 64). It also included provisions for financial support aimed at developing and maintaining the culture and languages of about eighty groups. In the years that followed, multicultural policies continued to develop. Most importantly, when the Constitution was patriated in 1982, the Charter of Rights and Freedoms (adopted as part of the Constitution) made explicit reference to "the preservation and enhancement of the multicultural heritage of Canadians" (section 27). Multiculturalism had become part of Canadian identity.

The 1982 patriated Constitution was a significant moment in Indigenous/Canadian relations not only because it moved away (somewhat) from the "two founding races" myth, but more notably because it "recognized and affirmed" the existing rights of Indigenous peoples. For Métis specifically, it was important because it recognized Métis Indigeneity. As stated in section 35.2, "In this Act, aboriginal peoples of Canada include Indian [i.e., First Nations], Inuit and Métis peoples of Canada." This recognition for Métis was the result of a great deal of lobbying and the hard work of Métis people under the leadership of Harry Daniels; more generally, the recognition of Indigenous rights was fought for by numerous Indigenous leaders (see Teillet 2012, Bulbulian 1987). Yet, the Constitution left the definition of Métis open to interpretation.[15] Furthermore, the inclusion of Métis in the Constitution was not understood as indicative of the federal government's obligation to engage in a nation-to-nation relationship with Métis peoples (Kermoal and Andersen 2021, 2). As a result of this lack of clarity, the recognition of Métis in the Constitution has led to numerous court cases aimed at determining who counts as Métis and what their inclusion means from the standpoint of Métis/Canadian relations.

Two court cases are particularly notable. The Powley Case (2003), centred on the right to hunt, established ten criteria – known as the Powley Test – used to determine whether a person has a legal claim to Métis rights. Though seen as a victory by many, it has been criticized for "fail[ing] to consider the right of self-definition of the Métis people itself, presuming instead to accord a right to every little community to decide who will have the constitutionally protected rights of a people" (Chartrand 2008, 35). In essence, it has opened the opportunity – or at least a sense of opportunity – for any group to make a claim as a (supposedly) Métis community, regardless of their connection, or lack thereof, to Métis peoples. The second court case is *Daniels v. Canada*. In 2016, the Supreme Court of Canada ruled that Métis and non-Status Indians are "Indians" as defined in section 91(24) of the Constitution Act of 1867. This much-misunderstood decision means that the federal government (rather than the provincial governments) has a legal responsibility to Métis people. Instead of turning to the provincial government for access to health programs, education, land rights, and more, Métis have the right to negotiate with the federal government. Ultimately, the Daniels decision acknowledged that a nation-to-nation relationship exists – and has always existed – between Canada and the Métis. Recent nation-to-nation "framework agreements" between Métis organizations and Canada since the Daniels decision suggest that it may have sparked a new era in Métis/Canadian relations (Kermoal and Andersen 2021, 4).

Contemporary Métis Gathering(s)

This introduction began by emphasizing settler relationships to Métis music – how settlers have used Métis music for their own purposes, whether to emphasize the (supposed) coming of civilization, or to set Canada apart as a Métis nation – a kind of possessive claim to Métis identity. It then provided a brief history of Métis/Canadian relations to situate the musical relationship between peoples within its broader context. One key goal of this book is to understand the shifting relationship between Métis peoples and Canada through music. However, a second equally important goal is to turn attention to Métis-created spaces for music and dance to understand how they provide a significantly different vision of and for musicking. Later in this chapter, I consider what these different viewpoints might mean by drawing on the work of Indigenous theorists, but before that, I want to offer a short vignette focused on the 2022 Back to Batoche Days event to bring the contemporary vitality of Métis peoples to life – a kind of counterpoint to the general historical context just provided. This vignette draws attention to the work being done by Métis people in the twenty-first century through Métis cultural festivals, and through music and dance, which are foundational to these festivals. To still be gathering, dancing, musicking, and visiting as Métis people was no easy feat; and I hope this vignette emphasizes the continued vitality of Métis peoples while beginning to highlight the connection between music and dance, and issues of recognition and resurgence.

22 July 2022 – It is the second day of the annual Back to Batoche Days. Unable to attend in person, I am sitting in a tiny hotel room in Portugal when I hear about an historic announcement made moments earlier; from then on, I am glued to my computer screen, intent on seeing as much of the streamed event and news stories as possible.

The sound of the "Red River Jig" (a popular Métis tune and dance considered by some to be the Métis anthem) echoes through my speakers as I watch a clip of the opening procession (the lead up to the big announcement), the tune providing a foundational soundscape for the opening ceremony. Toes tap and hands clap as an infectious energy spreads through the large crowd seated in the bleachers and in chairs brought by attendees. (Arriving at the event early – certainly by day one – and staking out a spot with your own chair is the only way to be assured of keeping one of the best seats near the stage and the dance floor throughout the event.) While the Back to Batoche opening ceremony is always a time to express joy and celebration, the excitement is especially notable this year when, after the officials have made their way to the stage, Métis Member of Parliament Dan Vandal steps up to the podium to make an announcement: after five years of negotiations, and 137 years of Métis insisting that they are still here, the federal government has agreed to give 690 hectares of land at the Batoche National Historic Site back to Métis Nation – Saskatchewan. Though it feels unprecedented (and certainly it is unprecedented in some ways), this transfer was preceded in 1996 by a small land transfer back to Métis ownership, namely, the Back to Batoche Festival grounds, a small parcel of land two kilometres north of the Batoche National Historic Site. Land back[16] began with the festival grounds.

In the midst of so much joy and celebration, it is the efficacy of Métis cultural festivals that, this year, resonates throughout the opening ceremony and through the days and weeks that follow as mainstream news outlets break the story of land back. (The *Globe and Mail* published the story that day, as did local papers across the Prairies.) Returning year after year in an expression of "still being here" was not just a celebration of culture and community – though that work was, and continues to be, important. Instead, it is clear today that returning year after year to fiddle, sing, dance, and visit as a peoples was, and remains, an activation of Métis sovereignty.

Performing Recognition in the Settler State

> Recognition is the gentler form, perhaps, or the least corporeally violent way of managing Indians and their difference, a multicultural solution to the setters' Indian problem.
> – Audra Simpson (2014, 20)

As already described, a fundamental shift occurred in Canada's political landscape in the late twentieth century. Rather than policies of assimilation, the new approach to underrepresented communities revolved around the recognition of these communities as integral to Canadian identity. This shift is addressed by philosopher Charles Taylor in his widely read essay, "The Politics of Recognition" (1992). In it, he argues that, by the time he was writing, the demand for recognition had become an increasingly common refrain within contemporary politics, especially in Canada. Explicitly linking recognition and multiculturalism, he makes several critical observations.

Recognition, he claims, is closely linked to identity, which is "something like a person's understanding of who they are, of their fundamental defining characteristics as a human being" (25). He further argues that recognition, lack of recognition, and *mis*recognition shape our identity. A central tenet of Taylor's work is, therefore, the concept of intersubjectivity: our individual identities are not self-made, but, instead, are dialogical (34). This includes dialogue within and against the cultural groups to which we belong. Perhaps most important here, however, is Taylor's suggestion that our sense of self-worth as individuals is tied to the ways in which the cultural groups (to which we belong) are (de)valued. As he writes, "[n]onrecognition or misrecognition can inflict harm, can be a form of oppression, imprisoning someone in a false, distorted, and reduced mode of being" (34). Nonrecognition, he furthermore notes, "can inflict a grievous wound, saddling its victims with [an incapacitating][17] self-hatred" (26). Recognition, for Taylor, is key to an equitable society.

While the politics of recognition have become foundational to the accommodation of difference in Canada, critiques have a long history, dating back at least to Franz Fanon's book *Black Skin, White Masks*, which was first published in 1952 (Chari 2004; Balaton-Chrimes and Stead 2017). Drawing heavily on Fanon, political scientist Glen Coulthard (Dene) has been particularly trenchant in his critique of recognition in Indigenous contexts. As he writes,

> the liberal recognition-based approach to Indigenous self-determination in Canada that began to consolidate itself after the demise of the 1969 White Paper has not only failed, but now serves to reproduce the very forms of colonial power which our original demands for recognition sought to transcend. This argument will undoubtedly be controversial to many Indigenous scholars and Aboriginal organization leaders insofar as it suggests that much of our efforts over the last four decades to attain settler-state recognition of our rights to land and self-government have in fact encouraged the opposite – the continued dispossession of our homelands and the ongoing usurpation of our self-determining authority. I suggest that this conclusion demands that we begin to collectively redirect our struggles *away* from a politics that seeks to attain a conciliatory form of settler-state recognition for Indigenous nations toward a *resurgent politics of recognition* premised on self-actualization, direct action, and the resurgence of cultural practices

> that are attentive to the subjective and structural composition of settler-colonial power. (2014, 23–4, emphases in original)

At the heart of Coulthard's critique is his accurate and astute observation that recognition "rests on the assumption that the flourishing of Indigenous peoples as distinct and self-determining agents is dependent on their being granted recognition and institutional accommodation by and within the settler-state apparatus" (2006, n.p.). In other words, recognition does not acknowledge Indigenous nations' sovereignty as entities that can and *do* function outside of the settler-colonizers' political structures, and it does not require significant modification of the colonizer/colonized relationship. This recognition is "still *colonial* insofar as it remains structurally committed to the dispossession of Indigenous peoples of [their] lands and self-determining authority" (Coulthard 2014, 151, emphasis in original). From this viewpoint, recognition is a conciliatory form of domination that does not so much break from past practice as repackage it; or, as Mohawk anthropologist Audra Simpson suggests, it is a "gentler form" of "managing Indians and their difference" (2014, 20).

Métis sociologist Chris Andersen is similarly critical of the politics of recognition, addressing issues that are especially pressing in the current context of (false) Métis identity claims. Andersen notes that the way in which Taylor uses the term *identity* "conceals a tension between 'situated self-understanding' and 'official classification'" (2014, 14). He notes that public recognition can create an impetus for a collective claim to an identity. That is to say, the bestowal of recognition, in some cases, can allow a collective identity to emerge. As such, misrecognition works both externally and internally, meaning that misrecognition can form the basis for the ways that a group understands itself as a collectivity. As Andersen articulates, "the very *claim* to recognition must be understood as a powerful animator of the groupness that much of the Canadian recognition literature already seems to take for granted" (189). The recognition of Métis in the Constitution in 1982, for example, provided a means for groups to begin a claim to Métis-ness. Some (non-Métis) Indigenous groups might believe that claiming a Métis identity is the only way to gain recognition and rights as Indigenous peoples, or they may legitimately believe that they are Métis, based on Canada's framing of Métis identity; in other cases, the reasons may be more insidious, as documented by Darryl Leroux (2019). Andersen ultimately points to the complexity of recognition within the Canadian colonial state. Without recognition, it can be difficult for Indigenous peoples to fight for rights to land and benefits guaranteed to Indigenous peoples. Furthermore, public recognition carries substantial symbolic and material resources. For this reason, recognition might be "necessary to make the subsequent 'turning away' from state-run social and political policies and programs even possible" (2014, 176).

While Coulthard and Andersen do not address music, music is often used in processes of recognition, and as Ursula Hemetek points out, both performers and ethnomusicologists-as-mediators might play a role in processes of gaining recognition – that is, "proving, documenting, and mediating 'cultural heritage' for minorities" vis-à-vis the state (Hemetek 2006, 52). Music-centred analyses of recognition, I would argue, complicate our understanding of what recognition is able (and unable) to accomplish. As Hemetek describes in a discussion of Romani music, "In the process initiated in 1989 of claiming political recognition in Austria, the public presentation of Romani traditional music contributed enormously to proving that a group of people who had been discriminated against and who formerly were merely seen as a social minority were in fact an ethnic one, with a distinct cultural heritage of their own" (2006, 35). This recognition required some strategic work by community members because Roma, having borrowed from diverse traditions, were viewed as having no music of their own. As Hemetek writes, "Their integration of different musical traditions especially challenges the idea of 'national folk music' that seemed so important in European folk music research and folklore studies" (37). Roma were initially denied recognition as a *Volksgruppe* (an Austrian political category that recognizes ethnic difference) because officials such as Austria's Prime Minister "did not see any 'cultural markers' that indicated an ethnic tradition" (44). The work of gaining recognition was done in part through festivals that "offered public proof of the existence of 'ethnic traditions' of Romani culture" (47). Applied ethnomusicologists facilitated this work through activities such as public presentations of Roma music, teaching, and other forms of cultural mediation. Hemetek concludes by noting that these processes were political acts that "prov[ed] that they [Roma] were there" (38).

Hemetek is not, however, entirely uncritical of the state process of recognition, pointing to the complex in-group dynamics that can play out within this climate of music for recognition. As she notes, "Austrian governmental institutions expected there to be one Romani culture to express cultural heritage, because all the Roma living in Austria were to be recognized as one *Volksgruppe*" (Hemetek 2006, 49). The Austrian government's expectation raised questions regarding whose music would be considered Roma music (i.e., the true or authentic music) and whose style of music would represent Romani culture in public-facing settings. As Hemetek further elaborates,

> Severe conflicts have arisen from this question, especially among musicians, fuelled in addition by jealousy and ethnocentrism … This might not be a problem for the ethnomusicologist who is an outsider, for all these styles can be the subject of research. It is not even a problem in public presentation, if you present them separately and always explain the distinctions. However, it starts to be a problem when one group wants to monopolize public presentation, which has a lot to do with intra-Romani politics and the perceived power of music as a means of cultural recognition … This problem had never occurred until the Roma were presented to the public, until applied ethnomusicology had found a new forum for these styles, until they had been staged for the Austrian public as the proof of a cultural heritage in a political process. (2006, 50)

What this means is that researchers and the public, in the context of a politics of recognition, play a significant role in shaping the musical practices of the "Other": how it is presented, what is presented, who gets funded, and so on.

Working with Franco-American fiddlers, ethnomusicologist Tom Faux provides a similarly rich critique of recognition. In the case documented by Faux, it is clear that recognition of the Franco-American population emerged just as the population (in the area he was working) was teetering on the edge of total assimilation into the Anglo-American majority. As Faux traces, the Franco-American people in Maine had, in previous generations, been faced with the tough choice between "losing their sense of community [and identity] and subjecting their children to second-class status" (2009, 40), an issue that resonates strongly with Métis experiences. By the 1980s, there had been a huge loss of French language and identity among Franco-Americans in Maine. Faux points out that "after nearly a century of social and political marginalization by officials of Maine's Francophones, a number of State agencies as well as non-profit organizations were turning their attention to what was perceived as a cultural crisis in the state's French communities" (2009, 38–9). Thus, the push for recognition only happened once the French Maine community had reached near assimilation (42): it was granted after the French community had lost almost all of their power, socially and politically. The new valuation of culture might thus be seen as a marker of acceptance and a (supposed) reversal of discrimination; but, it is one that is nonthreatening because there is little social and political power within the community (as a distinct community rather than a conglomeration of individuals) that might be used to challenge the mainstream. Just as significantly, Faux notes that "folkloric performances" (as recognition-centred performances tend to be) and "institutionally underwritten public events" may not actually be able to address the issue of community fracture or strengthen social relationships (43). This, of course, does not mean that music for folkloric performances and music for community-focused gatherings are mutually exclusive. Rather, it acknowledges that music as, or for, recognition may not be able to do the work most needed for community sustenance and continuation.

As suggested in the preceding overview, the term *recognition* has been used in a variety of ways. Simpson and Coulthard, for example, describe recognition as a neocolonial technique of difference management, while Hemetek, speaking specifically to the context of music, views it as having at least some liberatory potential. In this book, I take a critical stance on recognition, viewing it as far from the ideal that Indigenous nations seek and deserve; but my research with Métis communities has also shown that it is a tool that some Métis people use, perhaps as one possible pathway toward the "turning away" suggested by Andersen. In other words, this book engages with the complexity of recognition politics, rather than trying to flatten the complexity. As already noted, recognition of Métis music has not always reflected Métis understandings of musical practice. I would, in fact, suggest that Métis music has often been *mis*recognized as situated in the past, as unchanging, as limited or limiting, and even as *belonging to all Canadians*. These are themes that I address in further detail in chapter three ("Writing Métis Music in Manitoba Newspapers"), chapter four ("Exchange, Multicultural Compartmentalization, and the New Old-Time Style"), and chapter five ("Métis Music at Manitoba's Old-Time Fiddle Competitions"). At the same time, it is doubtful that Métis people would have been able to get land back if Canada had not, in 1982, recognized Métis as an Aboriginal people, and if the Batoche area had not been recognized as culturally significant. As I pointed out in the vignette about Back to Batoche Days, music can and does play an important role in gaining recognition – in being seen and *heard* as a distinct people. The strategic use of recognition is a theme that I take up in chapter six ("Cultural Festivals as Recognition and Resurgence"), though I propose that it is used alongside resurgent approaches to music making.

Resurgent Music

> Our liberatory and inherent theories of resurgence … do not tell us to persistently search through the web of colonial traps for settler political recognition and to gleefully accept white paper liberalism designed to redistribute resources and rights, placating the guilt of settler Canadians and neutralizing Indigenous resistance. Our inherent theories of resurgence are transformative and revolutionary. They are meant to propel and maintain social, cultural and political transformative movement through the worst forms of political genocide; and I think it is important to understand them as such.
> – Leanne Simpson (2011, 24)

> The art of resurgence seeks the recoherence of our fragmented existence in a dynamic return to presence, unity, and holism.
> – Jarrett Martineau (2015, 96)

Indigenous scholars began using the concept of resurgence in the 1990s. Resurgence has since become a foundational concept within Indigenous studies, especially among Indigenous activists and scholars working in Canada. Leanne Simpson (Michi Saagiig Nishnaabeg) has written in particularly compelling ways about the concept, both as something that is already happening and as a provocation to intensify resurgence movements. While resurgence is best understood as fluid and flexible – a process that each nation needs to make sense of on its own terms (Simpson 2011, 148) – the literature centred on the concept highlights several overlapping themes. Resurgence is, first and foremost, an act of refusal through which Indigenous peoples/nations transcend the colonial state. As Jeff Corntassel (Cherokee) remarks, "Resurgence means having the courage and imagination to envision life beyond the state" (2012, 89). Similarly, in her momentous book *Mohawk Interruptus*, Audra Simpson (Mohawk) writes that the Mohawk of Kahnawà:ke "insist on being and acting as peoples who belong to a nation other than the United States or Canada" (2014, 2). They refuse to be eliminated *as Mohawks*. This refusal marks a profound turning away from the settler state and what it demands of Indigenous peoples, such as being culturally different in a way deemed appropriate by outsiders (Povinelli 2002). Turning away is essential because, as Leanne Simpson points out, "colonizing governments and private corporate foundations are not going to fund our decolonization, because the colonial relationship serves their interests, and they remain the beneficiaries of colonialism" (2008, 77). Resurgence is thus "Indigenous at its core" (Simpson 2011, 17, 20).

Resurgence is not, however, about preservation in the sense of fixedness; rather, it creates a powerful and transformative past-present-future link that melds the continuity of traditional ways of life with regeneration, assuring the continued relevance of traditional practices in the context of contemporary life. Simpson provides a rich metaphor that demonstrates this connection, writing that "in our greatest period of destruction, our Grandparents resisted by planting the seeds of resurgence" (2011, 66). This metaphor is powerful because it allows for transformation (growth from a seed to a plant) without breaking from the past; it also acknowledges the agency of Indigenous ancestors who safeguarded knowledge for the survival of their nations. Continuity is essential because the purpose of resurgence movements is to ensure that each nation survives as an Indigenous nation. Thus, Simpson argues that "we [Indigenous peoples] need to be able to articulate in a clear manner our visions for the future, for living as Indigenous Peoples *in contemporary times* … In essence, we need to not just figure out who we are; we need to re-establish the processes by which we live who we are *within the current context we find ourselves*" (2011, 17, emphasis mine). As a challenge intended to propel the "re-envisioning and practicing of everyday acts of resurgence," Jeff Corntassel similarly asks, "How will your ancestors and future generations recognize you as Indigenous?" (2012, 88; also see Simpson 2008, 74). While carefully attending to the knowledge of Indigenous ancestors, resurgence nurtures revolution and Indigenous life for future generations.

Resurgence is, furthermore, about everyday acts, which are neither "glamorous [nor] expedient" (Corntassel 2012, 98) but, rather, assertive and active. As Corntassel writes,

> A *peoplehood model* provides a useful way of thinking about the nature of everyday resurgence practices both personally and collectively. If one thinks of peoplehood as the interlocking features of language,

> homeland, ceremonial cycles, and sacred living histories, a disruption to any one of these practices threatens all aspects of everyday life. The complex spiritual, political and social relationships that hold peoplehood together are continuously renewed. These daily acts of renewal, whether through prayer, speaking your language, honoring your ancestors, etc., are the foundations of resurgence. It is through this renewal process that commitments are made to reclaim and restore cultural practices that have been neglected and/or disrupted. (Corntassel 2012, 89)

It is these everyday acts that, according to Corntassel, have the best hope of disrupting colonialism and restoring Indigenous nationhood (88). Tying resurgence to decolonization, he continues noting that "every Indigenous person is in a daily struggle for resurgence. It is in these everyday actions where the scope of the struggle for decolonization is reclaimed and re-envisioned by Indigenous peoples … While decolonization and resurgence are often treated separately from each other in scholarly analysis … they are … interrelated actions and strategies that inform our pathways to resistance and freedom" (Corntassel 2012, 89). As the everyday assertion of Indigeneity, resurgence is a "call for Indigenous Peoples to *live* [their nations'] teachings and stories in the diversity of their contemporary lives" (Simpson 2011, 148). These everyday acts are about connecting Indigenous peoples with Indigenous ways of being in the world, with their homelands, with cultural memories and cultural practices, and with each other as individuals, families, clans, communities, and nations. It is about complete reconnection with all aspects of one's nation/culture (Corntassel 2012, 97). All aspects of Indigenous life – from culture to politics – are connected through resurgence and envisioned for the past-present-future.

Resurgence is a key theme in Dena'ina musician-scholar Jessica Bissett Perea's recent book on Indigenous music history in Alaska. Perea's interweaving of performance, resurgence, and sovereignty demonstrates how music is embedded in – indeed inseparable from – the social, political, and everyday lives of Indigenous peoples, past, present, and future. It furthermore does important work, that is, has a function that is beyond the aesthetic; it *sounds like* the complexity of Indigeneity. Perea thus argues for a "sound relations approach" that moves away from analyzing what Indigenous music is (i.e., the parameters of what counts as properly Indigenous or a checklist of elements or sounds that supposedly make it Indigenous) toward "an aesthetics of self-determination and resurgent world-making" (2021, 6). Referencing Coulthard and Hopi lawyer and ethnomusicologist Trevor Reed, she suggests that, within a framework of resurgence, aesthetic traditions should be placed alongside legal and political traditions because aesthetic traditions "are always already intertwined with Indigenous law and politics" (2021, 265). Put another way, she suggests that "aesthetic resurgence necessarily involves a reintegration of politics and arts as co-constitutive ways of being, knowing, and doing" (7). A resurgent approach to music history thus tends to issues of Indigenous density, which is distinguished by Perea (who draws on the work of Métis sociologist Chris Andersen [2009]) from Indigenous *difference* and the deficit-based analysis that often accompanies difference-based analyses; it allows for both the complexity of Indigenous being and "relationships with whitestream society" (Andersen 2009, 82). It also attends to relationality, including reaffirmations of "relations to lands, waters, and lifeways" (Perea 2021, 266).

Jarrett Martineau provides a similarly holistic discussion of resurgence and performance, emphasizing the visioning and anticolonial work accomplished through Indigenous creative practices. For Martineau, resurgent spaces for artmaking can reclaim presence and transform reality (2015, 5). He also emphasizes how art practice is "mobilized in creative contention with a violent system that continues to seek [Indigenous] assimilation and elimination" (3–4). Martineau's analysis therefore directly addresses how performance works *against* colonialism, noting that Indigenous arts can, and should, be used to confront colonialism. Martineau thus notes that he is guided by a "belief in the power of creative practice to transform the world" (10). As he writes,

> In my view, Indigenous artists are uniquely positioned to address the challenges and complexities of anticolonial struggle. Artists are not simply cultural producers; they are communicative tacticians able to embrace the chaotic flux of spectacular society while interrogating, re/visioning, remixing, and recoding Indigenous resistances in the midst of the mediatized present. Indigenous artists confront colonialism by asserting the resilient continuance of collective creativity and articulating lines of flight through and away from Empire's masked dances. Indigenous art-making is not inherently decolonizing, but it can activate and actualize forms of freedom through its deep connec-

> tions to acts of dreaming and creating. Songs, stories, art, music, dance, performance, and ceremonies are communicative forms of Indigenous art and *decolonizing media*—languages through which to glimpse visions, echoes, and refrains of decolonized realities. (10)

Martineau thus articulates the ways that artists enact anticolonial struggle through performance while creating works that contribute to the flourishment of Indigenous forms of life. A key thread that ties together Perea and Martineau's work is the assertion that artists are vital to Indigenous communities and within anticolonial work.

The issue of resurgent world-making and its intersection with recognition is a thread that runs through this book. As I pointed out earlier, the efficacy of spaces for resurgent musicking is not always understood and resurgent musicking is sometimes misunderstood or overlooked as an inauthentic expression of Métis culture. Resurgence is nonetheless at the heart of Métis cultural festivals and creative practice. These are issues addressed in further detail in chapter six ("Cultural Festivals as Recognition and Resurgence") and in chapter seven ("On Moving from *Louis Riel* to *Li Keur*"). As I suggest throughout, Métis music is a practice that gathers sound, movement, language, storytelling, community, history/historical knowledge, creativity and innovation, spirituality, and more in performative and everyday contexts; it is therefore central to Métis visioning of past, present, and future. As fiddler Brianna Lizotte succinctly explained, "[The fiddle's] been in my family since forever, and in my life since I was very little. I've been keeping that family tradition alive of playing the fiddle … I'm just really proud to be carrying my Métis heritage through music and making connections that way" (2022). When a fiddler steps onto the Back to Batoche stage, she carries with her and expresses (sounds) her family history, a collective and familial inheritance. She also refuses the representations created by non-Métis. In doing so, she invites attendees to join in a moment of transformative potential, whether through dance or by coming together as a community in celebration. She creates a space for the community to imagine how music and dance can once again function as celebration, competition, connection, diplomacy, prayer, or expression of spirituality. She creates a space – and becomes part of a space – that allows for a dynamic return to holism (Martineau 2015, 95).

An Ethics of Responsiveness

The themes of (non)recognition and resurgence highlight a degree of incommensurability (i.e., having no point of commonality or comparison) between how non-Métis represent and understand Métis music and how Métis themselves represent and practice their music culture (though there is not a singular Métis approach, and there are certainly moments of bridging and cross-cultural understanding). There are many examples in this book that point to this incommensurability. I have always been struck, for example, by the ways in which fiddling is approached at Métis-led cultural festivals versus how it is positioned within what I call, drawing on the work of music educator Ed Sarath (2018), the "multicultural compartmentalization" of fiddle styles (a theme taken up in detail in chapter four). Although it has never been my position that Métis music can and should be one thing (and in fact, I argue in previous work [Giroux 2020] and throughout this book that Métis music is diverse in sound and style, as well as function), it has become clear to me over the years that a compartmentalized "difference" approach has taken precedence over more holistic – and more Métis – ways of understanding and representing music and dance. It is easier, it seems, for many to understand Métis-sounded *difference* than to understand Métis musical density. Though I observe in this book's final chapter that change is already taking place, and that music can and will play an important role in this change, we are not there yet. Not even close. As a way to move closer to the vision that Métis creators have for Métis music, there is a need to engage with Métis music and musical creators in new ways, prioritizing and responding to Métis musicians', dancers', and creatives' "resurgent worldmaking" (Perea 2021).

The final theme of this book addresses the gap between the politics of recognition and resurgence, using the concept of an ethics of responsiveness as a starting point toward better relations. Developed by Tanja Dreher and Anshuman A. Mondal in their edited anthology, *Ethical Responsiveness and the Politics of Difference* (2018), ethical responsiveness attends to the limits of voice. With the rise of the internet and digital media more generally, voice has been foregrounded; there often is a sense that everyone's voice can be heard. Considering fiddling, for example, it has become increasingly easy for musicians to get their musical voices out there for all to hear through platforms like Facebook and YouTube, at no cost to either the performer or listeners. Though these platforms can make a positive impact on both the musicians and listeners, it is clear that – even though everyone *can* be heard – not all voices *are listened*[18] to or valued. Based on what I have seen in my field research and in conversations and interviews, these platforms have yet to make a significant impact on the general public's desire to consume Métis difference. Ethical responsiveness is a corrective to the overemphasis on voice and its efficacy, addressing "receptivity, attention, and response" as well as "listening, reading, and witnessing" (Dreher and Mondal 2018, 4). An ethics of responsiveness acknowledges that what is done with knowledge is as important as making that knowledge available. With a commitment to justice in the context of otherness and power, it shifts some of the responsibility from the marginalized who have to, and often do, make their voices heard, to those with privilege and power, who need to learn to listen with an intention to act on the learning gained through listening (Waller 2018, 228). Ethical responsiveness, therefore, addresses the continued failure of approaches that assume that "giving voice" will lead to change.

As I suggest throughout this book (in particular, in chapter seven, which addresses two recently staged operas where Indigenous voices were sought out and "heard" but often not really *listened to* or acted on), an ethics of responsiveness has the potential to radically change the field of Métis music scholarship and the relationship between arts organizations and Métis creatives. This potential is especially notable because Métis music scholarship – in the institutional sense, though certainly not at a grassroots level – is in its infancy, as is public engagement with Métis music (i.e., the arts sector and general public are only beginning to consider Métis music in a sustained way). Though this emergent state of public engagement and scholarship presents challenges – namely, a small number of individuals wield considerable power to define the boundaries of Métis music within mainstream spaces – it provides an opportunity to engage with Métis music and creators toward establishing a field of Métis music studies that is Métis led in every sense, and that is truly based on Métis approaches. Indeed, ethical responsiveness positions non-Métis as learners striving to act on the authority and knowledge generously shared by Métis creators and academics, and as learners working to listen differently. In this way, an ethics of responsiveness offers the opportunity to understand Métis music through Métis ways of knowing. This is not intended to suggest that non-Métis should have access to all Métis knowledge. An ethics of responsiveness respects the limits of what is accessible to non-Métis; even as it promises new ways of understanding Métis music, it requires accepting non-comprehension (Slater 2018), untranslatability, and incommensurability (Gaudry 2011, 115; Tuck and Yang 2012, 1; Snelgrove, Dharmoon, and Corntassel 2014, 3; Robinson 2020, 7) as part of a more ethical relationship.

Weaving Together Approaches

This book draws on my fifteen years of research with Métis music and musicians, an interest that developed from my experience as a competitive old-time fiddler as a child and then teen in Manitoba in the 1990s and early 2000s. When I began a PhD at Toronto's York University in 2008, I planned to complete an ethnographic study of Manitoba's old-time fiddle contest scene, one that seemed to be at risk as more and more contests permanently shut their doors. In fact, during the first decade of the 2000s, many of the contests that I grew up with – competitions in places like Austin, Miami, Holland, Carman, and Rathwell, Manitoba – stopped running. And so, I aimed to document Manitoba fiddle contests at a time that I viewed as critical. However, within my first year of research, I realized that old-time fiddling had a complicated, cross-cultural history: I grew up thinking of it as one of the most *Canadian* things anyone might do, besides, perhaps, playing hockey; yet – as I was starting to learn – old-time fiddling, at least in Manitoba, was in many ways created and maintained by Métis fiddlers. I quickly realized that it could not be addressed without considering the relationships between peoples implicated in the scene. I therefore began to think about old-time music as a site of encounter. And so, I began reading about Métis history and engaging with the work of Indigenous studies scholars.[19]

In the decade and a half since, my career has taken me across Canada. In Winnipeg (where I lived for five years during and after my PhD), I was surrounded by the deep meaning that the Red River region has for Métis people. It was here that the kinds of encounters that I had become interested in were most palpable, as everyone seemed to have *something* to say about Métis music (for better or worse); it was also here that I was most immersed in music and dance, attending everything from small jam sessions to large-scale, Métis-led festivals, to "multicultural" festivals. When I moved to Kingston, Ontario, where I spent two years as a postdoctoral researcher (2015–17), the context was very different, as few people had any understanding of, or even interest in, Métis history or culture. Even so, while I was there, I was able to connect with organizers and participants at Métis Heritage Celebration, a small gathering (by Manitoba standards) held in Oshawa, Ontario, that nonetheless connected people with their kin, often from quite far away. In Lethbridge, I found a similar lack of engagement with Métis culture and history; yet I was afforded the opportunity to build cross-border connections with Métis in Montana, providing me with a very different context for understanding Métis musicking and cross-cultural encounters. Throughout this career, I have always been committed to doing research in the places that I inhabit. These are the places in which I have the most responsibility.

Rather than emerging from a clearly delineated and bounded study in one place over a few years, this book, therefore, draws my varied experiences and projects together, sharing some of the ways of thinking about Métis music that I have come to know over the years. It is for this reason that I situate this book as stories rather than a grand narrative about Métis music and intercultural relations. These are the stories that I have come to know through my scholarly and personal life paths. In positioning these chapters as stories, I do not wish to devalue Indigenous storytelling, which I address in more detail in chapter two, and understand as "disruptive, sustaining, knowledge producing, and theory-in-action" (Sium and Ritskes 2013, ii). But what I also appreciate about storytelling approaches is that they emphasize the situated nature of knowledge, how knowledge emerges from relationships and is co-created by the storyteller and the listener. As I noted in the preface, my own knowledge of Métis music is embedded in a network of relationships and pathways that are unique to me. How this knowledge is understood will be shaped by the reader's own understanding and experiences. I hope that, rather than seeming disjointed (moving across both time and place), readers view these stories as an invitation to add their own to complement, challenge, or disrupt those that I share.

As an ethnomusicologist, field research has been foundational to my methods. Though it has been defined in a variety of ways (see Cooley 1997, 4; Pole 2005, xx; Winick and Bartis 2016, 4), descriptions typically emphasize direct, personal involvement with, and observation of, individuals and communities who are at the heart of the research study. It emerges from the belief that, through observation, field researchers can develop a "deep perspective on the lives and cultural practices of the people they study" (Gilman and Fenn 2019, 8). My field research included attending, and participating in, large- and small-scale music-centred events, both those advertised as

Métis and those advertised as "old-time," in the above-noted locations and in Saskatchewan, Alberta, and North Dakota. As an extension of my field research, I have also interviewed many individuals (fiddlers, accompanists, and organizers), all of whom contributed greatly to my understanding of Métis and old-time fiddle music. I furthermore completed numerous transcriptions and analyses of tunes as performed by Métis and old-time fiddlers. Although neither transcriptions nor tune analyses are included in the pages that follow, which aim to turn away from Métis music as primarily sound, they have informed my knowledge of Métis music; in particular, they have played a vital role in shaping my knowledge of the diversity of Métis fiddling, the stylistic nuances of fiddlers, and the relationship between old-time and Métis fiddling.

My research methods also included archival research. I drew, in particular, on archival resources held at the Archives of Manitoba and online newspaper databases. In reading archival materials, I quickly learned that I had to often "read beyond the words" (Podruchny 2006, 7–8). A good example is the use of words that Michelle Porter describes as "codes." Specifically, she notes that the Goulet men – her ancestors – were referred to by various names in newspapers: "descendants of the voyageurs … pioneers or fans of the old-time fiddling and jigging. Sometimes … French-Canadians" (Porter 2020, 69). As such, part of what I aimed to do in analyzing records was to understand the erasures – and the racism, classism, and sexism – and the broad patterns that emerged in the archive to "read around the overt intentions" of the writer, that is, to understand the underlying currents and tensions (Podruchny 2006, 8). Though I did consult some French-language newspapers, my ability to understand their nuance (especially those dating back a century) was insufficient to ensure accurate analysis. I suspected, though, that there were some differences in representation. Analysis of these French-language papers would be a fruitful area of further research and is one example of how other scholars may wish to complement or challenge the stories that I present.

As a non-Métis person writing about, or perhaps *with* Métis music, I view my role in part as someone who applies knowledge shared by Métis and other Indigenous peoples to the context of musical encounters. This application is often in the form of critique – what I understand to mean careful (re)consideration of something. Critiques that point to inequities, however, are often not easy to digest, especially when they respond to "good intentions,"[20] such as attempts to *include* Indigenous musicians or musics (as in the case study discussed in chapter five). Critiques are often seen as tearing down, destroying, destructive, and hurtful to those who meant well or worked hard to facilitate or create the encounter (an unwillingness to see the *good* in someone or something). Yet critique can be understood differently: drawing on the work of anthropologist Mayanthi Fernando, I understand critique as care. As Fernando notes:

> With this notion of critique as care, I am pushing against a distinction between critique and care that I notice hardening in how my colleagues and graduate students approach anthropology, a distinction inspired by Bruno Latour's essay "Why has Critique Run Out of Steam?" There, Latour distinguishes between the ostensibly haughty, self-satisfied work of critique that "has sent us down the wrong path, encouraging us to fight the wrong enemies," and a different kind of work "whose import ... will no longer be to debunk but to protect and to care." In this new dispensation, critique entails denunciation, destruction, and the foreclosure of livable futures; what we need instead, we are told, especially as the planet hurtles toward all kinds of species extinctions, is an ethics and politics of care. (Fernando 2019, 14)

Through a close analysis of the work of the late anthropologist, teacher, and mentor Saba Mahmood, Fernando's essay aims to show that critique can be a way of being present in the world, an expression of care for the world, for people who are being harmed or might be harmed in the future, and a way "to chip away at the present, to bring the glimmer of a different, more just, more livable world into view" (Fernando 2019, 17). Critique, then, can be understood as an act of care that creates, just as we care for our homes (repairing what is broken and renovating to make it more welcoming, perhaps more sustainable) or care for our relationships (taking time to build stronger connections and better ways of understanding each other).

Critique – the desire to create a "more livable world" – has, indeed, been an important part of my practice and process of becoming and being a researcher. Over the past decade, I have been personally and professionally changed as I learned about extraction-based research and engaged with Métis communities and Indigenous scholarship. Like many in my discipline, I have become increasingly critical and uncomfortable with field research as a method, including its zoological connotations (Robinson 2020, 149) and power dynamics. It is beyond the scope of this book to provide an overview of the history of field research, which might be represented as having emerged from a "yearning to know about the 'other'" (Pole 2005, xvii) or to detail the history of ethnomusicology, which is currently facing nothing short of a crises amidst calls to "dismantl[e] or significantly restructure" the discipline (Brown 2020; see also Amico 2020).[21] One of the pathways that this research has led me to is that of community-centred co-creation; this is where, I believe, the future of Métis music and dance research lies (see Gaudet 2019; and Gaudry 2021, 2011). My final chapter was, in fact, written through a much more collaborative process than the other chapters, in dialogue with Dr Suzanne Steele, whose opera is discussed. In other words, just as this book's foci move across time and place, my aim, especially in the final sections (though also in chapter two), is to highlight the need and appropriateness of new approaches – an ultimate critique that I hope can, in the coming years, bring new voices to the study of Métis music.

Chapter Overview

As already noted, this book addresses a wide range of spaces and contexts for Métis music, articulating some of its complexity as a musical, social, and political practice. Chapter two provides a historical account of Métis "fiddle dance," a term I adopt from the work of Sarah Quick to emphasize the essential connection between music and dance (2008; 2009, 178). Drawing on travel and fur trade narratives, I begin by adopting what I refer to as a "genealogical approach." This approach emphasizes European and Québécois antecedents to Métis fiddle dance while acknowledging First Nations elements added during the fur trade, creating a so-called "mixed" tradition. In the second section, I turn to Métis storytelling, demonstrating how these stories highlight place, social and political community, and kinship in the emergence of Métis music and dance. These Métis stories additionally position fiddle dance as a fully Indigenous practice. My approach to this chapter is inspired by Mi'kmaw Elder Albert Marshall's concept of Two-Eyed Seeing (Bartlett, Marshall, and Marshall 2012). While this generous framework emphasizes the importance of multiple perspectives, it also underscores how (hi)stories have sanctioned some voices, and silenced others. Drawing on the concepts of recognition and ethical responsiveness, I argue that we need to learn to listen differently to Métis fiddle dance history.

Chapter three focuses on Manitoba newspaper articles and advertisements to examine representations (or recognition) of Métis music from the late nineteenth century to the early twentieth century. I show that these representations demonstrate the fickleness of recognition. When Manitoba first became a province, many residents remembered when Métis held the balance of power – when Métis had a visible and majority presence in the province. To manage this continued, undeniable presence, Métis music, always positioned at a temporal, spatial, or fictionalized distance, was used to create a thrilling past. This added colour to settler history and bolstered the belief that civilization was triumphing over so-called savagery. Métis music was thus instrumentalized for colonial purposes. By the late 1920s, when Métis power in the region was an increasingly distant memory, recognition moved to nonrecognition. That is, newspaper articles rarely represented Métis music *as Métis music.* This erasure functioned as a way to prove the unfounded assumption that Métis people were disappearing. Strikingly, it took place even though Métis musicians remained popular performers – mainstream performers with their names documented in articles published in major newspapers – within Manitoba's music scene. The chapter ends as Métis begin to re-emerge as a cultural and political entity and as Canada moves from policies of assimilation to a new identity founded on multiculturalism. These changes led to Métis music being, once again, recognized as Métis music within mainstream spaces.

In chapter four, I turn to the old-time fiddle style, a style that developed at the intersection of musical exchange and mass mediation. I trace the history of several forgotten-by-many old-time radio fiddlers in Manitoba, and then use Andy Dejarlis (a Métis fiddler) and Don Messer (a fiddler from New Brunswick) to examine national exchange. In doing so, I situate Manitoba's old-time style within a long history of exchange and reciprocal musicality that pre-dates the arrival of Europeans, showing that Métis asserted their ongoing presence and performed their (Métis) modernity through old-time fiddling despite settler nonrecognition. I then turn to the way in which old-time has come to be understood as a seemingly neutral style, or a common language or dialect, for all Canadian fiddlers, analyzing it from the framework of multiculturalism. I argue that multicultural thinking has resulted in the compartmentalization of fiddle styles, which in turn has served to limit what counts as authentic Métis fiddling – something that anthropologist Carl Urion (Métis) refers to as "zero-sum" thinking (that is, an assumption that exchange or additions to repertoire or practice results in replacement). I conclude by considering the possibility of reframing old-time fiddling, especially Manitoba's unique, old-time style, through an emphasis on relationality. I draw attention to its Métis past and present while arguing that to understand its place and meaning, including the place of Métis fiddlers within the old-time style, definitions of the style need to move beyond features readily audible by outsiders.

Chapter five draws attention to the shift that began in the early twenty-first century, as a growing number of Manitobans claimed Métis-ness for Manitoba. To better understand this shift, I focus on old-time fiddle contests that have added Métis-style categories, thereby explicitly and intentionally including Métis music. Many participants and attendees position these categories as a positive step forward, marking an opportunity for increased recognition of Métis people in Manitoba's fiddle scene; and certainly, the shift is significant in the context of the erasures seen through much of the twentieth century and described in previous chapters. I argue, however, that these competitive categories contain Métis reemergence and resurgence, creating boundaries around what Métis fiddling should sound like to be considered authentic. I conclude that Métis-style categories allow the settler public to perform a (settler-defined) Métis identity – and indeed claim Métis identity as their own – without ever having to engage with the Métis Nation, with Métis people, or even with Métis music. Métis-style categories therefore create the semblance of cultural exchange and knowledge transfer, and the semblance of giving a voice to Métis music and people, but they do not require, or even facilitate, meaningful and ongoing relationships with Métis people.

Though Métis people have always gathered for political and cultural events, the 1970s saw the rise of large-scale, Métis-led and -attended cultural festivals like Back to Batoche. This emergence was in part due to the work of newly formed Métis political organizations but was also a result of the affordances of recognition, specifically funding available for cultural events that demonstrated Canada's diversity. Chapter six focuses on some of the festivals that emerged during this time, and which continue to this day. Centred on music, dance, and other cultural activities, these festivals embrace both the unity of Métis and the distinctness of place-based communities and histories. Drawing on my ethnographic research at Back to Batoche Days (Batoche, Saskatchewan), Oshawa Métis Heritage Festival (Oshawa, Ontario), and the Métis Music and Art Festival (Choteau, Montana), I describe these contemporary Métis cultural gatherings to show how they centre Métis resurgence while engaging with the settler state in complex and shifting ways. In particular, I use these events to demonstrate the strength, vitality, and self-determination of contemporary Métis peoples; to elucidate the difference between spaces that centre recognition (as performances for the gaze of outsiders) and spaces that centre resurgence; and to address the ways in which Métis use recognition strategically. In this way, this chapter addresses music- and dance-centred cultural events that enact, sometimes simultaneously, engagement with and turning away from the settler state.

The final chapter looks to the future, using two case studies to consider the issues of erasure, (mis)recognition, (mis)representation, appropriation, and resurgence through the frame of ethical responsiveness. The first case study is Mavor Moore, Jacques Languirand, and Harry Somers's opera *Louis Riel*, which was written in 1967 and restaged during Canada's 2017 sesquicentennial celebrations. The restaging attempted to update the opera, adding a "silent chorus" of Indigenous people and integrating some Indigenous people into the production. It became clear, however, that the opera – in terms of Métis representation and from the perspective of *listening* to Indigenous people – remained a failure. The second case study is Suzanne Steele, Alex Kusturok, and Neil Weisensel's dramatic musical work/opera, *Li Keur: Riel's Heart of the North*. Premiered in 2023, it demonstrates an alternative mode of creation within Western art music. Though this work has been exhausting for Steele, who has had to constantly push back against the status quo (including persistent erasure of her name and work) and educate non-Indigenous collaborators, the priorities embedded in the opera, which centre relationships and value process over product (what might be considered resurgent approaches), provide an opening into the kinds of work that primarily white legacy institutions need to do; and it is one possible model for how creators (Indigenous and non-Indigenous alike) might approach intercultural work. This final chapter is intended to provide hope – and some possible pathways – for a better future, even as it points to the continued struggles of Métis creators.

2

Fiddle Dance in the Fur Trade and across the Métis Homeland

> We configure the events of the past into causal sequences, in the process ordering and simplifying things and giving them new meaning … We wield what Cronon calls a "rhetorical razor," separating relevant from irrelevant, significant from insignificant, story from non-story. In the very act of making these decisions, in sanctioning some voices and silencing others, we exercise enormous power.
> – Brown and Vibert (1996, xviii)

> We must remember that not all stories are given equal time. We cannot separate the telling of history from issues of power. It is still a fact that those who have power still get to write their version of the story and have it accepted as "truth" to have other plausible stories pushed from the table, so to speak.
> – Newhouse (2005, 49–50)

This chapter responds to histories of Métis fiddle dance – including those that I have written – that place a strong emphasis on tracing the origins of Métis repertoire and style. These histories typically highlight European or Quebecois antecedents that arrived in the Prairies through the fur trade, where they "mixed" with Indigenous musics. I begin by using the method that I, and other scholars (see, e.g., Quick 2009, 135–9) have used in the past, focusing on accounts of music making found in the writings of fur trade employees and travel writers. Following the work of historian Carolyn Podruchny, who notes that fur trade documents present limited and biased representations,[1] I attempt to read these sources "against their grain" (2006, 7–8). That is, I aim to understand what the texts reveal if the known and probable biases are peeled away, or otherwise made less opaque. In the context of representations of fiddle dance discussed here, the writers' biases emerged from their overt prejudices related to the intersecting issues of race, class, and sex, as well as through the ways in which they were musically attuned – how their ears had been trained (explicitly or through enculturation) to hear and understand music. A corrective strategy of "reading against the grain" thus means reading with eye and ear turned, or tuned, to silences, looking for what is missing, and to stereotypes or mishearings, including understanding descriptors such as "scraped" and "sawed" as a reflection of a fiddler's perceived *low* status and race (which are, of course, intersecting issues), rather than a reflection of the fiddler's sound, style, or skill.[2] In this first section, I also discuss secondary sources, specifically some of the scholarly writing on Indigenous fiddle dance.

The second section aims to restory (Regan 2010, 6) academic histories of Métis fiddle dance by re-placing[3] Métis storytelling at the centre of Métis fiddle dance histories.[4] In turning to Métis storytelling, I affirm the value of stories not only as entertainment (though they certainly can be and very often are entertaining), but more importantly as modes of knowledge transfer; of theoretical analysis; of (expressing) relationship; and even of creative rebellion. I affirm their value as a methodology that calls both storyteller and listener to act – to respond to – the knowledge that is being shared toward building one's own understanding of the stories and acting on the knowledge shared for the benefit of future generations (see Cajete 1994; Dorris 1979; Howe 2002; Iseke 2013; Iseke and Brennus 2011; and Sium and Ritskes 2013). Though I cannot claim to comprehend Métis storytelling methodology or the stories themselves in their full depth, I aim to show that Métis storytelling can teach us to listen differently to Métis fiddle dance history and thereby gain a deeper understanding of its complexity, depth, and richness, as well as a more complete understanding of the meaning it holds for the Métis peoples.[5] While fur trade and travel writers' accounts, as well as past academic scholarship, provide a compelling look into cultural exchange and the movement of tunes across the Atlantic and North America, Métis storytelling that references fiddle dance (as it is most often only part of a more holistic story) highlights the centrality of place, social and political community, and kinship in the emergence of Métis music and dance; as such, these stories position fiddle dance as *an Indigenous practice* that arose at the heart of the continent with the emergence of the Métis peoples.

My approach to this chapter is inspired by Mi'kmaw Elder Albert Marshall's concept of Two-Eyed Seeing. As he explains, "Two-Eyed Seeing is the gift of multiple perspectives … it refers to learning to see from one eye with the *strengths* of Indigenous Knowledges and ways of knowing, and from the other eye with the *strengths* of Western knowledges and ways of knowing … using both these eyes together, for the benefit of all" (emphasis in original, Bartlett, Marshall, and Marshall 2012, 335). This generous framework (i.e., generous toward a knowledge system that has been used to discredit Indigenous Knowledges) thus emerges from the realization that "no one person ever has more than one small piece of the knowledge" (336). In this way, Two-Eyed Seeing makes room for, and values, a polyphony of voices in the process of knowledge-seeking and -sharing and encourages learners to adopt multiple methodologies. It also draws attention to whose voices histories have sanctioned (in the case discussed here, voices of non-Métis drawing on Western epistemologies), and those that have been overlooked or silenced (in this case, Métis voices and epistemologies). My aim, then, is not to suggest that there are only two ways to tell Métis fiddle dance history. Similarly, I do not want to suggest that the two approaches used in this chapter are always separate and easily distinguishable, or that they always result in distinct narratives. Rather, I am primarily interested in understanding what might happen and how we might come to understand in new ways if Métis storytelling is positioned as relevant – perhaps even foundational – to the telling of fiddle dance history.

Fiddle Routes/Roots in Fur Trade Country

European-derived fiddles began shaping Turtle Island's soundscape in the seventeenth century. The first known reference to a fiddle-like instrument in New France is from 1640, when a newly arrived Ursuline nun, Sister Anne de Sainte-Claire, wrote a letter to sisters in Paris noting that Mother Marie de Saint-Joseph was teaching her wards to sing and play hymns on the viol (cited in Gallat-Morin and Pinson 2003, 232). In a letter dated the following day, Mother Marie de l'Incarnation wrote that twelve-year-old Agnes Chabdikouechich – an Indigenous girl – was one of her most gifted viol students

(233). The next known reference to a fiddle is from 1645, in a description found in the *Jesuit Relations* of a wedding in Upper Canada, near Quebec City, where "there were two violins, for the first time" (Thwaites 1898, 13). By the mid-1700s, fiddles were frequently heard in New France, with some musicians performing as a professional activity (Gallat-Morin and Pinson 2003, 302). Fiddles and fiddle-like instruments soon moved beyond New France's settlements. In 1678, a note in HBC records indicates that a "violl and shell and strings" had been sent to HBC governor Charles Bayley at Moose Factory in the James Bay area (Arthur, Chapman, and Massey 1949, 5). Then, in 1749, HBC records indicate that three fiddlers in Moose Factory provided evening entertainment, creating a "merry" celebration (cited in Wilkins 2013, 70). In the centuries that followed, fiddles were adopted by Indigenous peoples in the eastern regions of what became known as Canada, as evident by the still-vibrant Mi'kmaq fiddle tradition and Cree tradition in the James Bay region.

Traders and explorers soon brought fiddles to the Northwest, and they quickly became very popular instruments across fur trade country. Although they could be ordered through formal means such as Montreal merchants and the North West Company (NWC), as evidenced by supply and inventory lists, historian and sound studies scholar Daniel Laxer suggests that fiddles were more often brought across fur trade routes as "personal belongings of fur traders" or were imported via "informal networks" between fur traders and merchants (2015, 343). Fiddles were also sometimes handmade using local materials. The first written evidence of a homemade fiddle comes from a publication by Scottish apprentice clerk Robert Ballantyne, who, in a description of a Christmas ball held in 1843 in York Factory, noted that an "Indian" was playing a fiddle "of his own making" (2007 [1848], 163–5).[6] Because informal networks and homemade fiddles often leave no written record, some of the most compelling evidence of the extensive spread of fiddles across trade routes is perhaps the number of violin strings found on HBC and NWC inventory lists (see Commissions of Goods to Servants, 1787–1897, and Laxer 2022, 209–10). Yet even then, fiddlers likely made their own strings from gut or other materials. As fiddler Solomon Ballantyne (Cree) shared in an interview in 2001, he used locally sourced rosin (a sticky substance sourced from trees and used on a fiddler's bow) and carved a bridge from a moose shoulder blade; adapting local Indigenous materials to the fiddle has a long history, meaning that inventory lists for strings might underrepresent the popularity of fiddles in the early fur trade.

Although there are no eighteenth-century records of fiddling in the Prairies and northwest interior (roughly equivalent to present-day Manitoba, Saskatchewan, Alberta, and parts of the northcentral and northwestern United States), the fiddle may have arrived as early as the mid-1700s. It was during this period that the HBC set up forts in these regions, while French, Scottish, Orcadian, and English traders – including the less documented independent traders – travelled inland toward the Rocky Mountains.[7] Folklorist Nicholas Vrooman asserts that there was indeed a "mixed-blood" Prairie population at the Forks (present-day Winnipeg) before 1775, possibly having originated "as a legacy of La Vérendrye and his men who began to co-mingle with the local peoples in the 1740s" (Cree and Vrooman 2006, 38). The presence of a fort or a mixed-blood population does not guarantee the presence of fiddles in the eighteenth-century Prairies. However, the certain presence of fiddles in the 1600s in Upper Canada and their prominent place in fort life in the Northwest by the nineteenth century (described below) strongly suggests that fiddles were part of Prairie fur trade culture from its earliest years. In fact, in the early 1980s, Parks Canada uncovered art from York Factory dating back to the late 1700s depicting a fiddler and dancers, a testament to the importance of fiddlers in early fort life in what is now Manitoba (Adams 1982, 40–2).

Though often problematic for their prejudicial descriptions of Indigenous peoples and "judgmental descriptions" of music and dance (Quick 2009, 135), mid- to late nineteenth-century travel journals, letters, and books written by European explorers, adventurers, and fur trade employees are a valuable resource for understanding fiddle dance history insofar as they provide a sense of its pervasiveness; reading between the lines, they also give an indication of some of the features of fiddle dance in the fur trade era. These accounts show that "what had begun as a pastime for fur traders overwintering at the trading posts" had become "a culture of music and dance that was shared by the gentlemen, servants, local First Nations peoples, and Métis alike" (Laxer 2015, 357). One such account was penned by James Hargrave, who, in 1871, published a book about life in Red River, based on papers that had belonged to his father, a long-time HBC employee. In it, he wrote:

> Parties not studiously inclined[8] often pass their spare hours in exercising their skill upon one of the musical instruments. Of these the violin, on account probably of its portable nature, is most ordinarily selected,

> and the votary, after a series of years passed in sedulous practice, usually attains a certain ghastly facility of execution. Some are admitted to play well, but the style of music aimed at is not a high one. In Red River Settlement the performance of a monotonous jig is one of the most admired feats of musical art, and the performer usually while playing, beats time with his feet so vigorously as to render himself a very disagreeable neighbour overhead. Two storey houses are, however, not numerous outside of the forts. So common an accomplishment is fiddle playing in the service that violin strings are annually forwarded as part of the regular outfit for sale in the northern districts. (Hargrave 1871, 196)

While Hargrave denigrates the music as "monotonous" and the style as "not a high one," he also refers to fiddling as an "admired feat" and an "accomplishment," descriptions that highlight fiddlers' abilities (even if begrudgingly, through phrases like "ghastly facility") and the importance of fiddlers to life within the fur trade.

Eight years later, Henry Martin Robinson published parts of the above passage verbatim. As a travel writer, Robinson noted that he supplemented his writing with the work of other writers when his "personal knowledge ... has been at fault" (1879, iii). Presumably, though, he had a fair bit of experience with and knowledge of life in the Prairies prior to Manitoba joining confederation because he was a resident of Red River and was briefly the editor of the *New Nation* (a weekly newspaper that reported on the debates and discussions of the provisional government). In a description cobbled together from Hargrave's work and his own experience, Robinson offers the following picture of a dance at a Company fort:

> Under the inspiration of this instrument, it is scarcely to be wondered at that the few holidays of the year, and frequently the long evenings also, should be enlivened with dances, in which all the dusky maidens within hailing-distance of the fort participate. It is in the enjoyment of this pastime that the wearied clerk finds his chief delight; and he jigs and reels the hours away to the measures of monotonous and oft-repeated tunes. On such occasions the company is cosmopolitan to a striking degree, and all grades of employés mingle on the terms of the most democratic equality. (Robinson 1879, 103)

As hinted at by Robinson, dances were preeminent events in nineteenth-century fur trade social life, bringing people together across race (presumably the racist "dusky maidens" refers to Métis and First Nations women) and class.

A particularly instructive (though racist and sexist) description of a fur trade dance is found in Scottish author Robert Ballantyne's travel memoir, titled *Hudson's Bay, or, Life in the Wilds of North America*, which he wrote after spending five years travelling across fur trade country as an HBC employee. The dance takes place at a Christmas ball held in 1844 at York Factory, in what is now northern Manitoba:

> On benches and chairs sat the Orkneymen and Canadian half-breeds of the establishment, in their Sunday jackets and capotes; while here and there the dark visage of an Indian peered out from among their white ones. But round the stove – which had been removed to one side to leave space for the dancers – the strangest group was collected. Squatting down on the floor, in every ungraceful attitude imaginable, sat about a dozen Indian women, dressed in printed calico gowns, the chief peculiarity of which was the immense size of the balloon-shaped sleeves, and the extreme scantiness, both in length and width, of the skirts. Coloured handkerchiefs covered their heads, and ornamented moccasins decorated their feet; besides which, each one wore a blanket in the form of a shawl, which they put off before standing up to dance. They were chatting and talking to each other with great volubility, occasionally casting a glance behind them, where at least half a dozen infants stood bolt upright in their tight-laced cradles. On a chair, in the corner near the stove, sat a young, good-looking Indian, with a fiddle of his own making beside him. This was our Paganini; and beside him sat an Indian boy with a kettle-drum, on which he tapped occasionally, as if anxious that the ball should begin. (Ballantyne 1848, 163–4)

Ballantyne then describes a kissing/greeting ceremony, where the women follow the custom of kissing all of the men, after which the dancing began:

> This ceremony over, we each chose partners, the fiddle struck up, and the ball began. Scotch reels were the only dances known by the majority of the guests, so we confined ourselves entirely to them.

> The Indian women afforded us a good deal of amusement during the evening. Of all ungraceful beings, they are the most ungraceful; and of all accomplishments, dancing is the one in which they shine least. There is no rapid motion of the feet, no lively expression of the countenance; but with a slow, regular, up-and-down motion, they stalk through the figure with extreme gravity. They seemed to enjoy it amazingly, however, and scarcely allowed the poor fiddler a moment's rest during the whole evening. (Ballantyne 1848, 165)

This description positions fur trade balls as polycultural events, bringing together people from varied ethnic/cultural backgrounds, including an Indigenous fiddler and Indigenous dancers. And although Ballantyne is derisive of the Indigenous women's dancing – a harmful moment of racist and sexist writing that needs to be acknowledged – his description points to an Indigenized approach to dancing to the Scotch reels that the fiddlers were purportedly playing. That is to say, reading against the grain of Ballantyne's racism, his description points to a new style of dance created by Indigenous women within the context of the fur trade industry.

Christmas and New Year's were the most popular celebrations within trading posts' "annual cycle of carnival" (Podruchny 2006, 74–5). However, St Andrew's Day, Epiphany, All Saint's Day, and Easter were also reasons to gather and celebrate. For voyageurs, gatherings were especially important in the winter months when they had more leisure time and could "create new connections, form new families, and solidify a distinctive society in the Northwest" (174). As Podruchny continues, "Their celebrations helped them create new memories and new traditions rooted in their new locations" (174). In some cases, traders would travel great distances to attend a dance. Archibald McLeod, for example, describes a New Year's party that he hosted at Fort Alexandria (near present-day Sturgis, Saskatchewan) in 1801 that brought out traders and hunters from Red River and Fort Des Prairie, near present-day Edmonton. McLeod notes that the attendees included servants (employees) of the company and voyageurs, as well as Iroquois and "Free Men," or retired voyageurs (cited in Laxer 2015, 330). Using journals written by Daniel Harmon, Laxer also references a dance that took place at Mouse River near the Qu'Appelle Valley, noting that men from the HBC, NWC, and XY companies put commercial rivalries aside to come together in music and dance (Laxer 2022, 199). To some degree, at least, fiddle dances challenged the social hierarchies created by fur trade companies.

While fiddle dances remained important to fort life through the mid-nineteenth century, they moved beyond fur trade forts, becoming part of Indigenous soundscapes and practice. The importance of the fiddle in early Métis communities is noted in a description of a Métis buffalo hunt in 1840, found in William James Healy's book, *Women of Red River*, based on Healy's interviews with some of Red River's oldest residents. In it, Healy notes that the "fiddles always went with them on their buffalo-hunting expeditions; and in their camps, they would sing and dance at night" (1923, 73). A much more colourful description of music making during a fall hunt is found in Robinson's travel book, where he writes – with a racist flair – about fiddle dancing during a Métis buffalo hunt:

> Perched high on a cart-wheel, farther on, sits a long-haired Paganini, drawing rude melodies from an antiquated and fractured violin. About him are congregated a crowd of delighted hearers, suggesting new tunes, requesting the loan of the instrument long enough to exhibit their own skill, or, seized with the infection, suddenly breaking into an improvised break-down, or executing a *pas seul* the very embodiment of caricature. (1879, 143–4)

Though again the description is not flattering, especially in its reference to "rude melodies" and the suggestion that the dancers had no agency (i.e., they were "infected" with a desire to dance), it does point to a fiddle *culture*, not just a singular event. In particular, Robinson indicates that there was a known repertoire (i.e., listeners requested tunes) and that there was proficiency among more than one fiddler. His use of Paganini as the European parallel is also an explicit recognition of outstanding ability.

As evident in some of the documents referenced above and in the brief mention of fiddle dance in eastern First Nations communities, fiddle dance – even as it came to be primarily associated with the Métis – was (and continues to be) a practice shared among Métis and First Nations peoples. In an account written between 1802–03, apprenticing clerk George Nelson writes of his surprise seeing Anishinaabeg west of Lake Michigan dancing, as the dancing "was near an imitation of us *white people*" (quoted in Laxer 2015, 334). Much farther to the northwest, fiddling gained popularity among Gwich'in in the second half of the nineteenth century. In his book *The Crooked Stovepipe*, Craig Mishler provides a fictional, though historically based, account of the arrival of the fiddle in Gwich'in territory, identifying the establishment of Fort Yukon in 1847, and HBC employee Antoine Houle's purchase of two coils of violin strings in 1848 and another three coils in 1850 as pivotal moments. Born in 1827, Houle was raised in Fort Halkett on the Laird River (in current-day Yukon Territory) and was recruited by the HBC at age fourteen to live with Loucheux chiefs and learn the Gwich'in language (Mishler 1993, 17). Although Mishler describes Houle as French Canadian, Lawrence Barkwell, a preeminent scholar of Métis history, indicates that Houle's father was French and his mother Métis (n.d., 1). In Mishler's account, the tunes played by contemporary Gwich'in are the direct descendants of those played by Houle, and possibly those of Orcadians working in Fort Yukon at about the same time as Houle. Passed down for more than a century, these tunes were still played in Gwich'in territory in the 1990s, albeit (re)indigenized with Gwich'in names (1993, 16).[9]

In the northeast, European and American whalers likely introduced the fiddle to Inuit in the early or mid-1800s. As Dorothy Harley Eber writes:

> [The whaling ships] appeared suddenly in 1817, north of Baffin Island in Lancaster Sound. For over a hundred years there had been whaling in Davis Strait in the waters off the Greenland coast, but previously the whalers had not found a path through the dangerous ice-pack of Baffin Bay. Soon other British whalers followed, daring the dangerous passage to exploit the waters around North Baffin. (1989, 3)

While whaling "spawned wealth for Britain and for the American eastern seaboard" (Eber 1989, 3), ethnomusicologist Frances Wilkins notes that it also led to "sustained cultural contact between whalers and indigenous populations," especially once whalers began overwintering onboard their ships in the 1860s (2013, 11). The subsequent "regular and prolonged socializing" between European whalers and Inuit during this period led to many shared social activities, including dancing, with the fiddle, concertina, and button accordion being the predominant instruments used for this purpose (Johnson 2012, 116). Soon, Inuit were playing these instruments, and by the turn of the twentieth century, European fiddle dance music was common among at least some Inuit (Johnson 2012, 117). Though this overview of the spread of fiddle dance is in no way complete (especially in its treatment of traditions outside of or on the borders of the Métis Homeland), it shows that by the early 1900s, fiddle dance music had become popular across many Indigenous communities in the vast land that was now known as Canada.

In the 1980s, scholars began writing about these Indigenous fiddle dance traditions.[10] These academic works tended to focus on the origins of the style and repertoire, tracing movement from Europe, across the Atlantic, and then across Canada (an approach similar to what I have done above). In the earliest analysis of this type, Roy Gibbons compared "La grande gigue simple" (a traditional Quebecois tune) with the "Red River Jig," a popular Métis fiddle dance tune. Gibbons began his article noting that "La grande gigue simple" was brought to the Northwest by voyageurs and French Canadian homesteaders, and that "over the years, this traditional step-dance melody was altered and transformed into [the] 'Red River Jig': a Métis expression typifying the 'welding together of European and Indian cultures'" (1981, 40). Gibbons provided many transcriptions of both tunes to support his argument. Ethnomusicologist Anne Lederman's foundational research on Indigenous fiddle dance in Manitoba expanded this approach, including a section categorizing the origins of about one hundred tunes recorded by ten Ojibwe and Métis fiddlers (1986, 59). She ultimately divided the repertoire into Métis tunes (i.e., tunes for which she could not find antecedents), tunes with roots in Quebec, tunes with Scottish Irish roots, tunes with Ukrainian origins, and tunes from early America. She also attempted to identify which stylistic elements could be traced to Ojibwe songs.[11] As such, Lederman argued that the Métis fiddle tradition is a syncretic tradition, an argument that at the time was in some ways groundbreaking because, as she noted, some ethnomusicologists believed that Indigenous musics were *too different* from European musics to mix (1986, 2).

Though Gibbons and Lederman were not alone in adopting an emphasis on origins and mixing, they are perhaps the best examples of what I think of as a genealogical approach.[12] The genealogical approach to fiddle dance music is linear, looks for tune/dance antecedents, and tends to focus on the structure of the tune (its "blood" or DNA) as proof of genealogy. I used this approach in writing a brief historical overview of Métis fiddle dance in my dissertation (Giroux 2013) and in my more recent book chapter on Métis (style) fiddling (Giroux 2020. Citing Lederman, my book chapter adopted her emphasis on the connection between fiddlers in the Northwest and Scotland, as well as influences from French Canadian voyageurs and coureurs de bois who were, in turn, influenced by Scottish and Irish fiddling and Indigenous music. My dissertation makes similar connections while also including references to the influence of Ukrainian fiddling in the Prairies and possible influences of Norwegian fiddling (2013, 152). These genealogical accounts are likely mostly accurate – although determining tune origins is perhaps more difficult than is sometimes acknowledged since tune pathways can be complicated (e.g., a result of ongoing rather than one-way exchange) and similar melodies may sometimes come from different origins (see Quick 2009, 225 for an excellent critique). They are furthermore helpful insofar as they provide a compelling look into cultural exchange and the flow of tunes across the Atlantic and across North America. However, a genealogical approach to tracing Métis tunes obscures, at least some of the time, a fundamental aspect of the music: it could not, and would not, sound as it does – nor would it have come to have the kinds of meaning it does to Métis people – if it were not for its presence in the Métis Homeland. It is these encounters *within place* that are often emphasized in Métis storytelling about fiddle dance.

Storytelling Fiddle Dance History in the Métis Homeland

> If stories are archives of collective pain, suffering and resistance, then to speak them is to heal; *to believe in them is to reimagine the world.*
> –Sium and Ritskes (2013, v; emphasis mine)

Emerging from an understanding of (Indigenous) storytelling as "disruptive, sustaining, knowledge producing, and theory-in-action" (Sium and Ritskes 2013, ii), the remainder of this chapter turns to Métis stories – both personal stories and stories with mythical elements (Kovach 2009, 95), some published in articles or books, and others from interviews – to better understand Métis approaches to, and perspectives on, fiddle dance history. As a starting point, I consider all academic work about fiddling to be, in a sense, stories; they are shaped by each scholar's hand – by what they choose to include and choose to exclude – and they then shape a larger (and often publicly accepted) narrative. As Métis scholar Yvonne Poitras Pratt writes in her book on digital storytelling, "As life reveals, some stories call out to us, some stories lay hidden in the recesses, and still others overtake all else – it is this living quality of stories that make them such a potent tool of transformation, and of domination. As the Métis people of Canada, we have only to think of how our history has been taught in schools to affirm this reality" (2020, 6). Onondaga scholar David Newhouse similarly highlights how some stories are given more weight and importance than others. As he writes, "We must remember that not all stories are given equal time. We cannot separate the telling of history from issues of power. It is still a fact that those who have power still get to write their version of the story and have it accepted as 'truth,' to have other plausible stories pushed from the table, so to speak" (Newhouse 2005, 50). My purpose, then, is to understand the stories that are not centred or pulled to the forefront in the academic telling of Métis fiddle dance history – at least, not in the ways in which genealogical accounts are centred. In pulling these stories into my account of fiddle dance, I aim to take these Métis stories seriously as oral histories that help us understand what fiddle dance music *means* for Métis, and to draw attention to how we might learn to know fiddle dance differently. In so doing, I also ask what it would mean to move beyond narratives of Métis music as mixed, that is, to move beyond narratives that constantly aim to find what percentage of tune DNA comes from European origins and what percentage comes from Indigenous origins.[13]

Though Indigenous stories can be a form of entertainment (Iseke and Brennus 2011, 249), Indigenous peoples understand storytelling as much more. As Gregory Cajete notes, "[s]tory, expressed through experience, myth, parables, and various forms of metaphor is an essential vehicle of Indigenous learning" (1994, 30). Michael Dorris similarly notes that oral tradition is "the vehicle through which wisdom is passed from one generation to the next and by which sense is made of a confusing world" (1979, 156–7). As a form of oral history, Indigenous storytelling is generally event-centred and is "recited in relationship to specific landscapes, waterscapes, and skyscapes" (Howe 2002, 162). As Howe writes, "Communities, then, made sense of their worlds by recounting events that in some fundamental sense related them to their surroundings – to other humans, to plants and animals, to landmarks and constellations. Such narratives recognized and reinforced webs of relationship that connected all entities of a community's spatial domain, and then related that domain to their cosmos" (2002, 163). In the contemporary context of colonization, Indigenous storytelling also works to "subvert and re-create what the Western academy puts forward as valid ways of knowing" (Sium and Ritskes 2013, iii). As Aman Sium and Eric Ritskes continue, "Contrary to liberal notions of stories as depoliticized acts of sharing, we must recognize stories as acts of creative rebellion. Decolonizing the very act of storytelling means breaking from liberal notions of stories as a kind of multicultural 'show and *tell*'. It means closing the false gap that often exists between *speaking* and *acting*" (emphasis in original, 2013, v). Fundamental to the concept of speaking and acting is the role of the listener who, as a witness, is called upon to reflect and act in accordance with what has been shared, in recognition that it is "intended not only to inform a present audience but [also] to be passed down to the next generation and for seven future generations" (Iseke 2013, 568–9).

It is, of course, somewhat of a contradiction in method to use stories – an oral tradition – in a book, a space and context where the "relationship between the reader and the storyteller is conceptual, not tangible" (Kovach 2009, 101). As Margaret Kovach further explains, "in oral culture, story lives, develops, and is imbued with the energy of the dynamic relationship between teller and listener" (101). In written contexts, this dynamism and relationality is literally inaudible and only comes to the surface through an active effort on the part of the reader to engage with the story and the storyteller beyond the page. Weaving story into this chapter is also (potentially) problematic for the way in which the story becomes finalized, and – following academic convention – analyzed "in declarative form [… which] conflicts with the interpretive teaching method assumed in Indigenous stories" (Kovach 2009, 101). Furthermore, stories are intended to be holistic, rather than pulled apart to meet the needs of Western academic scholarship. As Winona Stevenson writes, "It often is the case in mainstream scholarship, that once a story is shared and recorded, 'facts' are extracted and the remaining 'superfluous' data set aside. The bundle is plundered, the voice silenced, bits are extracted to meet empirical academic needs, and the story dies. In the process, the teachings and responsibilities deriving from the social relations inherent in student-teacher relations are forgotten" (Stevenson 2000, 79). By pulling out references to music within longer stories (in some cases), there is a sifting through – a curation – of what matters. Not all of these issues can be adequately addressed in the context of the written word; they are an inevitable downside to the approach taken in this chapter. However, it is worth noting that the stories included are ones that have already been published or are publicly available as transcriptions on the Gabriel Dumont Virtual Museum website. The storytellers have already made them available to the public, possibly with the understanding that new methods of passing on stories need to be adopted to address the contemporary needs of Indigenous peoples (Thomas, cited in Kovach 2009, 102; see also Oster and Lizee 2021). I have also tried to avoid too much interpretation, leaving this to the reader, although I do highlight how the stories have shifted my own understanding of fiddle dance history. Most importantly, I encourage every reader to seek out the original story to better understand it in its fullness, and to read Métis stories not referenced below as a way to add further context and nuance.

Restorying Métis Fiddle Dance History

> My grandma used to always say, "Kikino askiy ooma ka'takwanimahk," you know, we carry our home inside. And the kind of lifestyle we had, I mean, hunters and trappers, you didn't have big things to carry. You had to travel light. You could either put it on the canoe, carry it on your back, or on a red river cart, so everything was small and compact and if you had too much, well, you left it because somebody else would be coming and they could use it, and so, home was those stories and that music.
>
> – Maria Campbell (in Coyes 2002)

The first stories shared here – penned from the recited memoirs of mostly Métis men – follow, in large part, the formal structures of the travel writing and fur trade accounts discussed above. A key difference, however, is that they are shared by people who have deep relationships to the land and to the peoples described in the narratives and thus typically provide more significant insight into the relationships that constitute Métis fiddle dance music. One such account is found in Métis teacher, interpreter, guide, and fiddler Peter Erasmus's book *Buffalo Days and Nights*. A keen fiddler who was raised in the Red River Settlement, Erasmus describes being eager to attend a Christmas dance held in 1856 at Fort Edmonton. After receiving reluctant permission from his employer (a minister who allowed him to attend as long as he did not drink), he joined in the night-long festivities:

> The dance that night I thought upheld Bill's [an employee with whom he shared a room] claims; in fact he had slightly underrated it. Borwick [Bill], being an old-timer in the area, seemed to know every person there and soon made me acquainted with a number of his friends … A big lunch was served at midnight in the homes of the married couples, where the guests had previously left their contributions of food … At last the guests were all served and started drifting back to

> the dance floor ... There was very little rest for the musicians between dances, and there were plenty of fiddlers among the French Metis people from Lac Ste. Anne. Having too good a time dancing I did not offer my services that night, but later on I happened to mention to Bill that I liked playing the fiddle, and thereafter on Borwick's insistence I had to do my share ... The settlement guests all left for their homes at broad daylight. After dancing all night they had to run behind dogs for another forty miles before they would have any rest or sleep. (1999, 41–3)

Erasmus's praise for the fiddlers is implicit in his note about the good time he was having dancing (presumably to musicians who were *good dance fiddlers*). He also confirms that there "were plenty of fiddlers." I was particularly struck, however, by the comment – almost in passing – that emphasizes fiddling as a social *responsibility* ("I had to do my share").

Following a similar "personal story" or memoir approach, Métis freighter, scout, and interpreter Louis Goulet provides a more detailed description of a fiddle dance in a Métis winter camp that similarly emphasizes sociality and relationality:

> The evening began with a feast. People outdid themselves to see who could serve the best meal. During the feast, there'd be a big singing contest and after that would come the dancing. Talk about every kind of reel and jig you can imagine! Fiddles, drums, accordions, guitars, jew's harps and mouth organs, anything was fine as long as it went along more or less with the rhythm. At a shindig like that it was always a contest to see who could play the best, who could dance the best, who could sing the best, who could wear through his moccasins first, who'd be the first to cripple up with cramps in the legs.
>
> If the house had a wood floor, it would be creaking under the steady rhythm of dancing feet. If there was no floor, which was usually the case with those winter houses, the bare ground took all the stamping from our moccasins and the spectators were forced out many times in the evening for a beat of air because the dust inside would be suffocating. I often think the Red River Jig (*Oayâche Mannin*) was invented on evenings like that when sometimes the only instrument was an Indian drum.

> One night we were all jammed into Omichouche Godin's house in the Judith Basin on the Missouri River. The dance started. There was no wood floor and I don't remember any other instrument than an Indian drum. Some men were sitting on the ground around the drum, pounding away like mad to the rhythm of the Red River Jig while the dancing men and women took turns with wild enthusiasm. Spectators sat on the ground all around the room with their backs to the wall, almost completely invisible because of the dust and pipe smoke. The dancers kept time by clapping and snapping their fingers over their heads, adding an extra touch to the rhythm of their dancing feet.
>
> Broken by pauses when we sang, the dancing went on into the wee hours of the morning. (Charette 1976, 44–5)

Goulet highlights the importance of reels and jigs – the tunes associated with fiddling – and the importance of dancing and music making more generally. However, I found this description to be especially remarkable because Goulet includes the possibility of dancing the "Red River Jig" to an "Indian drum," in effect tying its rhythm (the repeated one-beat feel) and its very origin (its "invention") to older forms of Indigenous music; and of course, it situates the emergence of the Red River Jig within Indigenous community gatherings – to cold but joyous evenings in a Métis winter camp.

Though the "Red River Jig" has been tied by scholars to "La grande gigue simple" from Quebec (as noted earlier), the most frequently told Métis stories about the origins of the tune echoes the overall sentiment expressed by Goulet – that it emerged in the Métis Homeland and was central to relationships within Métis and other communities. One version, told by Arnold Asham, describes how it developed in the late 1700s as a way to ensure that fur traders would stop at the Forks (present-day Winnipeg); that is, it developed as a way to improve trade relations. As he noted, the fur traders would "whip down the ice and wouldn't stop in winter. So, the Métis developed these dances and danced by the river. The traders stopped, stayed the weekend and then the week for the festival. People would jig all night" (quoted in Robbins 2009, 3). Crediting Andy Dejarlis with the story, writer Mary Mindess provides the following more detailed story of the emergence of the "Red River Jig":

> The tune was born at the Forks, coaxed from the strings of a fiddle that had been bought with furs.

> Back in the far-off years when the first people settled along the Red – Scots on the west bank, French and Métis on the east – the melody that was to express the heart of old Red River came into being on a sweet spring night.
>
> […]
>
> In the early years, so the story continues, the Scots used to sit by the river on fine evenings and listen to the music of the bagpipes. Often the folk across the water listened, too.
>
> One night a man over on the east bank fingered the bow of his fiddle, then played a cadence slowly, in imitation of the pipes. He listened, then repeated the strain. There was a sadness in the thread of melody, a yearning for home across the waste of seas.
>
> So then – because it was spring and the river was open, because the prairie was wakening into new, green life – he brought his bow down on the strings and swung into a rollicking beat. So infectious was the rhythm that another man nearby began to dance.
>
> And thus, Andy says, the Red River jig was born: that tantalizing melody, with its mild, irrepressible gaiety combined with a haunting undercurrent of sadness. (Mindess 1966, 25)

Though this was printed in 1966, and it is not entirely clear how much Mindess adapted the story from Dejarlis's telling, versions of the story are repeated still to this day with the key features (the river, the bagpipe, and a Métis fiddler) intact across the stories.[14] What strikes me about this story is how it centres place and coming together through music. In this particular version, the importance of dance is also emphasized, just as it is in Goulet's story.

While Goulet and Erasmus share personal stories, the story about the emergence of the "Red River Jig" moves toward the mythical. A number of Métis mythical stories include reference to musical practices – sometimes as a central thread of the story. Two of these stories come from Jeanne Pelletier, a Métis square dance caller, dance instructor, and musician from Crooked Lake, Saskatchewan, shared in a powerful interview with Maria Campbell and Clementine Longworth. Though these stories are Pelletier's original stories, she explained to me that they are, in fact, "half and half" her own, emerging from the traditional stories (the "old stories," as she explains to Campbell and Longworth). She pieced these stories together to create her own stories and then asked her mother to check them for accuracy.

This was very meaningful to Pelletier because her mom – who passed away shortly afterwards – told her that they were perfect (J. Pelletier, interview, 2021). One of these stories recalls the emergence of the Rabbit Dance:

> The one story I have written down there is about a family, a Michif family, and how they used to gather every year to celebrate after harvest and to celebrate the coming of Jesus. And that's where they all got married or found partners for one another, and that's where they told their different stories and traded the different things. Where they come from, they traded [with] one another or, that was the gift giving. And the dances they did, and this old man, he was a very good old jigger, and he went out and he had work to do, like his ordinary chores to do, and he sent his family ahead to go to this celebration. He had to go and pick his traps and come back, and every year he used to show a different jig step. This year he was kind of tired, he didn't want to. He wanted to do something else, but he didn't know what. So, coming home, he learned a new jig step. So that's what he was going to do, and when he got closer to the place, he seen these rabbits and these dogs barking at one another. And then he noticed further down here there was a line of rabbits and a line of dogs, and this rabbit here. And a rabbit by this window, a big window where you could see the people dancing, like the images. And then this rabbit would run to this rabbit and tell him something, and the dog would do the same. And they'd go down here, and these ones were doing exactly what they were being told. It was just like a relay, you know. They're relaying the message of what was happening in this house, and that's how one of the dances were created. Because this old man was watching them, and he couldn't believe his eyes that he seen this dog and these rabbits dancing together. So, when he went, when he, when they were finished, they were all sitting down all happy, and when the music stopped up here, he went to the house and everybody was glad to see him, because that's when the jigging would start because he was a very good jigger. And then he told them that he wasn't going, he, like, they wouldn't believe in him, what he seen happening, and then he said, "Long ago, remember when we were told that the animals used to talk and, and work with one another, and, well, I just seen that." He said, "I seen these rabbits and these, and these dogs, they were dancing, and if you don't believe me,

> I'll show you the dance that they were doing." So that was the start of the rabbit dance. (Pelletier, Longworth, and Campbell 2004)[15]

Pelletier also shares the origins of the "Duck Dance," which is both a dance and tune by the same name. Taken from the same interview, the story of the Duck Dance highlights similar themes:

> This is the origin of the Duck Dance. It has been told generation after generation. There lived this kind and spirited old Métis man everyone called Uncle Louis. He was tall, skinny, and had long hands. When he spoke, he always made gestures. Everyone I grew up with enjoyed the stories he told. To get him to, to start one story, one of his stories, it seems like an eternity. During the month of August on a long and summer hot evening as we sat by the outside, we watched Uncle Louis walking close, slowly by the riverbank. He was coming toward us. As he approached, he began to wave his hands for us to meet him. We met him by the wagon trail between the hills and the river. He was very excited. "Tomorrow morning at 4:30, meet me by the riverbank beside those willows over there." He pointed with his long hands. He pointed with his lips. "I have a good story to tell you young people. I must warn you, be very quiet and patient. In this story it is very, very important with that." Then he left. The following morning was warm and beautiful. The sun was just shining and the birds were chirping as we came near the willow bushes by the river. We saw Uncle Louis. He was motioning us to be quiet. We sat beside him. He pointed with his long fingernails to look toward the river. At first, we couldn't see what he was pointing at. Hidden between the reeds and cattails in the water, we saw many of those ducklings and beautiful drakes and females, their parents. "Pssst," Uncle Louis, Uncle Louis began in a whisper, "Watch quietly and you will see the mallard duck and the female come out of the water," he said. "They will swim forward and backward about three times. The others will follow in straight lines." There were drakes on one line and with little ducklings, females on the other line with little ducklings, too. "Look," Uncle Louis said, "See them splashing their wings? Extending them and, and going quack quack quack, but others will be swimming down the centre under the splashing wings. They always gave turns so gracefully and so respectfully." Suddenly we heard

> a big loud bang. Jumping to his feet, Uncle Louis said, "Look at that duck now, look at the ducks now." They were waving and swimming in circles, which means the formation of the figure eight, and all were gone. To this day, it has been, to this day, this has been the beginning of the Duck Dance. (Pelletier, Longworth, and Campbell 2004)

Both of Pelletier's stories speak to the emergence of new forms of fiddle dance through Métis people's interactions with place and, in particular, their interactions with animals. The stories also speak to sharing teachings with the community and using what one learns from the animal nations to create stronger social bonds.

In a story published by Nicholas Vrooman, Frances Cree of Dunseith, North Dakota, draws on similar themes of place and community, powerfully recounting a story titled "The Fiddle I Give." The story – which is much too long to include here – begins by describing how the French king commands a "lazy guy" who was bragging about knowing where to find a cow whose horns light up, to go and bring back the cow. The lazy guy sets out on this journey, where he meets three (Indigenous) grandmothers, each of whom gives him an item that he will need to be successful on his voyage. The third item is a fiddle:

> By gosh, that evening, he come to another little tipi. Now, this one was a real old lady, real old. She could barely talk. "Ah, grandson, grandson," she says, "come on in, come on in. You must be tired," she said. She fed him and told him, "Now, grandson, tomorrow you're going to hit your journey, tomorrow, you're going to reach your journey. She said, "I'm going to help you. The reason why I'm going to help you, my sisters, you came down and seen them, they all helped you. I'm going to help you. I'm the oldest one of us three girls." She said, "I'm going to give you this little fiddle." She give him a little small fiddle, about that big. Little small miniature fiddle. She said, "I'm going to give you this. Okay, today, when you come to the shore, what your grandma showed you to use, you use that, see." (2006, 36)

What's striking about this aspect of the story is that the fiddle comes from the (Indigenous) grandmother, again pointing to the music as *Indigenous* music. The grandmother then explains how he should use the items provided to him by the grandmothers, including the role the fiddle will play in his success in capturing the cow. This foretelling plays out when he reaches his destination, where he joins a celebration taking place:

> Pretty soon, they ask him to play. My gosh, he took his little fiddle out, told his partner, you stay with me, stay with me here. By gosh, he started just like he was tuning his fiddle, boy that sound just got their attention. When he started playing that music, holy mackerel! Ever hear that kind of music, before? Maybe that was just rock 'n roll. (laughter) Boy, got everybody's attention on this music he was playing. Jiminy Crickets! Everybody flocking in, played quite a few tunes in there, you know.
>
> So then he told his partner, "Say," he said, "take and play this fiddle for me while I go out and relieve myself." This guy said, "I don't know how. Sure you know how, try it." He handed it to him, this guy played. By gosh, boy that guy played just as good as him. Made good music, man, the people start coming in, you know. So he snuck out. From there, he took off. He know the directions already where the cow was, the barn and everything. Surely enough when he got there, there was no guards there, so he opened the door. When he went in there, by gosh, he seen this cow in that manger, his horns were lighting, just like a light both of 'em. (Cree and Vrooman 2006, 37)

The story ends with the man, who is now understood as "not just a lazy guy" (Cree and Vrooman 2006, 39), using the other two items provided by the grandmothers (a stone and a rope) to lead the cow back to the king, who provides him with half of his kingdom.

In the interpretation that follows the story, Cree and Vrooman write:

> This Métis story has mixed origins. It has a basis in French folk tales, but it's more than that. It is uncontrovertibly American Indian in its narrative style and usage. The story has been mixed to serve a new purpose from the European side of its antecedents. It is a story that really tells us of three fundamental changes that occurred in Aboriginal life on the Northern Plains in the late eighteenth century. It is about Indians taking on Euro-American culture, and acquiring it on their own terms, thusly choosing how they become mixed culture people. It is about controlling the forces of change. It is about the Metis receiving cattle into their culture as a symbol and enabler of wealth. And it is a story telling us of the power of that new acquisition in material culture,

> the fiddle, and its relationship to magic and the centrality it holds in Metis culture for ameliorating the distance between what is and possible futures. (2006, 38)

Cree and Vrooman continue their interpretation of the story, noting that it "tells us the Metis took the fiddle and made it better, used it more fully, than even the people from whom it came" (2006, 39). They also note that an important theme of the story is listening to women – the Indigenous side of Métis heritage. In reading this story, I was particularly struck by the way that the story gives grandmothers a role in fiddling, threading women into a history that has generally only paid attention to the role of men. And while it may be easy to interpret this story metaphorically, Cree and Vrooman note that the places referenced in the story are the Red River Colony and Prairie du Chien, Wisconsin, and that the "king" is a Chief Factor. Here, I might add that there are ways to read the connection between women and the fiddle beyond the metaphorical: as central actors in trade, without women, the fiddle could not have found its way into Indigenous communities in the ways that it did.

Both the emergence of tunes from the people and land and the spiritual origins of fiddle dance tunes are clear themes in Maria Campbell's story "La beau sha shoo" (the beautiful song) from her book *Stories of the Road Allowance People*, a story written in such a way as to expresses the rhythm and nuance of the spoken language. Early in the story, Campbell recounts how "Ole Arcand" learned his tunes:

> Well you know
> dis Ole Arcand
> he was one hell of a fiddle player.
> Boy he can play anyting
> an he makes up hees own songs too.
> He always have a good story about how he got dah song.
>
> He say he got one song from dah wind at Batoche
> anudder one
> he say dat his horse he give it to him.
> But one good song he have
> dat was dah bes one of all.
> He call dat one La Beau Sha Shoo. (Campbell 2010, 55)

The story continues noting how, one night, Ole (Jonas) Arcand, floated up to heaven. There, he meets Jesus, who pours him a glass of wine. Jesus and Arcand enjoy the wine together, and Jesus shares his love of the fiddle with Arcand, saying,

> "You know Jonas" dah Jesus say
> "You're a damned good fiddle player.
> Me I always wan to play dah fiddle
> But I never have a chance.
> When da Lucifer he get kicked out
> He take all dah fiddles wit him an all we got now is harps.
> But me Jonas
> I got a hell of a song I been hearing in my head.
> I'll give it to you
> an you learn to play it when you get home."
>
> Ole Arcand he says him and dah Jesus
> dey finish dah wine an dah Jesus
> he make mouth music an teach him dis song.
>
> You know
> Olde Arcand he always stop hees story here
> an he take his fiddle out of dah flour sack
> where he keep him an he would start playing.
> Ooh
> he was a hell of a song!
> He was kinda wile
> full of high stepping an growling
> an we could shore dance to him
>
> An when he finish playing
> He would look at us an say,
> "Yes Sir dah Jesus Chrise he give me dis song."
> He say "Jonas you call dis song La Beau Sha Shoo
> an you play it for all dah peoples when you get home"
> (Campbell 2010, 62–3)

When I first read this remarkable story, I was struck by the way in which it melds learning from animals and the natural world with learning from the spirit world. I was also struck by the call to play "La beau sha shoo" for the people in his community – emphasizing the importance of the social aspect of fiddle dance. In my understanding, it is a story that melds the "natural" world with the spirit world, all in the context of kin and community.

Two-Eyed Seeing for Fiddle Dance (His)Story

> The exercise, then, is not so much to straighten out the "facts," but to understand how different ways of knowing generate distinct analyses of social processes and distinct interpretations of events, each with its grains of truth and its insights into the actors' various outlooks.
> – Brown and Vibert (1996, xix)

As noted at the start of this chapter, fur trade accounts of fiddling – including references to the adoption of European fiddling styles within Indigenous communities – provide insight into cultural exchange and the flow of tunes across the Atlantic and North America. They indicate that the European fiddle arrived in what came to be known as North America by the mid-1600s, and that traders and others working within the industry soon dispersed fiddles across fur trade country. Fiddles quickly became the pre-eminently important instrument within the fur trade and within Métis (and some other Indigenous) spaces. These accounts also indicate that fiddle dance brought people together across the lines of race and class. Reading against the grain (i.e., around or beyond the biases), they hint that the fiddle was shaped by the land (e.g., in the creation of homemade instruments) and that a new dance style emerged. It is these "hints" that become full-fleshed and central aspects of understandings of fiddle dance in Métis storytelling – even in the written form of storytelling provided above, which diminishes the dynamism and relationality of oral storytelling.

The Métis stories about fiddle dance shared in this chapter centre on the importance of social relations and responsibilities enacted through fiddle dance and emphasize musical connections to the land (including its peoples and animals). They furthermore link fiddle dance to the spirit world, an element of music and dance practice that is completely absent in fur trade and other non-Indigenous accounts. These stories (along with a becoming story from Suzanne Steele's new opera, which will be described in chapter seven) thus emphasize Métis fiddle dance music as deeply rooted and of *here* – of the Métis Homeland and of Indigenous territories. Specifically, they create a narrative that centres fiddle dance as a Métis form of musicking (not just a mixed form of musicking[16]) that emerged through Métis practices and worldviews. My aim here is not to question the veracity of histories that trace fiddle dance origins, but rather to pull Métis approaches to sharing about fiddle dance to the forefront, and to show how these stories might better address Métis *thinking about music – or Métis music as thinking*. In this way, I am pointing to what we could learn if we took Métis fiddle dance storytelling as seriously as we take genealogical analyses.

Returning to the concept of Two-Eyed Seeing, the goal of this chapter has been to consider the strengths of both knowledge systems and to allow them to coexist side by side. As historians Jennifer Brown and Elizabeth Vibert write in their introduction to *Reading Beyond Words*, there is no way to pull these "disparate perspectives into a coherent synthesis; nor is that a desirable aim" (1996, xviii). Each approach has value, has strengths, and each tells part of the story, providing a glimpse into the outlooks of the various actors and peoples whose lives come together through fiddle dance. At the same time, Newhouse reminds the academic world in particular (but also the broader public) that "not all stories are given equal time" and that the telling of stories – including, and perhaps especially, academic (his)stories – are entangled in issues of power (Newhouse 2005, 50). And so, it is my hope that the Métis stories shared above are the ones that readers will take with them and that these stories will be brought to the forefront of academic storytelling about Métis fiddle dance.

3

Writing Métis Music in Manitoba Newspapers

> Viewed as a whole and in the absence of an expert ability to disentangle historical fact from fiction, the reportage [in Canadian newspapers] collectively tells us little, certainly nothing accurate, about Aboriginal people *per se*, but it tells us a great deal about Canadiana, that is, the Canadian mainstream imagination, about Canada as an "imagined community," as well as how Canada's newspapers operate ideologically.
> – Anderson and Robertson (2011, 14)

The first section of the previous chapter addressed the recognition of Indigenous fiddle dance in fur trade and travel writing, as well as the interest in Indigenous fiddle dance that emerged within academic circles in the 1980s. This chapter turns to a very different representational context, namely English-language newspaper articles and advertisements published in mostly southern Manitoba between the late nineteenth and early twenty-first centuries. It is based on research made possible through the digitization of thousands of newspapers now available and searchable online through the database, newspaperarchive.com. I looked for references to "Métis music," "Métis song," "Halfbreed music" (since the term "Halfbreed" has been used to describe Anglo-Métis), "Red River Jig," and "Jigging," as well as names of known Métis musicians. As an example of how digitization made the analyses in this chapter possible, a search for "Red River Jig" resulted in well over 1,000 hits from Manitoba newspapers alone. This large number of references allowed me to see patterns in representation emerge. Yet even as it draws on such a large body of items and offers an interpretation, I position this chapter as just one way to read the archive. Indeed, one of the challenges of this work was that representations of Métis people are often inconsistent, perhaps a reflection of their very existence challenging colonial categories of "Indian" or white. Further complicating the interpretive process, I was often struck by what was *not* being said. Many articles required a kind of decoding based on knowledge of both music and Métis histories. Perhaps the clearest example of this is that most of the 1,000 mentions of the Red River Jig did not reference Métis people at all. The interpretive element thus included trying to decipher the erasures – what was left unsaid.

This need to "disentangle" newspaper representations – the stories told in individual articles and through the broader narrative arch – is not surprising, given a long history of Indigenous peoples being misrepresented and stereotyped. As Anderson and Robertson note, reportage "tells us little, certainly nothing accurate" about Indigenous peoples, or in the case here, about Métis musicking (2011, 14). But it does tell us something about the writers and their (perceived) audience. I would further add that monolingual (mis)representations from one region of the Prairies are only part of the story. As such, the analyses offered in this chapter are not meant to be necessarily applicable to representations in other provinces or regions of Manitoba, or in other languages. I would argue, however, that they are valuable *because* of their specificity and emplaced-ness. In particular, they offer considerable insight into the stories that English-speaking, mostly urban Manitobans have told about Métis music, that is, the ways in which they have selectively recognized or erased Métis music within the collective imagination. More pointedly, I observe that representations of Métis music in these papers demonstrate the fickleness and instrumentalization of recognition; in other words, recognition can, and did, easily shift to erasure (it is fickle), and it furthermore can be used for the benefit of non-Indigenous peoples (it can be instrumentalized) rather than to uphold and champion the artistry, value, and contributions of Métis musics and musicians. I begin by considering representations of Métis music in newspaper articles from the late nineteenth and early twentieth-century, focusing first on what I call distancing strategies and then on the euphemizing and erasure of Métis music *as Métis*. I then turn to late twentieth-century reemergence of Métis peoples and the subsequent framing of Métis music within *multicultural* Canada.

"Those Good Days Are Certainly Gone": Tales of a Distant (but Thrilling) Music

When Manitoba joined confederation in 1870, its population was largely Indigenous. Although the number of First Nations people in the area is unknown, out of a documented population of 11,400, about 9,800 residents of the postage stamp province were Métis (Dickason 1992, 263). In the years following confederation, the demographics of the region rapidly shifted, with non-Indigenous people soon vastly exceeding the Métis population. By 1880, Manitoba's population had increased to 66,000, and by 1910, the province was home to 450,000 people.[1] As noted in chapter one, despite the promise of substantial land grants for Métis residents and their children through the scrip system, delays, speculation, and theft meant that few Métis people occupied the lands that the federal government had guaranteed in the *Manitoba Act* (296).[2] In the years that followed, some Métis people left Manitoba, trying to escape the violence and discrimination they faced in Manitoba. Those that remained were quickly overwhelmed by the predominantly white, English, and Protestant settlers (often Anglo-Ontarian immigrants). As such, during this period, Métis people were being literally pushed out of Manitoba, while those that stayed in the province were being pushed out of positions of social and political power. By the early twentieth century, Manitoba's population had shifted from predominantly Métis to predominantly non-Métis.[3]

During this early period of creating Manitoba, English-language newspapers frequently referred to Métis people. Yet they created a sense of separateness between peoples through their approaches to representation and recognition, specifically through what I refer to as temporal, spatial, and fictional distancing.[4] Temporal distancing denotes modes of recognition that place people(s) in the past, far back in time from the contemporary world. Spatial distancing denotes representations that emphasize geographic distance between peoples. And finally, fictional distancing denotes representations in the realm of fiction, or the explicitly not-real – a relegation to fictional worlds that is especially problematic when these representations are presented alongside temporal and spatial distancing. Though these modes acknowledge, or recognize, Métis people, they do so in ways that foreclose on connection and relationship to non-Métis in the here and now. While numerous articles on a variety of topics published in Manitoba newspapers in the early twentieth century point to forms of distancing (see, e.g., *The Gazette* 1906, 3; *Manitoba Morning Free Press* 1899, 9, 14; *The Gazette* 1924, 7), focusing solely on articles that address music, as I do in this chapter, is useful because doing so draws attention to some of the nuances of recognition that may not otherwise be evident.

Temporal distancing is perhaps the most used strategy of creating separation between Métis and non-Métis people during this early period of Manitoba. At the start of the twentieth century, articles printed in Manitoba's newspapers often used Métis music to emphasize a thrilling history interrupted by the perceived arrival of culture and progress. One such article, published in 1899, is titled "The Red River Cart: 'The Race Has Almost Perished.'" This article emphasizes sound and music in striking ways, using it to create a romanticized description of life on the plains. The unnamed author begins by taking the reader back to his[5] childhood in a long and nostalgic introduction that concludes with the author declaring that he is "living in the old past," and that he "feel[s] at home with the old things" (*Manitoba Morning Free Press* 1899, 9). He then notes that "as the old cart is a native of the west it has become a part of myself" (9). The nostalgia for the past runs deep in this article, as is evident in the author's description of the musicality of the cart:

> For many years the cracked voice of the old cart has been singing its weary song with none to listen but the tawny faced master, and an occasional passerby … How often I have wished that some musical genius could have heard the chanting of the cart, and transcribed the music for the good of posterity … One cart has a deep bass voice and another is a fine tenor, one resembles a cathedral organ, another is like a fiddle, and another has the tinkling sound of a pair of brass cymbals. There were none who could interpret the music of the cart so well as the man who kept fellowship with it all over the monotonous plains. Once in a while in a merry mood, a hardy half-breed mounted the vehicle – having caught the key-note – and sang a song of the prairie, like Thespis, who "at country wakes sung ballads from a cart." (9, 14)

The author continues by explicitly suggesting that Métis music, culture, and land might serve as a resource for a great artist, who could "immortalize" and "preserve" an "effete civilization":

> The gypsies of the prairie are the Egyptians of the west, the Metis of other days. The melancholy eye of the men, and the beauty full and fine of the young women lent a charm to their unpoetic life. The romantic habits of these western nomads have not yet been fully described. The world is still waiting for a Liszt to immortalize their music, and a Scott and Barrow to give them their true place in history and poetry. A Metis poet? Yes, there is abundant material for thrilling romance, love songs and a great poem, and there may be sheltered in one of the lodges a sturdy youngster biding his time, who will some day stir our hearts with song and story, and preserve the glorious deeds of the heroes of an effete civilization. What tales these men have told in French, Cree and English, as with careless gait they walked by the cart-brigade across the plains, and at the close of the day, gather in one of the lodges around the cheerful fire, and renewed the thrilling stories of love and war … Look down ye angels upon this prairie scene, worthy the brush of a master artist, a picture which Raphael, Da Vinci or Millet might covet to immortalize on canvas. (14)

The article ends by reinforcing the idea that both the Red River cart and Métis are of the past:

> It might not be an ideal cart, yet the owner was proud of it, as we are all contented with things of our own making, though the artist and skilled mechanic may detect many blemishes. And this is well, for there are needed stages of culture for the man, and stages of perfection for the thing, as there are stages of civilization for nations. The old cart still lingers among us, a relic of other days, and a lost civilization … The city has come, the locomotive is here, and the Red River cart has fled. You may find a stray skeleton, but the race has almost perished. (14)

This representation emphasizes supposed temporal distance, while insisting that Métis culture and ways of life can be an inspiration for high art – presumably for settler creators and a settler audience (since Métis are described as "perished" and the cart *ours*, or "part of myself" [9]).

While this unnamed author uses music and sound somewhat peripherally, critic Charles W. Handscomb's descriptions of two musical performances published in the *Manitoba Free Press* in the early twentieth century are succinct expressions of temporal distancing that focus primarily on music. The first, a review of a performance by the Chicago symphony, is ultimately a declaration of Winnipeg's progress:

> It means something, this great orchestral festival, to those of us who here have labored and waited – to those of us who have seen this Winnipeg grow from a mud-hole to a metropolis, from an unesthetic little hamlet to a populous centre of music and art ... there is in the coming of this celebrated organization a fulfillment of hope, a reward of patient endeavor – a recognition of the attainment of metropolitan status, musically as well as commercially. And though the waiting has been wearisome and the discouragements a many, still as we look back over it all must we not admit that our progress has been remarkable? Why, Winnipeg was born after Theodore Thomas [conductor of the Chicago Symphony] had become famous in artistic maturity – it is scarcely more than two decades from the Red River Jig of the Metis fiddler to the classic Blue Danube waltz [recently performed in Winnipeg] of the world's greatest orchestra. (Handscomb 1903, 1)

Published on the front page of the newspaper, along with other glowing reviews of Chicago's orchestra, the *Manitoba Free Press* editors gave the article prominence of place – marking it as especially noteworthy and ensuring that it would be seen and read by many.

Three years later, Handscomb expressed a similar (and just as fancifully expressed) sentiment in his description of an opera mounted in Winnipeg:

> Wagner opera with eminent soloists, superb orchestra and chorus, elaborate costuming and sumptuous stage mountings! Well, well, how this young town of ours away out here in the wild and woolly west does take on metropolitan airs to be sure. Why there are good people still with us who recall the days when the only music was the weird beating of the Indian's tom-tom and it seems but yesterday that our most classic melodies were those scraped by the Metis fiddler for a Red River Jig. What changes a few fleeting years have brought – how rapidly we have evolved from the wail of the ungreased ox-cart,[6] the plainsman's sing-song and the beaded moccasin to grand opera, special trains, Wagner tone dramas, and swallow-tail coats. (Handscomb 1906, 8)

Handscomb continued noting that the performance was the "most remarkable event of our musical history" (8), explicitly positioning Western art music as a replacement for the "classic [Métis] melodies" of yesteryear and a natural indication of "Winnipeg's material prosperity and musical appreciation" (8). Although this review did not make the front page, it was a featured article illustrated with photos.

While the above articles expressed one person's opinion, other representations from this period similarly positioned Métis music at a temporal distance, taking for granted a belief in the disappearance of Métis music and ways of life. For example, in 1917, an advertisement for the Pantages Theatre in Winnipeg used the "Red River Jig" (a Métis tune and dance that has a long history within Métis communities) to emphasize what used to count as entertainment. With a tagline of "In ye olden days," the advertisement stated, "Winnipeg's public entertainment was limited to an occasional dance – the Red River Jig. Then came the early amateur theatricals at the Princess, the Bijou Opera House and other theatres long since gone. Now-a-days Winnipeg goes 20,000 strong every week to Pantages, The Universal Entertainment" (*The Winnipeg Evening Tribune* 1917, 9). Although this advertisement did not mention the Métis, and it in fact erased Métis people completely (a theme addressed below), like Handscomb's articles, it positioned the "Red River Jig" within a linear progression of Winnipeg's musical and theatrical evolution; furthermore, it is likely that readers at that time would have understood the "Red River Jig" as at least connected to Métis peoples. This advertisement thus created temporal distance between the settler population (of the present) and Métis communities and musical practices (of "ye olden days").

Though representations such as these were common in newspapers at the turn of the twentieth century, so too were representations that emphasized the (supposed) physical distance between Métis people and settlers. This spatial distancing is most evident in quasi-ethnographic articles printed in the early 1900s that report on Indigenous gatherings. The first that I will describe here is a long, detailed account – covering almost three pages of the newspaper – of a Sundance ceremony held in Saskatchewan by a "band of Indians." These "Indians" are depicted as having "eluded the vigilance of the mounted police" and the laws of Canada[7] to partake in a custom "to which the old and grizzled warriors cling" (Benham 1907, 24). Near the end of the account is a section titled "A Strange Anomaly," describing the music and dance of "half breed" participants:

> In another part of the grounds on an improvised platform, the half breeds danced gaily to the strains of a raspy violin played by a dusky musician. Many a ball room dandy might well have envied the step dancing of the light footed, nimble participants in the Red River Jig or favorite quadrilles where dusky belles and beaux balanced under the directions of the master of ceremonies, whose "calling off" recalled the joyful memories of a sugar bush or a barn-raising away back East when the West was young. Every little while over the din, in broken accents would float the familiar "address your partners," "right and left and all grand change,"[8] or "swing your honey." He had all the popular terms and the slang which form half the fun of a square dance. As there was no shade nor covering over the platform, the half-breeds had a sun dance of their own. In close proximity a thrifty "breed" had a refreshment booth where he gave a commendable imitation of a circus barker vending pink lemonade and peanuts, as he pushed his sales amongst the dancers and merrymakers. The picturesque whole was truly a strange and ludicrous mixture of civilization and barbarity. (Benham 1907, 25)

Though this remark in fact tells us nothing about the actual identities of the fiddlers and dancers (that is, they might have identified as First Nations or Métis, or both), it is clear that Métis peoples and culture were being used to tell a particular story: their presence served to highlight perhaps not the death of Métis practices (although they were hardly recognized as Métis practices at all, described as they were as recalling the "joyful memories … away back East"), but the end of "Indian" practices; Métis practices (positioned as happening now but at a distance) were presented as a stepping-stone between the dying culture of "Indians" and the civilizing influence brought by European colonizers. As the article noted in closing: "At sunrise the camp began to break up, each band going their own way, either back to the reserve or taking the homeward trail to Canada or Fort Totten. The offerings lodge was left just as it stood when dancing ceased, not a twig being touched by desecrating hands, for what may be the last sun dance in the history of the Chippewas, if not of the Indian race, was over" (Benham 1907, 25).

The scene described by Benham is strikingly similar to an article written five years earlier depicting a gathering of "Indians" during treaty days at St Peter's Reserve (north of present-day Selkirk, Manitoba, on the shores of the Red River). The unnamed author began by detailing his journey on a boat from Winnipeg to the reserve and the picturesque scene to which he was treated: "The fresh breeze from the lake sweeps up the river, making the sultry sun enjoyable as the steamer threads its way between the forest-clad banks and through the murky waters of the Red, revealing at every turn a landscape of loveliness where every spot is surrounded by a halo of romance of the days of the voyageur and the pioneer" (*Manitoba Morning Free Press* 1902, 24). Like the previous article on the Sundance ceremony, a section of this article titled "A Point of Special Interest," described a dance that took place during the treaty days' celebration:

> Passing down the streets of tents by the busy traders to the centre of the grounds one comes to not the least interesting attraction of the whole – the dancing platform – where the dusky devotees of Terpsichore work off the exuberance of youth. It is partially covered with boughs to protect the "orchestra" from the rays of the sun, but the dancers seem to enjoy the heat, which without exertion, makes the pale face long for an icehouse. A wrinkled old halfbreed, whose white locks curl from under his slouch felt hat and cluster around his face, bronzed by winter snows and summer suns, sat on an old packing case in the corner, dispensing music fast and fearsome from a squeaky old violin which he sawed with an industry worthy of a better cause. His moccasined foot beat ceaselessly on the floor and a continuous smile illumined his countenance, but whether it resulted from the contagion of happiness from the dancers who were tripping through the maze of a quadrille or from the joke he was perpetrating on "The Girl I Left Behind Me,"[9] may never be known. ("Paying Treaty" 1902, 24)

The author continued noting that, "A few moments afterwards the strains of the 'Irish Washerwoman' rent the air and instantly the platform was the scene of phenomenal animation, for the real 'Red River Jig,' danced as only the Metis can dance it, was in fast and furious progress. As a boy I have often watched the buck dances on the plantations of the South, but seldom indeed have I seen the same amount of energy, enthusiasm and perspiration thrown into any form of diversion or dissipation of the kind as those tawny children of the prairie threw into that jig" ("Paying Treaty" 1902, 24). The Métis (or Indigenous people who were represented as Métis) were elevated somewhat in this article (as "dusky devotees of Terpsichore"), but they were nonetheless positioned within the context of a dying remnant of savagery. In true romantic fashion, the author suggested that Europeans had a corrupting and demoralizing effect on the "Indian" and that "Indians" were disappearing quickly, with the younger generation only having a trace of Indian blood.[10]

This article is fascinating for the way in which it emphasized both *spatial* and *temporal* distance. Although St Peter's Reserve was not far from Winnipeg – and perhaps because it was not far – the author made a point of recounting his travels; he created spatial distance between the city and the "Indians" by taking the reader on his journey away from Winnipeg (where so-called civilization had already arrived). He then reversed this process at the end of the article, describing the journey home after the gathering: "We were still watching this interesting spectacle when the coarse whistle of the excursion steamer called us hurriedly on board for the delightful return trip, leaving us all still wondering at the sights we had seen where civilization and the remnants of barbarism commingle" (24). While spatial distance was thus clearly established, the author, somewhat more subtly, also created temporal distance, in this case appealing to the romantic days of yore, that is, the days of the "voyageur and the pioneer." Thus, even as contemporary Métis music was positioned *as Métis* (that is, performed and enjoyed by Métis people), the article emphasized spatial distance and, to a lesser extent, temporal distance between St Peter's and Manitoba's capital city.[11] Two years later, St Peter's Reserve – a community that had had considerable agricultural success (something that is in fact pointed to by the author of this newspaper article) – was moved further north by the government, becoming what is now known as Peguis First Nation.[12] It was, it seems, too close to the city, and too successful, to be tolerated by the growing settler population.

While the two articles described above could be classified as at least partially fiction, based perhaps on half-truths, others from this period were more overtly written as fiction. One example is a story by Alexander D. McLeod titled "A Daughter of the Ranch: A Story of Romance and Adventure of Western Pioneer Days." Published in 1924 in numerous Manitoba papers,[13] this fictionalization of early Anglo/Indigenous/Métis/French relations is particularly adept at representing a "thrilling" Métis past,[14] focusing on a budding romance between Mary, a young, (presumably) white woman[15] and her suitor. A substantial part of the narrative takes place during a "shindig" held in Mary's honour. The "shindig" begins as a gathering of the region's English-speaking inhabitants, but soon includes "Indians" and five half-breeds or French Canadians (the author does not distinguish between the two) who are travelling through the area. The story describes the half-breed/French men attracting "unusual attention" by demonstrating dances unknown to the guests. Before long, they begin an impromptu "Red River Jig" competition. The author describes how Joe, "feeling the intoxication of the dance … was not quite satisfied" and, desiring more, said to his companion, Napoleon Dore: "Poleon by tonaire, I beat you on de Red Reever jeeg, ah?" Dore, quick to agree to the competition, states, "Ba gosh, Joe la Tour, I tak' you on dad sure, me." With these words, a "Red River Jig" competition begins as spectators watch, "some in silent admiration; some keeping time with their toes; and some with the clapping of the hands" (McLeod 1924, 6).

The story's use of language, in particular the "Indians'" complete lack of language and the thick accent that distinguishes the French/Métis men from the English attendees, creates a chasm between white settlers and the Indigenous other. Furthermore, the description of the "Red River Jig" competition positions the Métis (and "Indians") as colourful additives, the thrilling part of an otherwise dull history. As McLeod writes, the contestants, "quickly responded to the rhythmic motions indicated by the time and tune. Arms swinging, hands twitching kept time with the rapid motions of the feet. Faster and faster the time increased, faster and faster the feet moved in unison as they cut small circles in the centre of the floor. 'Plus fort! Jean, Plus fort!' shouts la Tour. Quickly in response, the time gained speed, and the feet kept time. On, on the furious pace kept on without sign of relaxation … Though drops of perspiration trickled from the brows of the nimble contestants" (6). McLeod continues by describing the guests taking all of this in, watching with interest as the competition unfolds. Most telling is that only the "Indians" are pulled down to the French/Métis men's level of supposed wildness. As the author notes, "Even the squaws,[16] swaying to the intoxication and held in the grip of the exciting contest, first beat time and, finally, yielding to the call of their own wild music, gave way to a droning refrain that intensified in pitch as the music and the contest continued" (6).[17]

The tone of the story changes significantly once the competition ends and the instrument played by the (presumably) white fiddler[18] is "put into commission" for a waltz (McLeod 1924, 6). A sudden shift in imagery demarcates the relationship between the Métis and settler attendees, and thus points to the reason why Métis characters were included: "This was the first waltz Ronald and Mary had during the evening. All at once they seemed to be the centre of attraction as they gracefully glided in and out among the dozen or more couples now occupying the floor. Both were good dancers. Ronald, tall and athletic, guided his graceful partner through the maze of other dancers with the skill and grace required with much practice" (6). The stark contrast between the athleticism, grace, and skill of the non-Indigenous couple and the somewhat wild dances of the Frenchmen/half-breeds is telling. It is clear that the exoticized others are simply a thrilling diversion. Thus, when Ronald and Mary became not the centre of "unusual attention" as described by McLeod in reference to the Métis but the "centre of *attraction*," they became representatives of an ideal "civilized" culture (cf., the civ/sav dichotomy described in LaRocque 2010, 37). Although the guests are enthralled by the "exotic" performance of the Métis/French men, the exotic otherness is contained through the fictional genre and historical setting, and thus does not pose a threat to contemporary life.

It is evident in all of these accounts that Métis music and people were understood as having no place in the present or future, and no place in so-called "civilization." It is fitting, then, to end this section with one last excerpt, this one from an article published in 1903 in the *Winnipeg Daily Tribune*. The article quotes W.G. Fonseca, referred to as "Winnipeg's grand old man, who remembers those happy days [thirty years ago] quite clearly" (3). Apparently quoting him verbatim, the article shares his description of Christmas celebrations in the Red River Settlement:

> After mass they would depart in companies, and then the revelry started and lasted often for three and four days. The company would gather in the largest house and the whiskey and other luxuries would be opened and feasting would be in order till all were satisfied. Then the dancing would be started. I suppose you have heard of the Red River jig? No! Then it is impossible to explain it. You must see it to realize what it is. With the fiddles going and the moccasined feet moving, this dance was continued for hours and hours. When one dancer tired another took his place. Those good days are certainly gone. (*The Winnipeg Daily Tribune* 1903, 3)

Most remarkable is that even as proclamations such as these were being published, Manitoba's newspapers continued to report on contemporary Métis music, although it was rarely written about *as Métis music*. Articles such as this and those described earlier instrumentalized recognition to create a thrilling past while creating distance between Métis music and contemporary urban centres; yet many Métis people living in urban areas like Winnipeg could and did still dance and play Métis music. This erasure of Métis music is taken up below.

Euphemizing and Erasing Métis People and Music

> Backward, turn backward, for thoughts to my song.
> Make me to cherish those days that are gone.
> Memory turn back through the years that have flown –
> To those good old days of old. We Old Timers have known.
> […]
> Turn back to those days of our soft Indian shoes.
> Our twice-yearly mail and six-month old news.
> Our fresh meat, how scarce, when the buffalo were far.
> Though whitefish and rabbits were still at the door.
> Our pemmican, "richeau"[19] was grub good enough.
> […]
> In those old-fashioned days, We Old Timers recall.
> – Poem titled "Song of the Old Timer" (*Edmonton Daily Bulletin* 1911)

> There are a handful of words used to describe Goulet men in these newspapers that are like codes. They call the Goulet men descendants of the voyageurs. They call them pioneers or fans of the old-time fiddling and jigging. Sometimes they call them French-Canadian.
> – Michelle Porter (2020, 69)

The newspaper articles described in the first part of this chapter used Métis music to create an image of Métis people that served the needs of newcomers – marking a divide between then and now, here and there, real and fictional, and ultimately positioning Métis as incompatible with modern, urban, real life; in effect, these representations served to contain Métis music within certain places, times, and contexts. Hand in hand with this process of distancing, early twentieth-century newspapers wrote about Métis musical practices without referring to them as Métis; or else by euphemizing these practices with code words like pioneers, as noted by geographer and creative writer Michelle Porter (Métis), or as I have found, old-timers. This erasing and euphemizing were especially notable in contexts where distancing was not possible (e.g., when describing an event in a place with a large settler population). Although this is evident even in Manitoba's earliest publications, erasure and euphemizing became an increasingly common practice by the 1920s, at which point mainstream newspapers rarely referred to Métis music as Métis music at all.

The erasure of Métis music and musicians was most often subtle, and a reparative retelling of Métis presence usually requires reading between the lines (or against the grain, as Podruchny [2006, 7–8] suggests), applying knowledge of Métis music, history, community, and kin to understand what was left out. However, to illustrate, it is valuable to begin with a striking and unapologetic example of erasure found in an article on the Calgary Folk Festival published in 1930 in the *Manitoba Free Press*. The article mentions a group of "half-breed" dancers (possibly Joseph Dion's group described in more detail by Quick [2009, 145–6; forthcoming 165–73]) from St Paul de Métis[20] who were performing at the festival. Before describing the dances and dancers, the author quotes the performers who exclaim: "We are not French-Canadians. We are of French and Indian blood" (*Manitoba Free Press* 1930b, 13). Yet the article's author then continues, noting:

> These old dances are a fascinating study, as these willow-swaying women and lithe men take steps from Louis' court and in some way touch them with the tom-tom of the wigwam. Pure French, that face. Brush out and curl his hair, put ruffles at his wrists and buckled shoe for his moccasins, and the ancestral painting will have stepped from its frame. That girl, too – she who goes through the Red River jig on her toes – she is French. She flutters a handkerchief with the coquetry that was never born in a tepee. This is Canada. Western Canada. ("The Folk Song-Folk Dance Festival!" 1930, 13)

Although the dance may have been "touched" by Indian music, the reporter ultimately denies the dancers their Métis identity, claiming that the dances are French and that the dancers are performing Western Canadian culture.

The explicit erasure of Métis culture and people as *Métis* seen in this article is an example of a generally more difficult to notice approach to representation whereby settlers reframed the traditional practices of Métis people as pioneer, or old-timer, practices. For example, an article printed in

1911 in the *Manitoba Free Press* reported on an annual ball hosted by the Old-Timers' Association at the very posh Royal Alexandra Hotel in Winnipeg.[21] The author noted that:

> Formality was sloughed … and a glee and abandon rare in anything so conventional as a ball marked the gathering together in silk and broadcloth of those who had in ruder garments wrestled for the beginning of fortune, before the west had come into its own. The dance programme was shrewdly arranged; and, so that those who had come in state and with reserve to the function would not be jarred by the sudden obtrusion of jig and fandango, way was made by the easy foundation of waltz and cotillion to the climax of the fiddler and the Red River Jig. (*Manitoba Free Press* 1911, 9)

The article further indicated that Fred Genthon fiddled for the "Red River Jig," and that some of the guests had a "ruddy tan" suggesting that they were "guests from the country." Though not referred to as Métis in the article, Genthon was a Métis fiddler, with deep routes in the Métis Homeland.[22] He was, furthermore, one of the first fiddlers to record the "Red River Jig" (in 1940).[23] Clearly, Métis music was an important part of the Ball, and Métis people attended the event. And, while readers of the *Manitoba Free Press* may have at the time understood that these attendees were Métis, the impulse to erase Métis presence is strong, and it is a common thread found in reporting on these annual Balls.

The first Old-Timers' Ball took place in 1903, prior to the opening of the Royal Alexandra, where it would eventually become a keynote event. The Old-Timer's Balls created explicit ties between the present and past by making space for the embodiment of the music and dance practices of the Red River Settlement as they (may have) existed prior to the significant influx of newcomers. Focusing on the Ball of 1912, historian Jim Blanchard notes that the event was organized by the wives of Manitoba's political leaders along with "other women organizers [who] were not from the upper crust" but nonetheless respected because of their husbands' roles in "crush[ing] the rebel Riel" (Blanchard 2005, 255). As such, Blanchard suggests that the Ball "united people from different social levels in the common activity of commemorating the city's history, as seen through the eyes of the English Ontarians who had driven Riel out and assumed a dominant role in Manitoba" (2005, 256). Blanchard further proposes that "the ball seemed to make the history of the Red River settlement part of the Ontario immigrants' own history" (256), a process that Blanchard ties to historian Lyle Dick's notion of Anglo-Canadian newcomers claiming the Selkirk settlers as "imagined ancestors" as a way to justify their dominance in the area (Dick 1994, 69). Blanchard is likely correct in his assessment of *why* the so-called old-timers (i.e., newcomers) organized the Balls. As argued earlier in this chapter, Métis history and music were often used to create a thrilling history *for settlers.*

Yet, in writing a history of the Old-Timer's Ball, Blanchard makes the same mistake as reporters writing for mainstream newspapers in the early twentieth century, erasing Métis presence. Indeed, Blanchard's description of the Ball of 1912 makes no mention of Métis performers or attendees and can be read as explicitly excluding Métis given that the organizers are described as *antagonistic* to Métis. He does note that the evening dances included lancers and quadrilles, followed by "a mixture of Scottish dancing and local dances – the Red River jig, Highland Schottische, and eight hand reels" (Blanchard 2005, 256). Perhaps "local dances" is meant to indicate Métis dances, and he does of course note that the "Red River Jig" was performed, but again, there is no explicit mention of Métis presence. Blanchard furthermore does not mention that a fiddler was present (though this can perhaps be assumed given the music performed). Rather, he refers only to the Band of the 100th Grenadiers supplying the "program of twenty dances that were strictly 'old time' variety" (256). This is in direct contrast to a newspaper article printed the day after the Ball, which referenced dancing to "the music of a pioneer fiddler" (*Manitoba Free Press* 1912, 9). While I use Blanchard's writing to highlight this issue, this critique is not meant to place undue blame on his work; rather, Blanchard's work makes it clear that erasing Métis presence is deeply embedded in how we understand and write about Winnipeg's history. Blanchard simply did not question this erasure.

This is perhaps because, in most cases, the Métis-ness of people, tunes, and events is more difficult to uncover than in the article that refers to Genthon – who is widely remembered as a Métis fiddler. An article titled "The Old-Timers' Ball: A Glimpse into the Good Old Times of Yore," printed in the *Winnipeg Tribune* (1911), provides an example of the kind of work that would need to be done to understand the extent of Métis presence at the Old Timers' Balls. Describing events of a 1911 Ball, an unnamed reporter offers the following details:

> Needless to say, the programme of dances was thoroughly enjoyed by all and when it was whispered about that the Red River Jig was about to be danced, the great company thronged the big hall and formed a circle so as to get a good view of the performers. William Isbister, a real old Red River settlement fiddler, sitting on a stool, clad in a smock and devoid of collar, etc., struck up the familiar old jig tune which for half a century or more in the early days was wont to warm the cockles of the early settlers and start the crowd dancing with more vigor and animation. The scene last night brought back those prime occasions twenty or thirty years ago when John Norquay, Jack McBeth, Jack McTavish, Sam Bedson and a score more kindred spirits used to enter the ring and dance to their hearts content. (1911, 9)

It is possible that William Isbister was Métis, though that is difficult to determine without more information as there were several people with this name living in the early twentieth century and only some were Métis; certainly, he would have learned to fiddle in contexts where there were many Métis fiddlers. Whatever the case, the article appeals to the *past* dance practices of Métis through a reference to John Norquay, Manitoba's fifth premier, who was from a "half-breed" (Anglo-Métis) family.

As suggested in the name "Old-Timers' Ball" and made explicit in the poem included at the start of this section ("Song of the Old-Timer"), the term "old-timer" was, at times, a euphemism for Métis. An article published in 1924 describes different types of old-timers, specifically some from Ontario and others from the Prairies, pointing to some ambiguity in how the term was used:

> We weren't sure where the old-timers' ball was being held at the Royal Alexandra hotel last night but as we reached the second floor we noticed two men with the longest and finest whiskers in the world having a conversation, so straightway we handed in our coat and hat because we knew that we had arrived. There could be no doubt about it after a look at those whiskers that pushed themselves off into space; one set long and fine and reflective of the older and more polished culture of Ontario; the other strong and thick and bushy, home grown on the Manitoba prairies. (*Manitoba Free Press* 1924, 1)

As the article continues, it plays on the same trope of temporal distancing discussed earlier in this chapter, noting that "the rude forefathers of the hamlet that once danced the Red River Jig in cowhide moccasins and homespun suits and with countenances that gave Mr. Gillette, the razor man, his great inspiration have taken on quite a polish" (1). Like other articles about the Old-Timers' Balls, it is not clear whether there were, in fact, Métis attendees. Of note, however, is that while some of the music was supplied by an orchestra, the orchestra was supplemented by a fiddler described as quickly becoming the main act of the evening:

> The fiddler, Mr. A. Franks from Selkirk, takes his place on the chair at the centre of the room. He tunes a string and lets her go. The audience gathers around and sways to the quick jig time of the strings. Two dancers step into the circle ... the fiddle chases the years into the corner and vibrant youth slip in and sets the feet going. Winnipeg is again Fort Garry. Another couple cuts in, then another. These steps that have helped to rear a nation are not to be forgotten. There are cheers; the fiddler is right smart with his bow and his timing foot ... Mr. Wheilans, of East Kildonan, and a sprightly partner exemplify the fine points of the jig ... Mr. Wheilans is for doing away with the orchestra and keeping the fiddler altogether. (1)

It is almost certain that there was some Métis music and dance at the event in 1924; at the very least, settlers were imitating Métis music. Whether there were Métis participants at the 1924 Ball is more difficult to determine. Yet given other examples of erasure and the reality that many Métis people lived in Winnipeg (contributing extensively to fiddle culture, as described in the next chapter), it is likely that at least some of the participants were Métis, though they perhaps felt compelled to hide, or not speak about, their identity.

While the articles addressed above have focused on the Old Timers' Balls, they all also centre on one particularly noteworthy tune: the "Red River Jig." The "Red River Jig" was frequently mentioned in newspapers throughout the century; as noted earlier, I found well over a thousand references from Manitoba alone, with the greatest number of references from the 1940s and 1950s when it was often part of old-time fiddle competitions. Yet, other than a few instances described in the first section of this chapter, the tune was typically not explicitly tied to Métis culture or musicians, even though the musicians named as performers were often Métis. Reportage on the "Red River Jig" thus provides a significant example of the erasure of Métis music. During this period, fiddle and jig champion, Jellicoe LaFrenière, was especially well-represented, and his popularity was often a point of emphasis. In one article about the Manitoba Championships, LaFrenière was described as "the most popular entertainer of the night," regaling the audience with the "Red River Jig" (*The Manitoba Leader* 1948, 1). In an article from 1950, a reporter for *The Manitoba Leader* noted that LaFrenière created a buzz in the crowd:

> Many of the people in the audience were heard to remark at various times, 'When is Jellicoe going to do the jig?' When Mr. LaFrenière favored them with the Red River Jig halfway through the program they weren't disappointed. A master of this style of dancing, he is the present Manitoba champion. An even greater surprise was in store, however, when his two young children, Gary and Gwen, later appeared themselves and teamed up on the jig. They were the only performers the crowd insisted appear for an encore. (*The Manitoba Leader* 1950, 1)

Although others played and danced the "Red River Jig" for showcased performances at the 1948 and 1950 competitions, the praise showered on LaFrenière was unparalleled. None of the articles on LaFrenière indicate that he was Métis.

Given the large crowds (from 1,000 to 3,000 attendees in the late 1940s and early '50s),[24] the status of the competition as the provincial championship, and the overwhelmingly positive response, the "Red River Jig" had clearly become an important part of fiddle culture in Manitoba at the time. It served as a regional anthem that marked Manitoba's unique old-time scene. This importance is evident given the wide array of events that featured the tune and dance. In addition to fiddle and jigging contests, it was heard and seen at old-time dances, pioneer and heritage celebrations (including old-timer picnics), during movie showings, at Lord Selkirk Association of Rupert's Land gatherings, at a meeting of the Scottish Amateur Athletic association, at an event held to celebrate the Westminster Act, at historical pageants, and on live radio.[25] It was, furthermore, included on a Victor Company recording in 1930 ("Victor Company Records Pioneer's Red River Jig" 1930, 25), and again in a recording of Frédéric Genthon made in 1940 by CJRC radio in Winnipeg (see Johnson 2012, 91). In the 1930s, one dance company even advertised instruction in the "Red River Jig," claiming that it was a dance that "we all should know" (*Manitoba Free Press* 1930a, 31; also see *Winnipeg Free Press* 1935, 19; and *Winnipeg Tribune* 1906, 12). In none of these cases was the "Red River Jig" referred to as Métis. And in the case of the first recording of the tune, the performer – Métis fiddler, Robert Léon "Bob" Goulet – is not even named, much less named as a Métis fiddler. In another case, the fiddler (Andy Dejarlis)[26] is referred to as "French Canadian" (*The Manitoba Leader* 1952b, 6).

It is striking that the "Red River Jig" and the fiddlers who played it were not identified as Métis, especially given that the tune is now understood as an unofficial Métis anthem. As noted in chapter one, this period – from the late nineteenth to late twentieth century – was a time when some Métis, if they were able, "passed" as white as a means of survival. It is therefore unclear whether the general public, and the reporters writing about these events, understood that fiddlers like Dejarlis and Goulet were Métis. It is similarly uncertain if the fiddlers themselves were open about their Métis identity within these spaces. Certainly, Dejarlis did not completely hide his identity, at least by the 1970s (a couple of decades after these articles were written) when he was donating some of his earnings to the Winnipeg Friendship Centre (Watson 2002, 48). Writing about her great-grandfather, Bob Goulet, Michelle Porter furthermore suggests that, for some, doing so would be impossible. As she notes (writing in the form of a letter to her great-grandfather): "In the 1930s in Manitoba when you were performing with the Red River Echoes, the word Métis was a dirty word. Your family was so well-known that you couldn't escape the meaning of your last name, not in Manitoba. To hold the last name Goulet and to be the son of Maxime Goulet in that province and in those years was to be Métis in a way that carried you along like a fast-moving river … most everyone in Manitoba knew who you belonged to" (2020, 26). Later in the same book, she writes:

> Growing up I always heard how
> Pepé, Robert Léon Goulet,
> Wanted to protect his daughters
> From what it meant to be Métis
> In Manitoba in the 1930s.
>
> That's why they all moved to British Columbia. (95)

Perhaps not everyone knew that Genthon, Goulet, LaFrenière, Dejarlis, and other popular Manitoba fiddlers were Métis. But it also seems likely that they could not have been completely ignorant of this reality. Perhaps mainstream Manitoba, with its flourishing 1940s and '50s fiddle scene, was not willing to celebrate a *Métis* fiddler as Manitoba's fiddle champion – perhaps it was unspeakable (to some). Likewise, perhaps a tune that was heard at so many events well into the 1950s – a tune that should have signalled continued Métis presence, and certainly did to many Métis people – could not be recognized by the mainstream press as Métis for this very reason: it would have shattered illusions of the (only) fictional or temporally and spatially distant Métis. The "Red River Jig" and Métis music were thus represented as pioneer or old-timer music – music that reflected Manitoba's unique past and the spirit of its early immigrants, the "flavor [and thrill] of the old West" (*The Manitoba Leader* 1950, 1).

Re-emergence, Recognition, and Manitoba's Unique Heritage

> Although the Red River Jig may diminish in popularity, this unique Manitoba dance will remain an important part of our province's heritage.
> – David Bolton (1961, n.p.)

> The term "heritage" is both celebratory and strategically vague: "heritage" brings a dignified ring to non-specific notions of family, traditional food, dance and costume and, by implication, sanctions these non-controversial elements of the past as the substance of any given culture. Because "heritage" carries a positive and more specifically cultural connotation than the other lexemes excluded from the [contemporary discourse of multiculturalism], it represents a safer, less overtly political choice … "Heritage" can render the past slightly out of focus, sepia-toned, honey-coated, safely out of the realm of controversy.
> – Rachel Nash (2001, 122)

Though contemporary Métis presence was rarely acknowledged in early to mid-twentieth-century newspapers, change began in the 1960s as new kinds of Indigenous political and cultural organizations emerged (Quick 2009,

154–61; 2008, 82–5). For example, the Winnipeg Friendship Centre opened in 1959, providing space for urban Indigenous people to gather; both Métis and First Nations musicians were an important presence at the Centre from its earliest days. Although Métis have always gathered politically,[27] the formation of the Manitoba Métis Federation (MMF) in 1967 had a significant impact on cultural life.[28] Within six years of incorporation, the MMF began hosting Metis Days celebrations.[29] An MMF-sponsored event is first mentioned in 1973, in an article printed on the first page of both the *Dauphin Herald* and the *Swan Valley Star and Times*. The article noted that Camperville (in conjunction with the MMF) was to host a cultural event and that it was the "first of its kind in Manitoba" (*Swan Valley Star and Times* 1973, 1). Organizers hoped to make it an annual affair and indicated that it was a way to expose non-Métis to Métis culture, while bringing Métis people together to "meet and participate on a sociocultural basis" (1). The event included a fish banquet, jigging and fiddling, talent contests, sports events, and an artifact display provided by the Manitoba Museum of Man and Nature. Events such as these continued to grow, especially post-1982, when Métis were officially recognized as an Indigenous people; many of these events had government funding because, as Andersen notes, recognition carries both symbolic and material resources (2014, 176).

By the 1990s and 2000s, Manitoba's newspapers were including stories on a range of Métis gatherings. These included articles on Métis festivals like those referenced above, as well as settler-centred events that included Métis components (e.g., a Canada Day event).[30] While some of these articles focused on the preservation of Métis culture, others described their importance for expressing and restoring Métis pride (e.g., see Goranson 1990, 24, and Villeneuve 2006b, 7); and, of course, some emphasized both elements as dual aspects of Métis cultural events. In addition to being more abundant, these articles are markedly different from earlier references, emphasizing contemporary Métis presence and Métis modernity. One even described a Métis Days mud bogging competition where a mud pit was created to race ATVs (Goranson 1994, 12). This proliferation of public-facing events in the '90s and 2000s emerged from the hard work of Métis organizations, communities, and individuals in the late twentieth century; they marked the re-emergence and growing strength of the Métis Nation.[31] At the same time, the publication of newspaper articles about these events reflected settlers' new willingness to acknowledge Métis presence (or else they would not have been published). More importantly, they made the settler public aware that Métis culture was alive; that Métis people and ways of being were present in the modern world; that Métis people were teaching their traditions to their children; and that Métis people were moving from the deep shame (the "cultural closet") that had been imposed on them post-1885 to a renewed, and publicly expressed, pride in their culture.

This new (settler) recognition of living Métis musical practices opened the door for discussion about the place of Métis in Manitoba and a renegotiation of Métis/settler relations. This discourse is explicitly evident in an article printed in the *Winnipeg Free Press* detailing claims by some Métis performers that they were underrepresented at the Festival du Voyageur (Thompson 1986, 22). In it, Métis musician Ed Desjarlais notes that Métis are direct descendants of the voyageurs, the very people the festival is intended to celebrate. Louis Paquin, the festival's performance coordinator, responded to Desjarlais's comment in the same article, arguing that Métis musicians (such as Reg Bouvette) have participated in significant numbers; that most of the jigging and fiddling contest participants are Métis; and that, while the festival does not have a policy regarding the inclusion of Métis acts, the role of both "Native" and Métis musicians "has been given more thought recently" (22). By 1990, "native and Metis tents" had been added to the Festival du Voyageur, including a tent for souvenirs and a tent for music and dance described as adding a touch of flair. As journalist Stephen Ostick noted, "If being unique is a prerequisite for addition to the Festival du Voyageur, then the native and Metis tents at The Forks qualify with flying colours" (1990, 15). The inclusion of these tents at a French festival – one that has since been increasingly represented as a French/Métis festival – points to a reimagining of the place of Métis and other Indigenous people(s) at the Festival and, more generally, within Manitoba in the 1990s.[32]

This recognition is closely linked to the broader multicultural turn. By the late twentieth century, a growing number of articles reported on multicultural events that included Métis music. In 1982, a journalist reporting on the Winnipeg Folk Festival noted that the festival would include "special features devoted to ethnic and traditional songs and genres" and that the "flavors" included a program of "early Canadian and Métis music" (McIlroy 1982, 27). An article from the mid-1980s noted that Folklorama – an annual multicultural event in Winnipeg – was adding a Métis pavilion. Articles about the Métis pavilion at the Brandon, Manitoba, multicultural festival began to appear in the 2000s (Villeneuve 2006a, 39; Whiteway 1985, 17). In 2001, the *Winnipeg Free Press* printed an article about Back to Batoche Days, held in Saskatchewan. Although it is a Métis-run and largely Métis-attended festival, the article used it to emphasize Saskatchewan's multicultural heritage; that is, the reporter understood and wrote about it within a multicultural frame (*Winnipeg Free Press* 2001a, 30). A few years later, an article described a school program that involved pre-Juno award funding for schools which was intended to allow students to "celebrate various cultures by performing French songs, studying jazz, playing traditional drums from Africa and South America, writing an original song in French and performing Métis fiddle and dance music" (Lemieux 2005, 7A). By the turn of the twenty-first century, Métis music was increasingly accepted as part of the multicultural mosaic, integrated into the changing *Canadian* cultural landscape.

Through this multicultural turn, Métis music had become Manitoba/Prairie *heritage*, part of the region's unique but "non-specific" cultural mosaic. As evident in the article about the school program noted above, one of the features of many heritage performances is an aspect of play or dress up. This element was clear in an article on the Winnipeg-based group the "Forty Fiddling Fanatics."[33] The article noted that the young fiddlers (ages nine to thirteen) "specialize in Metis, French-Canadian, and old-time dance tunes" (Walker 1998, 5). "They are," the article continued, "so malleable, they can be bent from Metis fiddling to Celtic fiddling in the twist of a bow." And, as one group member declared, "We take off our sashes and put on our tartan hats." Reflecting on his love of dance music, this same group member also suggested that this "is perhaps unusual for a Mennonite" (quoted in Walker 1998, 5). An advertisement for the group's performance at the Festival du Voyageur in 2001 further confirmed this supposed ability to switch between styles, indicating that they would be performing French Canadian and Métis music (*Winnipeg Free Press* 2001b).[34] Though I do not wish to downplay the positive impact of recognition for those who now see their traditions featured on stages, the flipside is that Métis music can become – and did become, as I argue in the next two chapters – separated from Métis peoples: the multicultural turn framed Métis music not as something that Métis people do in and with community, but as a product or object. As a product, it can, and has in some contexts, become about "enriching" events for non-Indigenous people (see, e.g., Ostick 1990; cf. Robinson 2020, 6).

Representing and Recognizing Métis Music

As Anderson and Robertson write (2011, 14), articles from mainstream newspapers tell us little about Indigenous peoples. They are, nonetheless, a window into the Canadian mainstream imagination and the stories that we tell as Canadians. Read in this case with an eye to acknowledging the continuing presence of Métis in Manitoba, they tell us a great deal about recognition as a representational strategy. Though representations of Métis people were often inconsistent, I observed an instrumentalization of Métis music: that is, recognition and nonrecognition of Métis music *as Métis* were used strategically, reinforcing narratives of separation and distance, disappearance/erasure, and then, by the late twentieth century, multicultural Canada. At the time that Manitoba became a new province, many non-Indigenous residents remembered when Métis had a visible and majority presence in the region – and indeed had political, economic, and social power. To manage this continued, undeniable presence and power, or at least the memory of this presence and power (because it could not be ignored), Métis music was recognized, but it was recognized in ways that furthered colonial narratives. Specifically, representations of Métis music, fiddlers, and dancers were used to add colour to settler history, and to create an identity for settlers, while bolstering the belief that so-called civilization was replacing – and was destined to replace – Indigenous cultures. In contexts where distance could not be maintained (e.g., in articles that described events in Winnipeg) and as the memory of Métis power in the region faded, Métis music and musicians were simply erased *as Métis*. Rather than managing representations of Métis music, erasure signaled a *fait accompli* of colonial replacement; nonrecognition became more valuable to settlers than recognition. This erasure and nonrecognition occurred even as Métis musicians remained popular performers. In fact, Métis fiddlers, many mentioned above, remained mainstream performers in Winnipeg through much of the twentieth century.

By the 1960s, Métis began to re-emerge politically, socially, and culturally, regaining some power as Métis peoples and more openly expressing pride in Métis identity. In response, public discourse on Métis music began to shift with many articles once again recognizing Métis music, dance, and culture *as Métis.* Métis could no longer be ignored. A growing number of reporters began writing about Métis-run and largely Métis-attended cultural events, many of which took place in Métis communities and were led by Métis political organizations such as the Manitoba Metis Federation.

These articles made it clear that Métis peoples had not disappeared, and that Métis culture was being passed on to Métis children. Yet they also typically represented Métis music within a multicultural frame, in effect establishing Métis music as something that could be put on or taken off along with other cultural expressions – like a tartan hat or sash. That is, late twentieth- and early twenty-first-century newspaper representations picked up on a more than one hundred-year-old thread whereby Métis music was used to create settler identity. Just as early representations can be understood as a way to address the still-present-but-fading power of Métis at the end of the nineteenth century, modern representations might be understood as a way that Manitobans responded to, or "dealt with," Métis reemergence. Celebrating and appropriating Métis music, as part of a multicultural playground, for all of Manitoba (and perhaps all of Canada) is one way to (attempt to) take away its power for and to Métis communities; it is a "multicultural solution to the settlers' Indian problem" (Simpson 2014, 20). This notion of instrumentalization and, more specifically, multicultural containment is taken up in the next chapter, alongside a discussion of Métis fiddlers as mainstream musicians.

4

Exchange, Multicultural Compartmentalization, and the New Old-Time Style

> Most models for cultural exchange assume a process of acculturation, where an unequal balance in diffusion, or trait exchange, transforms both groups, one more than the other. I think that Indigenous protocols for song exchange provide a different model, one of reciprocity among and between groups that are situationally positioned as Others, in relational, instead of componential, terms. The consequence isn't necessarily replacement. Colonizers saw the "old" ways to be "dying" ways, and many attempted to speed up what they saw as a natural process of the loss of tradition while others sought to document it. An Indigenous outlook isn't zero-sum. Since early contact, Indigenous people have been incorporating musics that originated in White and Black settler societies into their own practice, including Christian, folk, popular, and art music. The music of the newcomers became involved through a process of musical reciprocity and exchange that have been going on since time immemorial. Vast amounts of traditional knowledge and music(s) have been lost, of course, but Indigenous people see that as the consequence of genocide and forced assimilation, not as an inevitable consequence of adding to a cultural repertoire.
>
> – Carl Urion, Métis scholar (2022, 24–5)

In his essay on the implication of some Cree precepts on music, Métis scholar Carl Urion notes that Indigenous peoples have, for thousands of years, been part of processes of musical and cultural exchange; rather than eliminating Indigenous cultural repertoire, exchange has been used to maintain distinct traditions *and* generate new expressions of creativity. As Urion notes, "the exchanges and reciprocal relationships among the diverse groups drive not just change, but continuity" (2022, 25). When the fiddle arrived in what is now Canada, it became part of this long history of exchange and reciprocal relationship, a part of the continent's soundscapes (see Wilkins 2013; Titus 2011; Mishler 1993 and 1974; Lederman 1988). It became part of an *Indigenous* soundscape. This chapter addresses a specific aspect and period of this musical exchange: twentieth-century fiddling within what are now known as Manitoba and Canada. In particular, I focus on the Canadian old-time style[1] that emerged in the twentieth century as a result of cross-style, cross-genre, and cross-cultural exchange. It is a style that has often been positioned as neutral or unmarked (as I have suggested in previous work [Giroux 2013]); it has even been positioned as overshadowing, or hastening the demise of, local traditions (Lederman and Smith 2014, n.p.; Quick 2009, 253–4; Trew 2009, 179). Drawing on Urion's scholarship, in this chapter, I aim to complicate this narrative, taking an additive (rather than zero-sum) approach to understanding Métis engagement with old-time fiddling in the twentieth century, while interrogating how multiculturalism, and scholarship that emerges from multicultural compartmentalization, has shifted our understanding of fiddling in Canada.

The first section addresses the interplay between the local (Métis and Manitoban) and the national as the old-time style was emerging. While old-time is sometimes understood as a common language or normative style for fiddlers across Canada, the Red River style is Manitoba's version of old-time fiddling, perhaps even Manitoba's normative style (just as the down-east style is a more localized version of the old-time style). Beginning with an overview of the exchange and technological advances that allowed old-time to emerge, I draw attention to the presence of Métis fiddlers within both local (Manitoban) and national (Canadian) old-time scenes. I also consider the impact of old-time/down-east fiddler, Don Messer, who is credited with creating a Canadian canon that influenced fiddlers, including Métis fiddlers, across the country. I then turn to the issue of old-time as neutral, or as a style that assimilates local styles. In doing so, I position late twentieth-century interpretations of the old-time style within the context of the multicultural frame that emerged in the 1960s and '70s; during this period, old-time fiddling and other styles of fiddling were being fit into the emergent idea of a multicultural Canada, resulting in what I refer to as multicultural compartmentalization. I conclude by turning to relationality, drawing attention to the old-time/Red River style's Métis past and present. I suggest that, to understand the place and meaning of old-time/Red River/Métis fiddling, definitions of these styles need to move beyond merely (readily audible) stylistic features (or features that are readily audible to outsiders) to centre relationality.

Old-Time Fiddling as Exchange

> Andy Dejarlis got up to the microphone with a fiddle ... he had seven thousand people in the palm of his hand. I never forgot it. It was an electrifying moment.
>
> – Interview with fiddler Jeanne Carlson (2012)

While the term "old-time" might bring to mind images of a bygone era, before electricity and the automotive, Canadian old-time fiddling is a relatively new fiddle style, though it was founded upon centuries of exchange. As examined in chapter two, exchange related to fiddle dance music in what is now known as North America began with the fur trade and led to the emergence of fiddle dance in many Indigenous communities, including among Métis peoples, who developed their own approach to fiddle dance. Exchange among peoples and communities has continued ever since, resulting in ongoing stylistic adaptations and the emergence of new approaches to (or styles of) fiddling. For example, in the late nineteenth and early twentieth centuries, lumber camps were particularly important spaces of musical exchange between and within Canada and the United States (see, e.g., Goertzen 2004, 340; Rickaby 1926, xix–xx; Leary 2015, 75–98). As Franz Rickaby wrote in his book on lumber songs,

> The relationship between the Northern lumbering communities of the United States and the Canadian provinces across the boundary was always close, not only in respect to the commercial exchange of the product, but in social ways as well. Migration took place in both directions; and, to a much greater extent, men from each side crossed over to work temporarily on the other, for profit, for a lark, or for both. The camps on both sides were similar, as were the logging operations themselves ... In the Golden Age of lumbering this cross-boundary visiting was most marked, particularly America-ward. Canadian "boys" came

> across in droves to work in American camps, especially those of Michigan. They brought their songs and left them in the memories and on the lips of the Americans. They learned American shanty songs and took them back across the Lakes. (Rickaby 1926, xix–xx)

Though Rickaby's focus is on the songs, fiddles were important instruments in the camps (see Leary 2015, 75–98), and, presumably, their presence would have led to a similar kind of exchange as that documented with the song tradition. Significantly, Métis were often employed at lumber camps – or built their own lumber camps; lumber camps were likely spaces that continued the tradition of Métis fiddle dance exchange, shaping Métis repertoire and playing.

Sheet music and travelling minstrel and vaudeville shows also shaped fiddle repertoire and style across the two countries, though these are vastly underresearched areas.[2] Laxer notes that sheet music arrived in York Factory with Swiss and German immigrants who, in 1819, left "a bound collection of waltzes for the fur traders, which influenced musical life in the Northwest over the following decades" (2015, 345–6). However, sheet music became much more important at the end of the nineteenth century, with the rising popularity of parlour songs. Although I have found in personal conversations that the impact of sheet music on Métis fiddlers is sometimes dismissed, as this chapter and chapter three document, many Métis fiddlers lived and fiddled in urban centres throughout the twentieth century; even if these fiddlers did not personally read music (though some likely did), these parlour songs were, undoubtedly, part of at least some fiddlers' soundscape. Vaudeville and minstrel shows were also part of this soundscape, although their impact on fiddling in Canada, or in the United States for that matter, is not well understood. Andy Dejarlis's former bandmate and biographer, Joe Mackintosh, does describe, however, how enthralled a teenage Dejarlis was when the Whiz Bang Review, a travelling vaudeville show, came to southern Manitoba in the late 1920s or early 1930s. Dejarlis, in fact, travelled to a couple of nearby towns, following the show for three performances (Mackintosh 2010, 47).

Many years earlier, a newspaper article reported on an "Ethiopian troupe" at St John's College in Stonewall (northwest of Winnipeg). As the article noted, "The St. John's College Ethiopian troupe gave a most successful minstrel entertainment at the town hall, Stonewall, on Friday night last. The well worn jokes, the old, old songs, the funiosities of Bones and Sambo, all went down with that large and delighted audience. Mr. W. E. Smith surpassed himself as a negro comedian, especially in his thrice encored banjo solo, and the Red river [*sic*] jig, brought down the house" (*Manitoba Daily Free Press* 1887, 4). Though it is difficult to know how the presence of these vaudeville and minstrel shows may have influenced the development of old-time fiddling in Manitoba, current old-time repertoire continues to include some tunes associated with Blackface minstrelsy, such as "Turkey in the Straw" (Studewell 1997, 58) and "Buffalo Gals." It is furthermore interesting that, in the article referenced above, the author refers to the Red River Jig. This connection may have been entirely fictional (e.g., the Red River Jig standing in for any tune at an up tempo), or there may have been a real connection, with the Red River Jig integrated into the minstrel show. Either way, it is clear that music associated with vaudeville and minstrel shows was part of the Manitoba soundscape in the late nineteenth and early twentieth centuries.

With the advent of recording technology and radio, contact between fiddle styles increased rapidly, as did contact between fiddle styles and other popular genres of music. Radio brought live and prerecorded performances of everything from opera to country music first to community hubs and then, as more were able to afford radios, directly into people's homes (Moir 2012). It was in the context of quickening exchange precipitated by technological advances that old-time fiddling emerged as something distinct – explicitly referred to as "old-time fiddle." In Manitoba, the first references to old-time fiddlers are found in newspaper radio listings soon after the advent of radio. These early old-time fiddlers heard over the airwaves included Bob Goulet, Del Genthon, Jimmy Gowler, and Andy Dejarlis. Jimmy Gowler (birth date unknown – after 1975)[3] and his group Prairie Schooner became frequent radio performers starting in 1925, continuing well into the 1950s.[4] Bob (Robert Léon) Goulet (1890–1955) was broadcasting with his orchestra by 1933, continuing until he left Winnipeg a few years later.[5] He made several recordings in the early 1930s, becoming the first fiddler in Manitoba that I am aware of to make a sound recording. Del Genthon (1896–1979), son of fiddler Frédéric Genthon (referred to in the previous chapter), similarly could be heard on the radio in the 1930s, continuing these radio performances well into the 1940s. His show, "Le Ranch," aired on CKSB, a French radio station based in St Boniface (Mackintosh 2010, 37). Genthon and his group, the Grainbelters, performed music on CJRC that was referred to in newspaper listings as "old-time and modern music" (*Winnipeg Free Press* 1942a, 21).

Though the radio was important to the careers of all three of these fiddlers, giving them a wider audience than they could have otherwise reached (including crossing provincial and national boundaries), performing for in-person dances was also a vital facet of their careers, sometimes helping them get radio gigs. As a brief article published in 1937 about Del Genthon notes, "His Grainbelters band was organized about ten years ago, and had already won quite a reputation playing modern and old-time dance music in and around Winnipeg before CJRC signed them up" (*Winnipeg Free Press* 1937, 26). Playing in dance halls, in some cases at least, allowed fiddlers to develop their reputation and then seek out radio engagements. While the term "old-timer," as described in the last chapter, emphasized an authentic connection to, perhaps even a re-enactment of, the past, the fiddlers playing for these dances and the radio were often described in advertisements as old-time and modern. This was noted above regarding Genthon and was similarly the case in many of the advertisements for Bob Goulet, for example, in a 1932 advertisement indicating that "Bob Goulet (Victor Artist) and His Orchestra" would be playing for an "Old-Time and Modern Dance" at the Norman Hall (*Winnipeg Free Press* 1932, 29). These fiddlers' music was, furthermore, thoroughly popular music, drawing huge crowds to the dance halls and other venues where it was performed. In fact, advertisements for dances, and short articles about the musicians, abounded in newspapers from the mid-1920s until midcentury, pointing to interest in the music and in the fiddlers. Through these live performances at dance halls and on radio, Gowler, Goulet, and Genthon gained popular and commercial success, becoming the foundational fiddlers of a new, old-time style that was emerging in Manitoba.

However, it was Andy Dejarlis (born Joseph Patrice Ephreme Desjarlais, 1914–1975) who became the most renowned of Manitoba old-time fiddlers; indeed, he is well-remembered today in Manitoba and across Canada among old-time fiddlers. Being slightly younger than Goulet and Genthon, he built his career as roads and access to personal modes of transportation were improving, when the radio and recording industries were becoming more established, and when television was emerging as a new medium; Dejarlis took advantage of all the opportunities that were made available through technological advancement. Born in Woodridge, Manitoba, Dejarlis and his sister Dolly,[6] a pianist and the first member of his band, began playing on a weekly radio program aired from the Royal Alexandra Hotel in Winnipeg shortly after they moved to the city in 1934 (Watson 2002, 11).

As Joe Mackintosh notes, Dejarlis won a Winnipeg fiddling contest shortly after arriving in the city. This gave him credibility as a proficient fiddler and gained him an audition and subsequent gig with CJRC radio in Winnipeg (2010, 49–51). He continued performing over the airwaves for many years afterwards, adopting what one reporter described as "old-time swing" (*Winnipeg Free Press* 1939, 4). Like Gowler, Goulet, and Genthon, Dejarlis was often described as playing "old-time and modern" music (*The Winnipeg Evening Tribune* 1935, 18), and certainly, as Mackintosh outlines, he was very conscious of making sure that his music was contemporary, even if rooted in the past (2010).

While radio was important to his career, Dejarlis – like other early to mid-twentieth-century fiddlers – built a large fan base by playing for dances. On Thursday, Friday, and Saturday nights in the 1930s and '40s,[7] he performed at Winnipeg dance halls, specifically the Trianon, Columbus, and Norman Halls. His groups were variously billed as "Andy Desjarlis and His Old Time and Modern Echoes," or "Andy Desjarlis and His CJRC Artists," or "Andy Desjarlis and His Red River Mates" (Watson 2002, 11 and Mackintosh 2010, 51–4). At the Norman Hall (also known as the Normandy), he would draw an estimated thirteen hundred dancers on Saturday nights. During the week, he played for dances in rural areas (including out of province), drawing attendees who had heard him on the radio (Mackintosh 2010, 51–3; Watson 2002, 13–17). Always aware of his audience, he would choose tunes that he knew locals would appreciate. As Dejarlis told Mackintosh in an interview, "Another thing, I used to surprise a lot of the Ukrainian folk. We used to make Dauphin our headquarters for the week. Do a little tour and then head back to Winnipeg. They were surprised because I was French and able to play their music. But south of Woodridge is all Ukrainians – Sundown, Caliento, Vita, Sandilands – and a lot of Ukrainians in Woodridge. Thus, I played kolomyjkas and polkas" (Mackintosh 2010, 50). In 1956, Dejarlis became the second Manitoba fiddler (after Goulet) to record commercially, releasing thirty-six albums by the end of his career. He made many of the tunes that he played available through his sheet music collections.[8] By the 1960s, Dejarlis's hard work was paying off in new ways as he began to gain national renown. During a brief stint in Montreal in the early 1960s, he led a band on a television show called *Chez Isidore* and, around the same time, made a guest appearance on *Don Messer's Jubilee* (Mackintosh 2010, 113–16).[9]

Dejarlis's repertoire was based on the foundation of old fiddle tunes, including many traditional Métis tunes that he had learned from family or heard while growing up in Woodridge. He also composed many tunes in the style of traditional Métis tunes. Yet Dejarlis did not shy away from incorporating his varied influences, including making repertoire choices based on specific audiences, as noted earlier. Dejarlis furthermore tried to keep up with the trends, adding "rock 'n roll numbers" to his sets (*The Manitoba Leader* 1957, 8; and Lecker 1965, 63). As Mackintosh notes, Dejarlis's band played a diverse repertoire, which "included swing and Dixieland as well as old-time" (2010, 56). Indeed, Dejarlis always aimed "to add more zing, something that would bring the band's sound to the forefront of contemporary music" (56). This was, according to Mackintosh, why Dejarlis hired Helen Lowe in the late 1930s. Lowe was well-versed in the music of Ella Fitzgerald and Billie Holiday and could sing the big band tunes that people were hearing on the radio. She helped bring a modern flair to Dejarlis's sound. Dejarlis also included saxophonist, Billy Nixon, and trumpeter, Les Finley, as part of his band, and played (and recorded) tunes that were popular on the radio, such as "Never on a Sunday" from the 1960 film of the same name, as well as "Latin" tunes.[10] In this way, he positioned himself as a modern performer, even if he was sometimes critical of new trends and acknowledged his affection for the old styles of music (see, e.g., Lecker 1965, 63).

As the large crowds in Winnipeg and his radio and television appearances suggest, Dejarlis's formula for success at the intersection of old repertoire and new technologies worked, and he became a local, and, to a lesser extent, a national sensation. Many made a special effort to catch his weekly radio program. As fiddler Henri Hince told me, "We used to walk – it was about three-quarters of a mile – to my uncle's. Andy Dejarlis had a program for fifteen minutes. I think it was on CJRC. Something like that. Anyway, he was playing at 11:00, I think it was 11:15 at night. So, we'd walk to our uncle's and wait for the programme, for the fifteen-minute programme" (H. Hince, interview, 2012). Hince revealed that he learned some of his repertoire from the radio, remembering tunes if they were interesting: "It would stick to your mind, you know. You'd go home and you'd try to play it" (Hince 2012). The effort that Hince made to catch the show points to both Dejarlis's popularity with fiddlers at the time and the impact he had in shaping repertoire. But Dejarlis also had a star quality. As his sister Dolly Desjarlais reminisced, "Girls wanted to date him. Some asked how old he was. Some girls wrote to ask if they could come and sing with the band, and some would send their pictures" (Watson 2002, 15). Joe Mackintosh similarly relates a story about a dance that Dejarlis was performing for and shares that two "exquisitely" dressed women in attendance were "hanging around his neck" (2010, 79). And as fiddler Jeanne Carlson told me, Dejarlis was able to hold "seven thousand people in the palm of his hand" (interview 2012). To this day, he remains Manitoba's best-known fiddler, and his original and adapted tunes are part of the common core old-time fiddle repertoire played in Manitoba and beyond.

The four fiddlers discussed so far – Gowler, Goulet, Genthon, and Dejarlis – were the most significant fiddlers in Manitoba as old-time fiddling emerged as a new style of fiddling. Notably, Goulet, Genthon, and Dejarlis were Métis, while Jimmy Gowler had long-time roots in Red River. Gowler's great-grandmother was the daughter of the English Lord Braybrooke, and his great-grandfather (Oliver Gowler) was Lord Braybrooke's butler. Jimmy Gowler's great-grandparents immigrated to Red River in 1836 after Oliver Gowler was contracted to work on the HBC's experimental farm in Red River. Jimmy Gowler's ancestors on his father's side, then, were early settlers to the region, likely with long-standing connections and cultural ties to Métis families.[11] Bob Goulet, in contrast, was Métis, the descendant of a well-documented Métis fur trade family. His father, Maxime Goulet, was the younger brother of Elzéar Goulet, a Métis leader killed by Canadian troops for the role he played in the Red River Resistance. Del Genthon also had deep kinship ties to Red River Métis families, with ancestors who married Cree and Métis women prior to the 1820s.[12] And Andy Dejarlis was from the Desjarlais family, whose ancestors included Métis singer-songwriter Pierre Falcon, best known for having written "La Chanson de la Gournouillère" (also known as "Falcon's Song") which is considered by some to be the Métis Nation's first national anthem. Métis fiddlers, then, had a significant impact on the development of a popular, professionalized, and commercial style of fiddling in Manitoba.

While these fiddlers were most significant locally, old-time fiddling developed concurrently on the national stage. The first nationally broadcast fiddler was George Wade and the Cornhuskers, who could be heard across the country in 1933 (Johnson 2012, 15). However, it was New Brunswick-born fiddler Don Messer (1909–1973) who took the national stage by storm. First broadcast in Saint John, New Brunswick, in 1929, Messer's radio show was being broadcast nationally by the mid-1940s. As he was building a national reputation via radio, he began touring the country on a nearly annual basis (17). Then, in 1959, Messer moved from radio to television, as CBC began broadcasting his show, *Don Messer's Jubilee.* The *Jubilee* quickly became one of the most viewed television shows in the country, though admittedly one of the only shows to watch given the limited number of available channels (Sellick 1969, 60). As folklorist Johanne Trew suggests, the *Jubilee* was "so popular that there was a sense that almost everyone you would want to know was watching Don Messer," creating a "sense of community across the country" (2002, 43–4). Focusing on his musical impact, Neil Rosenberg argues that Messer created a "national canon of repertoire and performance practice" (1994, 24). That is, his tunes and style became a musical practice shared by fiddlers across the country; and fiddlers and fiddle fans could imagine a sense of common ground even when literally playing or dancing together was not possible. As recounted by fiddler Lynn Mitchell (1922–2011), this influence was notably present in Manitoba:

> Well, I'll tell you, it's a lot of years ago, [Messer] went across Canada, twice, maybe three times[13] ... he was at Pilot Mound [Manitoba] one day ... He had [performed in] a big hall, or a big arena; they put a floor in there, and it was jam packed ... They came from as far as Winnipeg ... After the thing was over, [Messer] went down to Bill Delorme's house, and they finished the night out playing down there with Bill Delorme [a local fiddler]. And Bill just idolized him too, you know. (L. Mitchell, interview, 2008)

Mitchell's comment is valuable because it speaks to the distance people were willing to travel to catch Messer live and in person (over 180 kilometres) and to intimate spaces of exchange (i.e., jamming in a local fiddler's home) even in the context of a major, national tour.

Though Messer's influence was significant in Manitoba, it was not a one-way street; rather, local fiddle tunes and fiddlers – from coast to coast – had an impact on Messer's repertoire and approach to playing. In fact, Messer learned tunes from local fiddlers during his cross-country tours, and he had people send him tunes to play on his show (Johnson 2012, 18). Lynn Mitchell's story about Messer, continued from above, links this process to Manitoba: "he taped it. [Messer] taped all the playing that he did with old Bill Delorme. And you know what? There's a lot of numbers that Bill Delorme wrote, good old-time waltzes and different [tunes]. [Messer] taped them and then [commercially] recorded them. And then he sent him a cheque for two dollars. Minnie Delorme – that's his wife – she told me, she says 'I framed that, and I still got it, and it's going to be in my possession and then the kids can have it afterwards'" (L. Mitchell, interview, 2008). Trew notes that, by learning tunes that were being performed across the country, Messer "enabl[ed] Canadians from diverse regions [to] recogniz[e] their own particular tunes, to identify with his music overall" (2000, 187). Messer's adoption of tunes by Delorme would have made his performances more familiar to Manitobans, allowing them to "identify with his music" (187). Messer frequently performed Delorme's composition, "Pilot Mound Waltz," and included it on an album in 1958. He also played many of Dejarlis's tunes, recording a homage to Dejarlis in 1973, titled *A Tribute to Manitoba's Golden Boy*. The importance of Dejarlis's music "out east" is confirmed by fiddler Bill Guest who noted that Dejarlis's tune, "Manitoba Waltz," was one of the most popular waltzes in mainland Nova Scotia (1985, 11). There was something of Manitoba in Messer's music.

There was, then, overlap and exchange between the national old-time and the local old-time (Red River) traditions. But they did remain separate, at least to some. This separation is evident in an interview between Herb Lafferty and renowned Métis/Ojibwe fiddler, Mel Bedard (from Manitoba). Bedard begins by noting that he did not have access to radio when he was growing up, but that he heard fiddle everywhere he went, from birthday parties to weddings, so he "knew the tunes." He eventually began learning the guitar, and then in his early twenties, began learning the fiddle:

> HL: So, when you made the switch from guitar to fiddle you must have had a musical influence or a mentor or a fiddler that you were watching and following, could you maybe tell us about who that fiddler might have been?
>
> MB: Oh, yeah sure. It started with we were the first ones to have a radio in our community. We lived at the Little Black Reserve for a couple of years and Andy Desjarlais had a program on it on Saturday nights, so I heard that music but the people didn't, my dad [who was Québécois] didn't fall into it, he didn't care for it because he thought it was jumpy sort of a thing because he didn't understand, he had the other style in mind, the Don Messer style, it was more smooth, more even flow. I followed that to begin with until it went for quite a few years and I hear Andy playing every now and again and he was off during the war years

> and then I started hearing him again maybe in '48 or around there, so it went on and he started having a weekly half an hour program starting about '53 and then I could hear this Red River style of music; there was a few guys that played it, not everybody played the Red River style. I could actually name the guys. There was a clan called Wheelers and they were Metis, and everybody played the fiddle, all the boys, the father, and the girls played too. And they played this Red River style, distinctive notes, individual notes stick out in the playing sort of thing and all different length notes, so it differed very much from the down east style. The down east style is up tempo, and the Red River style is nice danceable tempo, so I changed after I met Andy Desjarlais. I switched probably about six or seven years later I started doing his stuff, and I took about two years to develop that style and the bowing is very different in it, very, very different. (Bedard 2001)

As Bedard makes clear, even though there was something of Manitoba in Messer's playing, and something of Messer's style in Manitoba – that is, there were years of complex "both ways" exchange – Dejarlis and Messer remained stylistically distinct fiddlers. More significantly, Bedard could trace the Red River style to certain (Métis) families who played in the style. This theme will be addressed in this chapter's final section.

On the Canadian Centre and Multicultural Containment

> Don has kept alive the best in our musical past – the expression of our thoughts, feelings, hopes and dreams. His is soul music carved from the rock from which we have sprung. He is perpetuating the roots of the community life in which he was born and reared.
> – Allison MacLean, quoted in Sellick (1969, 129)

> Don Messer is Canada. He belongs to Canadians, and they have every right to expect and demand that he continue with his blend of entertainment.
> – Ken Reynolds, quoted in Sellick (1969, 127)

By the second half of the twentieth century, old-time fiddling was becoming less popular. Demand for community-based entertainment decreased and musics such as rock 'n roll took over the dance halls where old-time music had formerly been a mainstay (Johnson 2012, 12). Dejarlis commented on this change several times later in his career, as rock 'n roll clearly impacted the social positioning of his music; that is, he acknowledged, with regret but also acquiescence, that fiddle dance music was no longer the popular music of the day. While its decreasing popularity was evident by the mid-1950s, the issue of old-time music's place within Canada erupted on the national stage in 1969 when *Don Messer's Jubilee* was abruptly cancelled. The reasons for cancellation were unclear and came as a shock to Messer, whose ratings remained high, leading to speculation about why the show was cancelled and emphasizing – perhaps even escalating – emergent tensions around Canadian identity. This section of the chapter addresses this complex social and cultural context and its impacts on how fiddling, in particular old-time fiddling, was interpreted and positioned by Canadian scholars and the fiddle community in the late twentieth century. I consider how, with the rise of multiculturalism, old-time fiddling has been constructed as neutral and unmarked, and how what I call multicultural thinking impacted perceptions of authenticity within Métis fiddling. I further suggest that multicultural thinking has led to the (attempted) containment of Métis fiddling, at least in some contexts.

In the 1960s, discussions of bilingualism, biculturalism, and multiculturalism emerged on the national stage. Canadian society was rapidly changing as more and more people moved to urban centres, and immigration policies became less discriminatory against racialized people. Perhaps because of the timing of these national discussions alongside the *Jubilee's* cancellation, Messer and his show became embroiled in identity debates. As historian Greg Marquis notes, some of Messer's fans felt that his music and show upheld a Canadian identity that was threatened by modernity; it was a needed antidote to the ills of modernity at a time of tremendous change. Thus, they "complained that the CBC was failing not only old-time music fans but also the nation" (Marquis 2022, 229). For Vancouver radio host, Vic Walters, "television without Don Messer is like Canada without John A" (quoted in Sellick 1969, 90). Regardless of how anyone feels about the first prime minister today, Walters's comment positioned Don Messer as foundational to music in Canada. Similarly, the town of Strathroy, Ontario, issued a proclamation stating that Messer had "developed a truly Canadian medium of entertainment" and that the *Jubilee* "represented the development of entertainment in the Canadian family and community from earliest pioneer days" (quoted in Sellick 1969, 131). Old-time fiddle fans, MacLean and Reynolds, quoted in the above epigraph, echo this view, emphasizing every Canadian's *right* to access Messer's music.

As the above commentary indicates, many people felt that Messer unified the country through his music. In a biography written shortly after CBC cancelled the *Jubilee*, Lester Sellick emphasized this very aspect of Messer's music:

> The title of Canada's Goodwill Ambassador which has been conferred upon him is well chosen, for he has promoted 'unity through music' among Canadians. He has learned and has played the music of the English, the French, the Scots and the Irish, as well as that of the new Canadians. With the help of the Buchtas [a dance troupe led by Peter and Irma Buchta, who immigrated to Canada in 1950], he has promoted European costume dancing and singing. He has promoted Canadian talent from all provinces, from the young to the old, from the little Indian boy from Edmonton to Catherine MacKinnon in Halifax. Daily his mail contains tapes or recordings of Canadians who would like to appear on his show. National unity is also stressed in the titles given to many of his tunes, from the *Banks of Newfoundland* to the *Fraser River Breakdown*, with the *Mouth of the Tobique*, the *Joys of Quebec* and the *Red River Reel* in between. Thus, Canadians in one area learn something of the culture in a region of their country many miles away. The highlight of course was Centennial year when an entire program was devoted to each province. On the spot tapings, too, have portrayed scenery in one part of Canada to other regions. Through his overseas radio broadcasts, he portrays Canada as a whole to the world. (Sellick 1969, 134–5)

While Sellick emphasized regional representation, others have pointed to Messer's approach to style and repertoire as the key aspect of his ability to unify Canadians. Specifically, Messer removed the most obvious and distinctive regional traits of fiddle tunes and played melodies in their simpler versions. Since specific elements of regional fiddle styles were often difficult for outsiders to successfully perform – such as cuts in Cape Breton music or foot work in Quebecois and Métis music – the result was a style that more fiddlers could perform. Thus, as Johnson noted, Messer's approach made it "easier for fiddlers from all regions of Canada to identify with and of all skill levels to learn by ear" (2012, 18). This, in turn, created a repertoire and style that connected people from coast to coast – a national canon (Rosenberg 1994, 24). The flip side of this image of Messer and old-time fiddling as unifying is that of Messer as a homogenizer, a fiddler "who did not represent the truly authentic fiddle music of any particular region" (Rosenberg 1994, 31). As Trew explained, some have even suggested that Messer hastened the demise of local styles (2000, 179). This perspective is evident in Lederman and Smith's article on fiddling in Canada, where they stated that radio and recording created "a new class of 'professional' fiddlers whose styles and repertoire tended to overshadow the more varied personal approaches of former times" (2014, n.p.). They also suggested that "people often abandoned [local traditions] in favour of what they were hearing through new media."[14]

Though Messer has been particularly criticized, so too has Dejarlis, pointing to the way in which old-time music (and not just Messer's music) was and is viewed by some as homogenizing. For instance, Lederman and Smith note that Dejarlis "employ[ed] the down-east model" while "adapting many older tunes from Métis repertoire, losing some of the highly asymmetric phrasing and establishing a smoother, 'professional' and widely-imitated version of the Métis tradition." Lederman and Smith furthermore suggest that some fiddlers and community members viewed (and still view) Dejarlis's style and repertoire, like Messer's, as "definitive." In other words, he is viewed by some as having created *a* singular style from local styles – a style that was then adopted by fiddlers in Manitoba and beyond (also see Quick 2010, 116–20).

The debate about whether Messer, and old-time music more generally, unified or homogenized, is striking because it echoes discourse around multiculturalism: that is, many have debated whether multiculturalism creates divisiveness in a country (it fails to unify) or supports difference (prevents homogenization). I believe that the close connection between discourse on multiculturalism and discourse on old-time music, along with the above-noted identity debates, indicates that, by the late 1960s, a multicultural framework was shaping how people were thinking about old-time music. When I first began writing about old-time, I drew heavily on the work of anthropologist, Eva Mackey. In particular, I found her concept of *Canadian*-Canadians helpful because it addressed how multiculturalism maintains a core, unmarked culture – a group that view themselves as mainstream or normative – against which all other cultures *become* multicultural (2002, 2). Within this frame, certain people are viewed as hyphenated Canadians (e.g., French-Canadians, Chinese-Canadians, etc.), and others as just Canadians, that is *Canadian*-Canadians. I applied her concept of an unmarked core to old-time; specifically, I examined how old-time absorbed a range of fiddle and popular music styles, removing key markers of difference, to create a normative, neutral, or 'regular'[15] fiddle style (Giroux 2013, 165–79). Indeed, I defined old-time as a *process of unmarking:* consuming music of ethnic and regional others, while removing markers of difference to create the old-time style. In this sense, I understood old-time as a homology of assimilation policy (Robinson 2020, 213).

Old-time fiddling developed, of course, prior to official multiculturalism in Canada, at a time when Canadian policies pushed for the assimilation of new immigrants, and limited immigration to those considered likely to assimilate. In this way, it makes sense that old-time music might have both developed with less attention to *difference*, and with a goal of expressing a unified, Canadian identity. One of the most vital points that Mackey makes, however, is that multiculturalism still requires – and reinforces – a core, unmarked culture. In this way, multiculturalism is not a change in policy vis-à-vis the white centre, but a repackaging of policy so it appears to address the erasures and imbalances of power that Canadians openly endorsed in the pre-multicultural era. As she writes, "it is useful to look beyond the so-called polarizations between left and right, between tolerance and intolerance, inclusion and erasure, and instead explore the power relations that nevertheless inhere through the continuities and flexibilities of projects. It is important to explore how inclusion and the seeming celebration of multiplicity and difference can also be expressions of power" (2002, xx). Instead of presuming that "the proliferation of cultural difference" necessarily rectifies past erasures and imbalances of power, she argues that we need to consider how "'threatening' and 'dangerous' differences are contained, controlled, normalised, stereotyped, idealised, marginalised, and reified" through multiculturalism and its adoption of tolerance and inclusion (6).

The adoption of multiculturalism as official policy was, of course, seen by many as a huge step forward, one that had the potential to open increased space for a diversity of voices; to provide opportunities to celebrate many ways to be Canadian; and to distinguish Canada from the growing monolith south of the boarder. Multiculturalism was, furthermore, funded; similar to recognition more generally, it carried and carries substantial symbolic and material resources (Quick 2009, 286–7). Opening these spaces and opportunities was and is, undoubtedly, an important avenue for the vitalization of cultural practices for Indigenous and non-Indigenous people alike. However, what I understand from Mackey's critique is that multiculturalism did not and does not change the power relationships among socio-politico-cultural groups, but reframes these relationships to make them appear as if they are significantly different than they were in the past. Just as pointedly, "the power to define, limit and tolerate differences still lies in the hands of the dominant group," and these limits "are defined by the ever-changing needs of the project of nation-building" (Mackey 2002, 70). In this way, through a positive framing of multiculturalism as the acceptance and celebration of difference, difference can be more easily controlled and contained. In my early work on old-time, then, I understood multiculturalism as accommodating old-time music as *the* normative fiddle style. It did not require old-time music to change, and in fact positioned it as a non-ethnic music.

However, since first writing about old-time as a process of *unmarking*, I have come to believe that old-time does not simply *reflect* Canada's changing identity politics; rather multicultural thinking changed discourse about fiddle styles in Canada, which in turn affected how fiddlers and academics perform or otherwise work with old-time and other fiddle styles. Specifically, viewed through a multicultural framework, fiddle styles became increasingly compartmentalized; there was a growing assumption that there are, and should be, clear containers for, or boundaries among, fiddle styles – defined largely in terms of repertoire and to a lesser extent ways of playing.[16] Because old-time fiddling was, in the unity/homogenization debates, treated as *non-ethnic*, the result was the creation of a series of hyphenated fiddle styles; there was fiddling (i.e., old-time fiddling), *plus* Irish-fiddling, Scottish-fiddling, Cape-Breton-fiddling, Ukrainian-fiddling, Québécois-fiddling, and more. There is certainly nothing wrong with emphasizing the Irish-ness or the Ukrainian-ness of fiddling (just as people may in some cases prefer to identify as French Canadian, Japanese Canadian, and so on), and, at times, communities may want to create boundaries of style as a way to claim something distinct, and in turn, clarify the distinctness of their community. Nevertheless, the point here is that our categorization of, and thinking about, fiddle styles is not neutral. Even if much of the fiddling in Canada falls into discrete categories (though I suspect that this was never the case – and certainly is not now), there is always movement and space in between; how we understand this space, and how or if we think about it, matters.

Drawing on both Mackey and music educator Ed Sarath, I am referring to the process of compartmentalizing fiddling as *multicultural containment*.

As Sarath notes, a multicultural approach places musics into "discrete, cultural compartments to be approached … one by one in aspirations to evolve an adequate diversity awareness" (2018, 27). While I would argue that this compartmentalization has affected all fiddle styles in Canada (and beyond), Métis fiddling is an excellent case study and is, of course, most relevant to ideas addressed in this book. Prior to the 1980s, scholars did not necessarily recognize Métis fiddling as a distinct style – and certainly those outside of Métis and other Indigenous communities did not know it as something distinct. Hogan and Hogan's overview of Canadian fiddle culture (1977), for example, refers to twelve styles/regions but does not include a category for Métis fiddling or any other Indigenous fiddle style. The authors do acknowledge, however, "Indian" *influence* in a region that they called the "Western Plains." As they write, "Western fiddle music is a mixture of styles reflecting the Indian, French, Scottish and Ukrainian communities. Western Swing, as played by King Ganam and Al Cherny, reflects the American influences. General Canadian, represented here by Frankie Rodgers and Grant Lamb, is also popular in the West. Whatever the style, Western fiddlers seem to adjust it to the prairie landscape and people. Western fiddling is free, easy and sometimes very wild" (1977, 75). Though this description is problematic (e.g., the statement "free, easy and sometimes very wild" speaks more to prejudice than to sound), it is interesting that Hogan and Hogan describes fiddling both in terms of distinct styles and regional approaches. In other words, the impact of place is readily acknowledged. Helmut Kallman's entry on fiddling in the *Encyclopedia of Music in Canada* just a few years later cites Hogan and Hogan but includes a list of only eight styles. Kallman specifically mentions Métis fiddlers (though not a Métis style per se), noting that they "have introduced elements of their own, unrestrained by strict metre or standard tuning" (1981, 326). In contrast, George Proctor's article titled "Fiddle Music as a Manifestation of Canadian Regionalism" refers to six fiddle styles, including the western provinces, with no mention of Métis or other Indigenous fiddling or fiddlers (1985).

Into the 1980s, then, there was inconsistency, or perhaps flexibility, in how writers categorized fiddle styles, with the number of styles/regions varying from author to author. Furthermore, writers either did not mention Métis and other Indigenous fiddlers or referred to them as contributing *influence* or elements of style within a particular region rather than as creators of a unique style. This was, of course, in part due to a lack of research on fiddling; lack of interest in Indigenous fiddlers; and the erasure of the Indigeneity of popular fiddlers as traced earlier in this chapter. Ideas about what constituted Métis fiddling began to solidify, however, in the 1980s, as researchers became interested in Indigenous fiddling. While Roy Gibbons (1982, 1981, 1980) and Nicholas Vrooman (1984) were the first to write about Métis fiddling (and in fact Gibbons was the first to specifically write about a Métis *style* and not just Indigenous influence), ethnomusicologist Anne Lederman's work was the most comprehensive early work on Indigenous fiddling in the Prairies, outlining how it constituted a distinct and clearly bounded style. Her research influenced the next generation of fiddle scholars as well as the public's understanding of Métis fiddling; by releasing some of her field recordings people across the country were able to listen to, learn, and hear the *difference of* Métis fiddling. Here it is relevant to note that not all the fiddlers and fiddle tunes that Lederman recorded in the 1980s sounded audibly different from other fiddlers in Manitoba; but in tracing the style's boundaries, she chose to emphasize examples that pointed to sonic distinctiveness. By the time I began my PhD, fiddle and folk music enthusiasts alike knew, at the very least, that there was a Métis style.

The shift toward recognition of Métis fiddling in the 1980s was, in many ways, extraordinarily important, addressing the long-time erasure of Métis and other Indigenous fiddlers in Canada and beyond. Yet, as Métis fiddling's difference became more widely recognized, the proximity of Dejarlis and other Métis fiddlers to old-time/Red River style fiddling, as well as to popular music styles, started to be used as a measure of a Métis fiddler's *inauthenticity*. In other words, the compartment that the style "Métis fiddling" created, left little wiggle room for understanding Métis fiddling as something other than just (or mostly) a collection of repertoire and performance practice. As Lederman wrote in an article that reflected on what she had observed over more than twenty years:

> So, "Métis fiddling" is on the map. Surely then, one would think, there must be some strong sense of what exactly "Métis fiddling" is to support such media attention. I maintain that, in spite of all of this activity, I was largely right in my fears of twenty years ago. All the recordings, books, interviews, web sites and fiddle lessons in the world do not seem to be able to prevent the loss of much that was distinctive in the old repertoire and style – the loss, in fact, of those very elements which, in my view, make the music Métis. The tunes one hears today in the hands

> of self-identified Métis fiddlers or even non-Métis players playing so-called "Métis" tunes are generally only occasionally and mildly asymmetric, the footwork is sporadic, fiddles are rarely re-tuned, much of the double-stringing is gone, fiddles have moved up to the shoulder, bowing is longer and louder. So, we are moved to ask, what is it that makes this music "Métis"? (Lederman 2009, 371)

Continuing, she noted that "in practice, it would seem that we are now dealing with issues of identity, not of music. In other words, a good deal of the time, the 'Métisness' of the music seems to go no further than the fact that it is being played by Métis people" (Lederman 2009, 371). Concluding, she stated that "Maybe it will simply be left to white girls like me to play this old crooked music, revelling in its unique beauty, while young aboriginal fiddlers are busy trying to sound as much like everyone else as they possibly can. After all, who could blame them?" (373). What is striking here, of course, is that Métis (or Aboriginal) fiddling, following Lederman's definition, can be completely removed from Métis communities – from the fingers, feet, minds, and spirits of Métis fiddlers – and still be Métis fiddling. In fact, the suggestion is that it might only remain Métis in the hands of someone other than Métis fiddlers.

In the first section of this chapter, I pointed to a lineage of mostly Métis fiddlers who were responsible for the development of old-time/Red River fiddling in Manitoba. Métis fiddlers were innovators in Manitoba's fiddle scene, though for much of the twentieth century the Métis-ness of their music was erased. The new erasure that is happening is to only include, as real Métis music, fiddling that sounds *distinctly Métis to outsiders* – to only include fiddlers who fit the boundaries of the Métis style as defined by a small number of scholars and folk music enthusiasts. This erasure is equally problematic, especially when the result is to situate so many of the Métis fiddlers of the twentieth and twenty-first centuries – who were and are doing important work as musicians in their communities – as not really playing Métis music; they, too, end up being erased as *Métis* fiddlers. Indeed, if many of the most important Métis fiddlers are left out of definitions of Métis fiddling, how academics define both old-time and Métis fiddling may need to be reconsidered. To be clear, I am not suggesting that the music Lederman recorded and wrote about should not be promoted and valued; it is part of a compelling and beautiful Métis tradition. However, I am disputing the idea encouraged through the multicultural compartmentalization of fiddling that the music of Red River style fiddlers is *necessarily* less Métis because of its proximity to old-time fiddling; after all, Métis fiddlers have always been innovative, melding various influences, and some might say that innovation and exchange is how Métis fiddling came to be. Furthermore, as Urion notes, "an Indigenous outlook isn't zero-sum" (2022, 24–5). There is room for many approaches to Métis fiddling. While the next chapter considers another context of multicultural compartmentalization, in the brief concluding section, I argue that turning toward relationality in both old-time and Métis fiddling offers one possible solution.

Relational Approaches to Red River/Old-Time Fiddling

In June 2022, I attended The Hills Are Alive Camp, a fiddle and Métis culture camp at Eagle's Nest Ranch, south of Medicine Hat, Alberta. While there, I had the opportunity to take group lessons in a team-taught class led by Alex Kusturok and Daniel Gervais. As is often the case in these classes, learning tunes by ear is interspersed with chatting and laughter, moving from jokes to more serious subjects. During one of these classes, a student asked Kusturok about his style, noting that it was not like anyone's that he had ever heard. The student wanted to know where he got his style – how he had developed it. In the conversation that followed, Kusturok noted that he can hear the unique style of each fiddler, whether it is the style of Garry Lepine (a Métis fiddler from Manitoba) or a fiddler from Quebec or Cape Breton. Gervais jumped in noting that Kusturok has gone through periods where he intensely studies the work of a single fiddler. Kusturok was quick to name fiddlers that he had learned from, most often referring to informal learning, a result of close listening and performing together. Most strikingly, he could play tunes in such a way that I could unmistakably hear those fiddlers (if I knew them) sounded through his fiddle, demonstrating his close listening to each musician (though here it is important to note that he did not, typically, play in a way that was intentionally emulative of any one fiddler but, rather, was demonstrating his knowledge of these fiddlers' own personal styles). Kusturok suggested that he does not play anything new – everything he plays has been done – but that he makes these influences his own. He fashions them together to create a personal style formed in and through a community of fiddlers.[17] This discussion of both aspects of personal differentiation and sounded connection to others sparked, for me, the understanding that, for Kusturok, every fiddler emerges from their musical relationships, whether those are relationships to people, to recordings, or to places and their soundscapes.

Kusturok's explanation made me think back to Mel Bedard, and how he positioned Messer and Dejarlis as very different and was able to hear kinship networks within Dejarlis's playing – something he made explicit by his *naming* of Red River style fiddlers. He could hear how Dejarlis's playing connected to Métis histories and communities and to a specific family. Though the Red River style might be dismissed by some as hardly Métis at all – as homogenized and homogenizing – Bedard's long-time relationships with community and Red River style fiddlers allowed him to hear Métis community, lineage, and kinship networks. What I am arguing for here, then, is moving beyond old-time, Red River, and Métis fiddling as merely stylistic categories, and instead seeking out the relationships that they sound – whether these are relationships of unmarking and assimilation (as may sometimes be the case in the old-time style) or of care and connection (as described further below). As discussed earlier, research on Canadian fiddling emerged alongside multiculturalism and has most often adopted a discrete styles approach (i.e., an approach that attempts to show the sonic boundaries among styles). While this approach can offer clarity about the most readily audible sonic differences, it is less successful in addressing the ways in which fiddling is embedded in flows within and across communities. Understanding relationality is perhaps especially relevant to old-time/Red River fiddling (though I suspect that it is important to all fiddling) because it emerged at the intersections of styles and, in the current day, has to engage with its perceived normativity. Indeed, Red River style fiddling had its roots in the music of Métis performers who engaged with mainstream audiences, often in non-Indigenous spaces. This made it possible to reach broader audiences (allowing Dejarlis to hold "seven thousand people in the palm of his hand"); but it also meant engaging in relationships with non-Indigenous people who did not, or could not, recognize the music's Indigeneity.

There are two lines of thinking with which I want to conclude. First, in writing about old-time/Red River fiddling, we need to consider networks of care for tradition and the people who practice the traditions. Early in my academic career I wrote that the fiddlers who were first heard on Manitoba radio stations, fiddlers such as Bob Goulet, are now largely forgotten (2013, 156). Seven years later, Goulet's great-granddaughter, Michelle Porter, proved me partially wrong in a compelling book that tends to her relationship with her late great-grandfather. He was not forgotten by his kin. As a way to show and engage in this relationship, Porter interspersed a series of letters to Goulet throughout her book (including one that I referenced in chapter 3). In one of these letters, she wrote:

> The names you went by, Pépé, and the stories that would unravel if you could tell me about each Bob and Robert and Leon. To your daughters and your grandchildren you were Pépé, and that's how I knew you, long before I knew your first name was Bob. Were there other names, Pépé? Those who knew you as a lover, a brother, a son, or a friend must have called you other names. The fiddlers you learned from, the fiddlers you played with, and the fiddlers who learned from you in the Métis kitchens, where soup and drink were passed around by the hands of mothers and sisters and lovers to keep the music coming on and to keep all the feet dancing together on the floor deep into the night and right into the next morning. You were one of the greats – I heard that from an interview with one of the last of the old-generation Métis fiddlers. When he was a boy trying to figure out how to hold a bow, you were in your prime, you could dance and fiddle and tell a story. Who were you those nights and what did they call you? (Porter 2020, 30)

Porter's work embeds the music in community as its most important element and is a model for how the old-time fiddle community might move beyond viewing fiddle styles as "cultural compartments" (Sarath 2018, 27) toward a practice of caring for relationships in our telling of fiddle dance stories; these musical kinship relationships might be understood as foundational aspects of what we commonly think of as style. As Urion expresses, "the music of the newcomers became involved through a process of musical reciprocity and exchange that have been going on since time immemorial" (2022, 24). Rather than making the music *less* Indigenous, I observe that reciprocity and exchange are foundational to Indigenous ways of being, and that is something that needs to be embedded in our analyses of so-called styles and more generally, our thinking about Métis music.

Second, Bedard and Kusturok show us that we can listen differently, including listening *through* (and with) kin and community. Both paid close attention to how they hear relationships. Music is an expression of that kin and community, though non-Indigenous peoples do not always listen for it. Or perhaps we cannot always hear it. Here I am reminded of Dylan Robinson's concept of listening positionality: we listen from the intersectional positions in which we inhabit (2020, 9–10). We also listen from within relational networks. I can hear Lepine in Kusturok's playing because I grew up listening to Lepine (and his son, Jason, who has a similar – though not exactly the same – style), but I would not be able to hear the Wheelers (i.e., the family Bedard mentioned) because I do not have a relationship with that Métis family. I do not hear those kinship ties. In other words, it may be hard to hear relationships – even impossible – because of our listening positionality and our (limited) relational networks. Yet listening, if we do place kinship at the centre of stylistic analysis, is essential work; and it is essential work if we wish to overcome the multicultural compartmentalization that positions Red River style fiddling as not quite Métis. Here again I wish to return to Urion, who points out that "an Indigenous outlook isn't zero-sum" (2022, 24–5). Red River and other versions of Métis fiddling all express the authentic relational experiences of the performers. While I remain convinced that this kinship-based work needs to be Métis-led because Métis musicians, dancers, and scholars are best positioned to hear these kinship and relational networks, I am moved by Robinson's suggestion that, by being attuned to how we listen, "we are better able to listen otherwise" (10–11). If so, this is work that we can all begin.

5

Métis Music at Manitoba's Old-Time Fiddle Competitions

> We are a métis civilization. What we are today has been inspired as much by four centuries of life with the indigenous civilizations as by four centuries of immigration. Perhaps more. Today we are the outcome of that experience. As have Métis people, Canadians in general have been heavily influenced and shaped by First Nations. We still are. We increasingly are. This influencing, this shaping is deep within us.
> – John Ralston Saul (2008, 3)

> It is Riel as the emblem of "in-between-ness" who expresses a most basic fact of the Canadian experience: that of cultural hybridity or, as I will choose to describe it, *métissage.* It is this hybridity that I wish to suggest rests at the foundation of an elusive Canadian identity.
> – Jennifer Reid (2012, 71)

The previous chapter considered the old-time/Red River style broadly. This chapter turns to old-time fiddling competitions, one of the most important spaces for the performance and continuation of old-time fiddling in Manitoba and across Canada. I focus in particular on the addition of Métis-style categories, which began to be included as part of some of Manitoba's old-time competitions in 2006. Drawing on Robinson and Kaminsky's scholarship on musical encounter, I read these categories from the framework of Canadians' shifting understanding of and relationship with Métis identity in the 2000s and 2010s (as evident in the Saul and Reid epigraphs above). As previously described, Métis music and musicians have always been part of the old-time scene; the addition of Métis-style categories at competitions might, then, be understood as recognition, rectifying erasures of the past. Yet they might also be understood as spaces of control and containment, positioning Métis fiddling as *merely* sound and separating it from Métis communities. I further observe that Métis-style categories may constitute a refashioning of distancing strategies, allowing non-Métis to claim Métis music as their own without having to engage with Métis people, or even with Métis music. That is, they may create the semblance of cultural coming together – the semblance of making space for, and giving a voice to, Métis music and people – but they do not *require, presume, or necessarily even support* ongoing or meaningful interaction or exchange, at least not beyond what was already happening for a century within the old-time scene. Adding to the previous chapter's discussion of multicultural compartmentalization, the Métis-style categories that I have attended in Manitoba point to one problematic outcome when Métis fiddling is understood as simply a series of readily audible stylistic features, while demonstrating the flawed nature of recognition.

Much of the research for this chapter was completed between 2009 and 2013 using participant observation and interviews, though I updated the research with additional interviews in 2016 and 2017; attending the Brandon Winter Fair competition in 2022, where I had the chance to talk to participants and organizers; and following conversations about the Métis-style categories added to the Festival du Voyageur fiddle contest in 2023. It is certainly true that much has changed in Canada since my first years of research with these categories, especially post-Truth and Reconciliation Commission (TRC). Canadians' understanding of, and interest in, cross-cultural engagement and building meaningful relationships with Indigenous peoples has grown exponentially. That these categories have remained relatively unchanged during this period (as I observed in 2022) may signal, however, that they reflect pre-TRC Canada's (limited) understanding of relational responsibilities. Their continuation relatively unchanged perhaps also reflects the difficulty many non-Indigenous people have applying, or being responsive to, new discussions and understandings of respectful relations (a theme addressed in chapter seven). Certainly, since starting this research, it has been clear that Métis-style categories were added and have been maintained with good intentions, often with a sense of celebration. I have no doubt that organizers and participants wish to support the preservation of all fiddle traditions in Manitoba and beyond. But, as many scholars have pointed out, good intentionality is not enough to prevent harm, nor can it be presumed to move beyond the colonial project (Haig-Brown and Nock 2006; see also Robinson 2020, 153). As someone who grew up with old-time fiddling, and who continues to take part in the old-time scene when possible, I feel a tremendous responsibility to address this issue and view my critique as an act of care that calls for a more socially engaged and just old-time community.[1]

Métis (Style) Fiddling at Old-Time Fiddle Competitions

Fiddle contests have been taking place in Manitoba since, at least, the 1920s. There is, in fact, documented evidence of a regional competition taking place in 1927, suggesting that a network of competitions was already established (since competitors had to win a local contest in order to compete at the regional one) by the mid- to late twenties (Giroux 2013, 194).[2] Throughout their hundred-year history, they have been held in a wide variety of venues and contexts: they have been part of outdoor picnics, town or school reunions, and large fairs or exhibitions; and they have been held in malls, in parking lots, and over the radio (195–6). Though the basic principles of the competition have remained consistent (i.e., playing solo fiddle for a prize), they have seen several significant changes over the years. For example, although weekend-long events were standard in the 1990s, throughout much of the twentieth century, contests were single-day events. The first reference to a weekend-long contest in Manitoba that I have come across only dates back to the 1980s (Giroux 2013, 195). In recent years (especially since about 2005), contests have, however, reverted to single-day events, a result of declining attendance as the older generation – the largest audience for old-time competitions – passes on. Repertoire expectations have also changed over the years. Prior to the 1950s, contests typically required a waltz, schottische, and a reel. This was the norm when fiddler Lynn Mitchell (1922–2011) began competing in the early 1930s (2008; also see *Stonewall Argus* 1930; and *The Manitoba Leader* 1952a, 1). Although I have not been able to determine the exact time when the repertoire changed, it occurred before the 1970s (Hince 2012, Snider 2012).

Another change that occurred was the addition of age categories. Until the 1970s, most fiddle contests in Manitoba had only one category, open to anyone, although the reality was that women and children typically did not participate, though there were exceptions. The eventual addition of youth categories may have been due in part to greater exchange with Ontario. As ethnomusicologist Sherry Johnson's chart on the origins of fiddlers competing in Shelburne, Ontario, indicates, the number of Manitoba fiddlers attending the competition was especially high in the mid-1970s (2006, 113). Accompanist Jean Snider (1923–2022) offered an alternate explanation, noting that a couple of teachers began giving fiddle lessons, encouraging their young students to attend competitions. According to Snider, contests added youth classes in response to youth interest (2012). Whatever the case, a major shift occurred in the late 1970s and early 1980s. At this time, it became typical for contests to include two or three youth categories (e.g., nine and under, thirteen and under, and eighteen and under), plus a championship (or open) category, plus one or two senior categories (e.g., sixty plus and seventy plus, or just sixty-five plus). A twin fiddles category (where one fiddler plays the melody and another plays the harmony) also became standard at this time, giving fiddlers an opportunity to play together and make some extra cash. By the early twenty-first century, contests included a combination of the above-noted categories, as well as, occasionally, an adult category (so that less skilled adults would not have to compete in the championship class against the most skilled fiddlers of all ages) or a first-time competitor category.

In 2006, the Miami Fun and Fiddle Festival, held in Miami, Manitoba, became the first Manitoba old-time fiddling contest to include a Métis-style category. As described in chapter four, the presence of Métis fiddlers in spaces for old-time fiddling – which includes contests – went unacknowledged throughout much of the twentieth century. This began to change in the 1980s and '90s, a shift marked by the release of Ojibwe/Métis old-time contest judge and contestant Mel Bedard's album, *Métis Fiddler* (issued circa 1981), considered the first fiddle album to include the word Métis. By the time I was competing in the 1990s, the presence of Métis fiddlers at competitions and other old-time fiddle events was increasingly acknowledged: Dejarlis and Bouvette were openly recognized as Métis fiddlers, and the father/son fiddlers, Garry and Jason Lepine, were considered important Métis fiddlers in the old-time scene. The addition of a Métis-style category in Miami, Manitoba, then, followed many years of growing acceptance and recognition. This addition was, nonetheless, a spur-of-the moment idea. As I was told in an interview with an organizer, it was suggested by the competition's master of ceremonies, Joel Lamoureux, as a way to include fiddler Sierra Noble, who had arrived too late to register for the competition

(2009a). Since the number of fiddlers was down that year, the addition of a Métis-style category furthermore helped to ensure that the contest would span the entire afternoon (anonymous, interview, 2009a).[3] The addition may additionally have been influenced by the John Arcand Fiddle Festival in Saskatchewan, which already included a traditional Métis category, though notably, it also included an Andy Dejarlis category.

Two years later, a Métis-style category was added to the Manitoba Open Old Time Fiddle Championships, the provincial fiddle championship organized by the Manitoba Fiddle Association (MFA) and held in Portage la Prairie, Manitoba (see table 5.1 for an overview of the categories). Unlike the Miami contest, this Métis-style category was planned prior to being offered, and in fact began after the MFA received sponsorship from the southwest division of the Manitoba Métis Federation (MMF), an official governing body of Manitoba Métis. This sponsorship arrangement was initiated because then-MFA president, Larry McLennan (who himself is Métis), felt that it was important to solicit the endorsement and sponsorship of the MMF prior to adding the category (2009). Significantly, Leah LaPlante, who represented the MMF in this negotiation, told me that the MMF's continued sponsorship would be on a year to year basis, contingent on its promotion of the true Métis style (interview, 2010). The Michel "Kiki" Bohémier Memorial Fiddle Contest held in Lorette, Manitoba, and the Royal Manitoba Winter Fair Contest in Brandon, Manitoba, followed suit, adding Métis-style categories in 2012 and 2013 respectively, both with MMF sponsorship (anonymous, interview, 2016; and personal communication, March 14, 2016). The sponsorship relationship between the contest organizers and local branches of the MMF created a sense of cross-cultural cooperation and, of course, helped ensure that there was funding for prizes.

Although fiddle competitions are no longer held in Miami and Lorette, Métis-style categories continue to be included at the Manitoba Open and the Royal Manitoba Winter Fair. Furthermore, the Festival du Voyageur added three Métis-style categories in 2023. As such, they are, as one organizer shared with me in 2016, increasingly an expected category at Manitoba's old-time contests, a statement that holds true today. Again, it is important to note that Métis fiddlers have always been a part of Manitoba's old-time contests, profoundly shaping old-time music; the addition of Métis-style categories does not, then, entail a movement from no Métis involvement to Métis involvement. But the expectedness of Métis-style categories by the 2010s does mark a significant shift: Métis music and fiddlers went from

Table 5.1
Manitoba Open's categories and prize money

CHAMPIONSHIP	**MÉTIS-STYLE**
1st Place, $400	1st Place, $100
2nd Place, $300	2nd Place, $75
3rd Place, $225	3rd Place, $50
4th Place, $200	
5th Place, $150	
6th Place, $125	
10 & UNDER	**14 & UNDER**
1st Place, $75	1st Place, $75
2nd Place, $50	2nd Place, $50
3rd Place, $25	3rd Place, $25
18 & UNDER	**19-64**
1st Place, $125	1st Place, $125
2nd Place, $100	2nd Place, $100
3rd Place, $75	3rd Place, $75
4th Place, $50	
5th Place, $25	
65 PLUS	**TWIN FIDDLES**
1st Place, $125	1st Place, $125
2nd Place, $100	2nd Place, $50
3rd Place, $75	
4th Place, $50	**PEOPLE'S CHOICE**
	One prize, $200

Source: by author.

having a somewhat hidden presence (though as I suggest at the end of chapter four, many people may have known that certain fiddlers were Métis all along, and by the 1990s, the Métis identity of some Manitoba fiddlers was more widely known and acknowledged) to Métis music being explicitly recognized within old-time contests. Thus, while old-time fiddle contests in Manitoba have always been meeting places between Métis and non-Métis peoples and musics – that is, spaces of copresence and interaction – over the past nearly two decades, this relationship has been signalled or highlighted through Métis-style categories. In the next section, I consider in more detail the nature of the encounter between peoples at old-time contests, and specifically the nature of encounter enacted through Métis-style categories.

Musical (Pseudo) Encounters

> Reid and Saul's ultimate shortcoming is their combined failure to envision what real relationships between Indigenous peoples and Canadians would look like *in practice.*
>
> – Adam Gaudry (2013, 82, emphasis in original)

> As fiddlers were warming up, I spent some time talking to [one of the organizers] … She noted that [a representative from the Métis local] was supposed to be there, but was sick … She also noted that [a Métis fiddler] is usually present to do a Métis-style demonstration, but she unfortunately couldn't make it this year.
>
> […]
>
> A Métis flag was hung behind the chair that the Métis-style fiddlers use to compete. But beyond that, this year there was no evidence of Métis presence except for a few individuals at the competition.
>
> […]
>
> After the competition, I spoke with [a Métis fiddler]. He didn't compete in the Métis-style category because he didn't quite feel confident with clogging [using foot accompaniment] … [Another Métis competitor] said that he didn't play in the Métis-style category because he was too nervous. He was relatively new to fiddle competitions (and the fiddle) and had a lot of other activities on his mind.
>
> – Fieldnotes (30 March 2022)

In this section, I query the kinds of encounters constituted by Métis-style categories. In so doing, I ask whether they constitute the "real relationships" Gaudry is envisioning (what I understand here to mean long-term relationships that respect Métis peoplehood), or if they fall short, constituting, perhaps, a mostly symbolic relationship. Many scholars and creatives have argued that music has a great deal of power; specifically, it brings people together, and, in so doing, can build positive relations. Some of these creatives and scholars have furthermore addressed music's potential vis-à-vis

Indigenous/settler relations, suggesting, for example, that musical collaborations "may stimulate dialogue and inspire a desire for change" (Avery 2012, 161; see also Wallace 2012). Suzanne Steele, whose opera, *Li Keur: Riel's Heart of the North,* is discussed in the final chapter, has similarly positioned her work as that of reconciliation. Viewpoints such as these express great hope – hope that may give musicians a sense of purpose and agency toward creating and supporting better intercultural relationships. Building on these positive ways of thinking through musical encounters, Métis-style categories might be considered an example of the power of music to not just reflect change but to bring about change. These were ideas that I repeatedly heard from participants in my research; many expressed enthusiasm for the categories, framing them as contributing to inclusiveness. As a fiddler who grew up in Manitoba, who loves old-time music and the old-time community, it is a sentiment that I understand, and a sentiment that I even wish to be true. In fact, this sentiment might be especially strong because so many people in the old-time community are genuinely warm, kind, and generous individuals who, I believe, want to live in a peaceful society.

Without wanting to dismiss this potential, if music has power, then all of its potentialities need to be considered, including its power to reinforce the status quo, or worse. I was always somewhat uncomfortable with Métis-style categories perhaps because it never quite felt right for me, as a non-Métis person, to compete, though I certainly could have competed along with many other non-Métis (and as is explicitly outlined in the Festival du Voyageur competition's rules). However, it was Dylan Robinson's early work examining musical encounters (2012a), further developed in his book *Hungry Listening* (2020), that pushed me to consider the structural aspects of fiddle competitions. At the heart of Robinson's work is a call to not assume that "nice" encounters – encounters that smooth over the "rough aggregates of difference and sovereignty" (2020, 117) – enact real change. His concept of *felt* reconciliation is also important here, serving as a reminder that the affect (or *feeling*) of reconciliation is not the same as transformation (201–32). Robinson's work is thus an analysis of the range of musical encounters that can take place, from performances that demonstrate "the colonizing impulse of integration" to those that "make audible the rough edges of difference" (2012a, 224). In expanding this idea, Robinson offers a four-model taxonomy: integration; nation-to-nation music trading and reciprocal presentation; trading that moves toward integration; and coexistence that avoids or blocks integration (2020, 122–3). I understand this taxonomy not so much as a tool to categorize all musical encounters but rather as a provocation to consider how performances might structurally enact intercultural relationships, for better or for worse. It is a call to address the "depoliticization of musical encounter as the simple coming together of difference" (Robinson 2020, 123).

To understand how Robinson's call can be applied to Métis-style categories, it is valuable, as a first step, to consider the issues of Métis presence, visibility, and voice. Although Métis-style categories are open to all who wish to participate, the Manitoba Open event has, at times, drawn out proportionally more Indigenous (both Métis and First Nations) fiddlers than the old-time categories (that is to say, more of the Indigenous participants at old-time contests have decided to compete in Métis-style categories, in addition to the age-based categories, than non-Indigenous participants). The contests that I documented prior to 2017 suggested that about fifty per cent of the participants and up to two-thirds of the finalists in these categories were Indigenous. Notably, this was not the case at one recent competition that I attended with no Indigenous fiddlers in the category. In all cases, the fiddlers competing in the category were old-time competition regulars, often with a long history of performing in contests prior to the inclusion of Métis-style categories; several at the Manitoba Open even had a parent or grandparent who was active in the old-time scene before they themselves began competing. These categories, then, have not brought out *new* fiddlers, or fiddlers who otherwise would not have competed, though they have sometimes made the presence of Indigenous fiddlers a bit more visible, even if just for a moment during the competition. This presence is important given the long history of erasure discussed earlier in this book. It might, in fact, encourage participants to ask questions about Métis fiddling and fiddlers, and be an opportunity to make the history and contributions of Métis and other Indigenous fiddlers more known.

While the performance of individual fiddlers in the category addresses one aspect of voice, there is also the issue of reaching out beyond the individual to the broader Métis community. As noted earlier, all but one of the competitions in Manitoba that have included Métis-style categories established a connection with the MMF before adding a Métis-style category, with the relationship typically centred on sponsorship.[4] In the case of the Manitoba Open, then-MFA president Larry McLennan, himself a citizen of the MMF, reached out to the MMF because he felt that it was a natural alliance (2009). The representative from the MMF's southwest division, Leah La-

Table 5.2
Brandon Winter Fair categories and prize money

Category	1st Place	2nd Place	3rd Place
OPEN	$300	$200	$100
NOVICE (10 & UNDER)	$50	$30	$20
MÉTIS-STYLE NOVICE	$50	$30	$20
YOUTH (11 TO 16)	$50	$30	$20
MÉTIS-STYLE YOUTH	$50	$30	$20
ADULT	$150	$100	$75
MÉTIS-STYLE ADULT	$150	$100	$75
SENIORS	$50	$30	$20

Source: by author.

Plante, noted the importance of relationship, suggesting that these categories could bridge some of the gaps between Métis and non-Métis peoples. She further indicated that the categories should be controlled by the MMF, citing their right to ensure that the judges are qualified, that there is no favouritism, and that the categories represent the true Métis style (2010).[5] Since the Manitoba Open established its Métis-style category (which is open to all ages), the MMF has pushed contests to include more than one Métis-style category, based on age of participants. As a result, the now defunct contest in Lorette included two Métis-style fiddle categories (though the MMF was pushing for three),[6] while the Royal Manitoba Winter Fair includes three Métis-style categories (see table 5.2). However, when I attended in 2022, the adult Métis-style category was not offered, simply because there were no competitors. The recently added Métis-style categories at the Festival du Voyageur have followed this model with three age-based categories. In this way, the MMF has been able to push for more equality in terms of categories.

The organizers of old-time contests have expressed, since at least 2008, a desire to involve the MMF as a representative of Métis Nation citizens in Manitoba in the creation and sustenance of Métis-style categories. Yet, in practice, this involvement has meant little more than the MMF providing funding. In fact, MMF representatives have not been in attendance at contests with the Métis-style categories that I have seen (though I have been told that there is often a representative in Brandon), likely due to a lack of resources and personnel to do this work.[7] Furthermore, although LaPlante asserted a right to control the category, there is nothing built into the structure of the competition that ensures – or even supports – Métis control over rules or judging. The issue of judging is, of course, paramount: the judges determine which competitors are the best Métis-style fiddlers. Unfortunately, I found that many who have judged are not qualified to judge that category (though this is perhaps changing). Indeed, early in my research, I asked judges about the Métis style; several advised me to talk to someone more knowledgeable – even though they had already judged the category at least one time.[8] When pushed further, they would give a vague answer about rhythm or feel or would mention a tune they considered "Métis." One judge said that she did what the other judges told her to do because she did not know much about the style, and that the category gets "boring" (anonymous, interview, 2009b). And when asked if the judges agree as to what constitutes Métis fiddling, one interviewee indicated that the judges "agree in their unsureness" while another commented that the judges just "sit and look," not quite knowing what to do (anonymous, interview, 2009h). Notably, one Métis participant felt that "some contests don't judge the actual Métis class like it should [be judged]" while another suggested that the judges are judging how well a tune is played, not whether it is in the Métis style (anonymous, interview, 2017). Though there are certainly some judges who are very familiar with the style (as was the case in 2023 at the Festival du Voyageur), and are Métis fiddlers themselves, this is not necessarily the norm.

Of course, how the judges determine winners is, or should be, closely related to the rules of the competition. In the case of Métis-style categories, rules – both formal and informal – were created in large part through the collective process of competition (cf. Scott-Maxwell 2013, 15). Initially, few or no rules were in place. As an organizer of the Miami competition shared, contestants would approach her to ask about expectations for the category. Since she was unsure, she asked a judge, who told her that he would have to discuss it with the other judges (2009e). Over the years, competitions have developed Métis-style category rules, often hand in hand with contestants informally coming to know what is expected beyond what is explicitly set out in the rules. For example, clogging was not initially required, yet fiddlers quickly came to understand that winning was tied in part to clogging, and by 2012, the Manitoba Open's rules required clogging (see table 5.3).[9] This change was made in part because the accompanists (who are hired by organizers) did not know how to accompany all the tunes, as was sometimes quite apparent to listeners, but it also reflected an emergent understanding of Métis fiddling. As one organizer told me, "Let the category form itself." Let it be shaped and moulded "as it will" (anonymous, interview, 2012). The process of competing was thus used to collectively produce the parameters of what, in the context of the competition, constitutes the Métis style. Though rules have since become more standardized, they remain relatively vague beyond requiring contestants to play a Métis tune, clog, and have good timing. Addressing some of these concerns, the Festival du Voyageur's "rules and regulations" for the Métis-style categories specifically states that "there will be two qualified judges," though it is not clear how or who will determine qualifications.

While the above suggestion is that the MMF has little say in the categories, even if representatives were engaged in all aspects, ultimate control over inclusion and rules would remain in the hands of a small number of organizers – most of whom are not Métis (though certainly some are). The MMF could withdraw financial support for prizes, but the prize money for these categories, especially in the case of the Manitoba Open with its single category, is relatively insignificant compared to the amount of money handed out in the other categories (just $225 out of $3,500 in prize money goes to Métis-style category winners)[10] and could likely be made up for in other ways. While the organizers have worked to include the MMF, should a disagreement arise, the contest organizers would have the last word on the category since the MMF (or notably, any Métis cultural group) is not an equal partner in the competition's organizational fabric. In fact, one organizer from the

Table 5.3
Manitoba Open Métis-style rules

1. The Métis-style fiddling contestants must play one tune of their own choice in the traditional style.
2. The judges will take into consideration: double stringing, double bowing, and timing.
3. No accompaniment except foot rhythms.

Manitoba Open Championships shared (after reading a draft of my dissertation, where I offered some of these same critiques) that she would continue including the category even without MMF support because it has been so successful (anonymous, interview, 2013). As this organizer's comment makes clear, the inclusion of the category is closely tied to its value to the competition as a whole rather than its acceptance by Métis peoples. Competitions can therefore add or drop the categories – that is, include or exclude – or change the rules, whenever it is beneficial for the larger competition to do so. Since the addition of Métis-style categories has not changed the structure of the competitions, they can easily be added or omitted without affecting the larger event.

What I have observed, then, is that the addition of Métis categories has done very little to enhance old-time competitions' engagement with Métis communities, especially beyond the level of individual fiddlers. Despite this, they are often (mis)interpreted as spaces of real cultural and inter-nation (Métis/Canadian) exchange, as if they express a "side-by-side" relationship of copresence. In fact, several participants suggested that the addition of these categories strengthens the relationship between Métis people and other Manitobans. Others view the categories as giving space to Métis music. Yet as noted above, Métis voices are heard in all categories, and non-Métis voices are heard in the Métis-style category (which raises the question of whether what the non-Métis fiddlers are playing would even qualify as Métis music [Derksen et al. 2019, 69], though it is certainly heard as such by at least some of the audience). What is perhaps most problematic here is that none of these expressions of "voice" require, in any way, learning from Métis people or community. Of course, in the case of Métis performers, it is likely that many are learning in and with community. However, some (non-Métis) competitors have shared that they competed with tunes learned from non-Indigenous sources (e.g., recordings of non-Indigenous fiddlers or from non-Indigenous teachers) – meaning that they have not even had to *listen to* Métis fiddlers to perform the (supposed) Métis style.[11] The category therefore makes it possible to play "Métis" music (and win) while at no time engaging with Métis music or people. Though I do not wish to suggest that the categories can *never* work toward relationship, my observations thus far are that they do not; certainly, learning a tune from a recording that sounds Métis (at least to a non-Métis fiddler) is insufficient.[12]

Returning to the question posed at the start of this section about Métis-style categories, my research indicates that they might be understood as integration (here referencing Robinson's taxonomy), because their addition has not changed the structure of the competitions. More problematically, they may create the semblance of copresence and the affect of alliance, without being or becoming spaces for meaningful intercultural exchange, much less spaces for inter-nation encounter (cf. Robinson 2012b, 122–4); that is to say, performing in and listening to a Métis-style category may *feel* like a meaningful encounter even if, as was the case at one contest that I attended, there are no Métis participants. Here, it is worth noting that some of the other categories at this contest *did* have Métis participants; these "old-time" categories therefore may have represented a more authentic encounter with Métis musicking, though this too should not stand in for ongoing and meaningful engagement with Métis collectivities. As such it is possible for Métis-style categories to displace the encounters and exchanges that occur in other arenas of the competition. Herein lies a key problem of recognition, as identified by scholars such as Chris Andersen (Métis) who highlight the issue of *mis*recognition: the category, in being named a Métis category, presumes that the fiddling in the category is Métis, even though it was created with limited engagement with Métis communities and can take place with no Métis involvement, and no learning with and from Métis communities. In my understanding of what Gaudry is suggesting in terms of "real relationships," meaningful engagement should mean greater entanglement – likely enough that the category could not run without significant Métis involvement. Certainly, MMF sponsorship cannot and should not stand in for broader engagement.

Containing Métis Music

Métis-style categories, as I have observed them, sit in contrast to Métis-run cultural events where creativity, vitality, diversity, and responsiveness to communities are vital. These events are centres of Métis resurgence and contemporary nation-building, serving as spaces for Métis people to unite as a healthy, vibrant community (cf. Simpson 2011, 12–13). The next chapter discusses these events in detail, but a brief overview is needed here to situate the issue of containment, the key theme of this section. Held across and beyond the Métis Homeland during the summer months, with smaller events held throughout the year, they embody creative and growing Métis traditions, and are responsive to the needs of contemporary Métis people. As a central component, the fiddling heard at Métis events reflects the diversity of a lived, Métis identity. It is not one thing, bounded within a restricted, narrowly defined style, but is varied and ever changing based on the lived experiences of the fiddlers. Certainly, the Métis fiddlers at these events play in styles that would be recognized by many as uniquely Métis, but they also perform in a multiplicity of Métis *styles* and draw on styles perhaps not typically heard as Métis. Fiddlers furthermore play with a variety of backing bands (although bands made up of guitar, bass, and drums are the most common), and mix their own local styles with country, bluegrass, Cape Breton, and other old-time musics. In this way, the fiddlers engage past and present Métis identities alongside contemporary influences and relational networks, while centring emergent understandings of what it means to be Métis (Giroux 2016). At these events, fiddling (as well as dancing) embodies transformation and alternatives and allows Métis communities to see themselves in action and represent themselves as a collectivity (Rice 2007, 35).

In contrast to Métis cultural events, the value of Métis-style categories, for many at least, lies in their sounded difference and their narrowly defined authenticity. Though Métis fiddling does often include sounded differences (even though this sounding is not always audible to outsiders, nor does it necessarily include the elements considered most important from the perspective of the multicultural categorization of fiddle styles, as noted in the previous chapter), in the context of old-time competitions, this difference is fundamental: fiddlers, audience members, and organizers need to be able to hear, or see, Métis-style categories as a unique addition because, without this visible or audible difference, they would be nothing more than additional old-time categories. As one judge told me, they were added because organizers wanted to include something new and interesting; they "added flair" (2009g). While as previously discussed, the rules that govern Métis-style categories remain somewhat vague, the rule that fiddlers must sit and clog with no accompanist is, in the context of these categories, the clearest marker of Métis-style fiddling's difference from the old-time style, creating both visual (the fiddlers are seated and use their feet) and aural (there is no piano, just foot accompaniment) markers of difference from the old-time categories. Fiddlers further mark this difference through tune choice, playing Québécois tunes (considered "somewhat interchangeable with Métis tunes," as one fiddler told me); iconically Métis tunes (e.g., the "Red River Jig"); tunes recorded or composed by Métis fiddlers John Arcand or Andy Dejarlis (e.g., "Victor's 39th Movement in G"); or tunes that are popular among old-time fiddlers, but typically not chosen by fiddlers in the old-time categories because they are too common or perhaps too "traditional" (e.g., "Big John McNeil"), a point I will return to below. Tunes are one relatively easy way to maintain difference because they can be easily identified and categorized as appropriate or not appropriate.

In addition to aurality and visuality, difference is also created through discourse that positions Métis-style categories as *more traditional* (a loaded term). This "traditionality" was mentioned by many participants who suggested that Métis-style categories give fiddlers who are good dance musicians but are not technically perfect, or who learned by ear ("in the traditional way") rather than through formal training, the opportunity to win (2009c; and personal communication 2016). This issue has been debated in the old-time scene for decades, certainly long before the addition of Métis-style categories, as I witnessed growing up in the scene; and it has been debated in the broader Canadian old-time scene (see Johnson 2006). Strikingly, though, it is not uncommon for the winner of the old-time classes to *also* win the Métis-style categories, meaning that mode of learning is *not* a key factor. Instead, one of the ways that so-called traditionality is expressed is through tune choice. In addition to tunes by Andy Dejarlis, many popular old-time favourites were mentioned as appropriate for the Métis-style categories, including "Whiskey Before Breakfast," "Big John McNeil," and "St. Anne's Reel." Although these tunes and those popularized by Dejarlis are part of Manitoba's and Canada's old-time canon and are thus frequently played by fiddlers across the country at jam sessions, dances, and concerts, many are not considered particularly appropriate for competing in old-time categories since they are so well-known. Old-time fiddlers (especially in the open or championship category – but much less so in the seniors' categories) prefer to compete with unique tunes that will make them stand out in the competition and, perhaps, that better reflect the contemporaneity of old-time fiddling, which, as previously discussed, has a long history of cross-style and cross-genre borrowing.[13]

Affirming "traditionality" in Métis-style categories is further accomplished through the rule that requires clogging. Certainly, clogging – footwork that imitates the sound of a horse – is deeply meaningful to Métis people. (This same sound is, in fact, heard in jigging, a form of dance primarily associated with Métis peoples.) In the past, clogging also added volume and rhythmic texture in contexts where accompaniment was rare, that is, prior to the arrival of pianos and guitars. In noting this, I wish to highlight how contexts continually shape musics, and attend to the idea that there is no one moment where Métis music was "most authentic" (e.g., prior to the arrival of guitars and pianos – which in itself varied greatly from place to place). Although many Métis fiddlers still clog, it is now often venue- and context-dependent. In large arenas, Métis fiddlers usually perform with amplification and a band; they are less likely to clog in these settings than in more intimate settings[14] (though some are reviving this practice, and I have even seen one fiddler use a more subtle form of clogging while standing). Change, then, is part of the Métis tradition. As one Métis fiddler told me in response to Métis-style categories and the expectations that they impose, it is important to look to the Elders to see what they played, but there is nothing wrong with "thinking outside the box" (2009d). The insistence that fiddlers must clog, along with a heavy focus on certain tunes, is thus problematic because it suggests that Métis fiddling can only be what it was in the past. (In Brandon in 2022, the rule requiring clogging ended up excluded one Métis fiddler who could not clog.) Not only is situating "authentic" Métis fiddling in one moment in the past inaccurate (see Quick, who traces shifts in Métis fiddling over time [2009, 265–6]), but it can also position Métis music as incompatible with change and modernity.

What I have observed about Métis-style categories, then, is that they define and delimit Métis music and in doing so, place it in a container that it exceeds. In reading and thinking with Indigenous musicians and scholars about conceptualizations of traditionality and modernity, I have learned that tradition is important – indeed vital – to Indigenous musicians, but it does not mean immutability; that tradition can be transmitting through ways of thinking and doing (not just specific ways of *sounding*); and that multiple ways of being musical can and do exist within Indigenous communities without the presumption that one way replaces the other (Urion 2022; see also Deloria 2004, Derksen et al. 2019, Knight 2015, Perea 2021). Speaking specifically to past practices, Heidi Senungetuk (Inupiaq) writes, "we don't see ourselves as old-fashioned; rather we exist in the present while invoking past and future generations. Bringing ideas from the past into the present is a way of 'Indigenizing' just about anything, including popular and classical musics by Native composers and singer-songwriters. New music challenges listeners to rethink static images of Indigeneity through expressive media that are at once forward-looking and of the present and that embrace the past" (2019, xiv). Knight similarly points to ways that Indigenous hip hop continues much older practices, such as storytelling and centring the drumbeat (2015, n.p.). These artists and scholars challenge assumptions about tradition and what that means in the context of music and musicking. They also explicitly position Indigenous musics as always modern (Senungetuk 2019, xiv). These ways of understanding and framing Indigenous musics resonate strongly with the practices at Métis cultural events; but not so much with Métis-style categories.

It is from this perspective that I view Métis-style categories as containment. I further posit that this containment meets particular needs at this moment in time for non-Indigenous people (who make up the majority of competitors and audience members at most old-time contests). According to Plains Cree/Métis scholar Emma LaRocque, an insistence on Indigenous difference and an obsession with authenticity can be tied to an economy of otherness. (And here, the use of the term "economy" is important given that the first Métis-style category in Manitoba was added because there were too few competitors and the organizers wanted to ensure that there was enough entertainment.) She points to the pressures put on Indigenous "artists and intellectuals to produce works expressly and manifestly different from the dominant culture," arguing that this fetishization of difference reflects "a continuing attempt to find a culture unspoiled by contact" (2010, 135; see also Quick 2009, 265). An insistence on difference, she ultimately suggests, "affords the colonizer the room to exploit Native culture(s) for economic, entertainment and even spiritual purposes" (138). Given the relative lack of engagement with Métis people, I do believe that Métis-style categories are a form of exploiting through contained difference. To be clear, in forwarding this argument, I am not making an assertion about the *intentionality* of organizers, who I believe simply want their events to be successful (here defined as sustainable over the long term) or participants (Métis or non-Métis), who I believe simply enjoy playing in the categories. Rather, I am speaking to the possible *function* and *result* of these categories, and the ways that they may reflect unspoken and unacknowledged assumptions, priorities, stereotypes, or relationships. In the final section of this chapter, I consider one additional possible function: the claiming of Métis music for all Manitobans.

Métis as Manitoban Identity

> I consider myself lucky to have the benefit of having had [a] positive and enriching experience with the Métis culture, and I even identify with it even though I am not Métis.
> –Manitoba Open fiddler and judge (personal communication 2017)

> At the heart of every Manitoban lies the spirit of the Métis.
> – Anonymous speaker during the opening ceremony of the Festival du Voyageur

In interpreting Métis-style categories and how they function, I read them alongside the changing relationship between Manitobans (and Canadians more broadly) and Métis peoples that emerged in the late twentieth and early twenty-first centuries. At the start of this chapter, I included quotes from popular philosopher John Ralston Saul and religious studies scholar Jennifer Reid, whose monographs embody, I believe, this changing relationship. Specifically, both authors adopt Métis-ness as a solution to the problem of an "elusive" Canadian identity. This appropriation of Métis identity is not new. It might, in fact, be dated back to the 1960s (as discussed in chapters three and four), as Canada struggled to emerge as a nation unique from both Britain – to which it had long-held political and cultural ties – and the United States, whose cultural exports (such as music, television, and radio) were becoming more pervasive.[15] As part of uncovering what it meant to be Canadian, there was an increased interest in Métis peoples, as many Canadians – and some non-Canadians – began drawing artistic inspiration from

Métis history and culture. This interest resulted in a flurry of settler-created cultural productions that focused on the story of Louis Riel, or to a lesser extent, Métis singer-songwriter Pierre Falcon, or that used Métis music, such as the "Red River Jig," to create something new.[16] While these works (especially those prior to the 2000s) might be best understood as representing exploratory or emergent undercurrents, it is clear, given Saul and Reid's work in widely divergent disciplines, that by the early 2000s, this undercurrent of interest in the potentials of Métis history and culture within artistic practice had turned into much more: Métis-ness was being *openly and unapologetically* used by two non-Métis authors (one widely read) to explain and create Canadian identity.[17]

As traced earlier, it was at about this time that Métis-style categories came to be an accepted and even expected part of Manitoba's old-time fiddle competitions. It was also at about this time that ethnomusicologist and scholar of Indigenous fiddling, Anne Lederman, noted that, "as a Canadian fiddler, I really want to be able to claim [Indigenous/Métis fiddling] for all of us, to be able to stand up and say, 'Look what was created here – look what we did – look at our beautiful new baby'" (2009, 368). Something was, I would suggest, shifting, and the success of Métis-style categories in the years that followed might indicate that they addressed an ongoing need among Manitobans/Canadians. The success of Métis-style categories is particularly notable given a failed attempt by the MFA to encourage the addition of novelty or own choice categories in the early 2000s – categories that are included at some contests in other provinces, and that certainly could have incorporated some Métis-style tunes, and lots of "flair,"[18] though here it is notable that they likely would not have addressed a desire for "traditionality." Something about Métis-style categories, *understood, defined, and limited* as such, made them particularly relevant to Manitobans at the turn of the twenty-first century. In this final section, I argue that the adoption of Métis-style categories marks a shift away from understanding Métis identity as something that should be placed at a temporal, physical, fictional, or perhaps even historical distance, to something that can, problematically, be claimed for all Manitobans. That is, I consider Métis-style categories as one way in which non-Métis began to claim Métis-ness as part of their identity *as Manitobans*. In doing so, I reflect on how Métis-style categories might benefit non-Métis, and especially white Manitobans, at a cost to Métis people, by creating a space where they can enrich their own cultural experience while consuming a "safe" form of Indigeneity.

While Robinson's work has been particularly important in developing my understanding of the structural and relational aspects of Métis-style categories, ethnomusicologist David Kaminsky's research on the appropriation of klezmer by Swedish musicians offers insights that help disentangle the *function* of these categories. In the case of encounter that Kaminsky identifies, specifically the Swedish klezmer boom, there is no physical encounter between peoples; indeed, Sweden has never had a large Jewish population (Kaminsky 2014, 256). Rather, Swedes encounter (supposed) Jewishness primarily, or even only, through performance. This, of course, is different from the context in Manitoba, as there is a significant Métis population in the province; however, it is similar in the sense that many non-Métis people do not regularly engage with Métis people *as Métis* (though this is rapidly changing); and it resonates with some non-Métis fiddlers learning supposedly Métis music from non-Métis fiddlers. Kaminsky offers two possible explanations for the popularity of klezmer in Sweden. The first centres "currency and propriety": as a hybrid music, cultural mixing is understood as authentic, and, having been born of European soil, it is viewed as belonging to Europeans. This resonates with the ways in which Métis music might be seen by some as Canada's "new baby." His second explanation is that klezmer is used to help Swedes "mitigate their anxieties" about increased immigration from the Middle East (2014, 254). It is "just exotic enough" (272). This explanation highlights how music, as a safe, controllable, and claimable form of otherness, can "bring comfort," in the context of racial tensions (256). This points to the possibility that Métis music – as a music that is proximate in some ways to European music traditions – might be seen by some Manitobans as a safer, *less Indigenous,* form of Indigeneity, that is, as *just Indigenous enough.*

The first line of thinking around the issue of "currency and propriety," was evident in the ways that many participants spoke about Métis-style categories, connecting them to Manitoba's history. When asked why the category was added, one organizer noted that "Métis people come from here" and as such are the "original Canadians" (anonymous, interview, 2012). In organizing the competition, she wished to promote music from here (i.e., from Manitoba), rather than music that was brought here from elsewhere. Both an organizer and a competitor at the Manitoba Open similarly told me that the addition of a Métis-style category was closely connected to place; these consultants noted that there are many Métis people in the area and that the addition therefore reflected this presence (2009i). More recently, judges and participants have told me that Métis-style categories have been added because Métis music "is an integral part of our society," and "is very much part of Manitoba's old-time fiddle history" (anonymous, interview, 2016) both statements that I agree with wholeheartedly. Participants further suggested that Métis-style categories allow Métis people to "showcase their heritage" and Manitobans more broadly to "show off *our* Métis heritage" (2016) – statements that I am less inclined to agree with (the first because it is not always clear that it is Métis people "showcasing" their heritage, and the second because it makes a move toward claiming). As such, they are positioned by some participants as "a way to pay respect to a people who have greatly influenced the Prairie fiddling style" (personal communication, 2016). As these statements indicate, participants tie the inclusion of Métis-style categories to Manitoba's Métis history and Métis population (both positive and legitimate reasons for inclusion). But they also make a subtle move toward *claiming* Métis music as belonging to all Manitobans ("I identify with it"), a way to position Manitoba as unique (cf. Mackey 2002, 102–3).

The appropriation, or claiming, of marginalized people's cultures for the purposes of (white) identity building has been addressed in the work of a number of scholars including sociologist Sunera Thobani, anthropologists Ghassan Hage and Eva Mackey, writer and scholar Sara Ahmed, and others who have written about multiculturalism as state policy. These authors point out that multiculturalism emerged at a time when marginalized people were gaining power and were more actively resisting domination; they could therefore no longer be excluded from social and political life (Thobani 2007, 155; Hage 2000, 101). Assimilation policies (as law or practice) could no longer work in the face of this heightened resistance, and, to address this, policies that nonetheless functioned to *govern* diversity (policies such as multiculturalism) were put into place (Hage 2000, 237). Eva Mackey's work is particularly relevant here because it highlights how the management of difference became a central means of identity formation for white Canadians. By managing internal differences, "the nation could be imagined as distinct and differentiated from external others such as the United States" (2002, 145). As a result, difference (especially cultural differences in the realms of food, music, and dance) has been tolerated and even advocated for; difference has come to be used for the "nation's sustenance and enrichment" (Thobani 2007, 164; cf. Deloria 1999). This tolerance of, and even advocacy for, Métis music (explicitly named as such, though perhaps not always an accurate descriptor) may indeed be a mode of sustenance and enrichment. In returning to the idea of traditionality and the ongoing fear among some in the old-time community that the real "old-time" style is being lost or always slipping away, Métis-style categories may fulfill a perceived need to sustain the most "traditional" elements of fiddling. (This idea recalls the Old-Timer Balls discussed in chapter three, where Métis fiddling and dancing, though at the time not named as such, were used to create a tie to "pioneer" life.)

While difference is in this way accepted and even positioned as valuable, authors such as Mackey have noted that it is often framed as acceptable "in terms of food and dancing" ("flavour" and "colour"), but that this tolerance has limits, and does not extend to anything that might be perceived as "special rights" (Mackey 2002, 100–1, 104–5). In the context of Métis-style categories, it is helpful to put these ideas in conversation with Kaminsky's framing of certain musics as "just exotic enough." It has certainly been clear to me that Métis-style categories are thought of as "flavour" and "colour" (or "flair," as often repeated). But Métis music might also be seen as "just exotic enough" *to appropriate*. To better explain what I mean, imagine the following scenario: a group of non-Indigenous (or perhaps mostly non-Indigenous) people decide to organize a powwow to promote music from here (Manitoba/Canada) and allow Indigenous people to "showcase their heritage." Now, imagine that many of the dancers, and maybe drum groups, are non-Indigenous; perhaps all the dancers and musicians are non-Indigenous. I suspect that most readers would consider this to be inappropriate.[19] Though I do not mean to suggest that Métis music is interchangeable with powwow dance and music, they are similar in that they are both social rather than primarily ceremonial forms of Indigenous musicking. Given that this is what happens through Métis-style categories at least some of the time (i.e., there are occasions where most or even all of the competitors are not Métis, and often many or even most of the organizers are not Métis), it seems that the performance of Métis music (or what is believed to be Métis music) by non-Métis is viewed as acceptable. Why might Métis fiddling be seen as a "safe" way for non-Métis to appropriate Indigeneity? Might it be a way to keep Métis-ness close (consuming identity and culture) while keeping Métis people at a distance (since it does not require engagement)? Or might it be because (white) Manitobans, by and large, view themselves as already somewhat Métis just by being Manitoban – holding that spirit deep within?

Concluding Reflections

> Composers [and musicians] who make works that represent Indigenous history, culture, and people have consistently failed to enter into a long-term practice of relation with the very people they create work about, as well as with the larger political history and present-day contexts of the communities they represent through their music.
> – Robinson (2020, 152)

The explicit and intentional recognition of Métis music at old-time fiddle contests marks a significant shift away from earlier practices of erasure within the old-time scene. There is no longer a sense that Métis individuals and musics need to be hidden in these spaces, to simply not be named, or to be referred to as "French." This shift is important and, in many ways, affirming; it makes room for an increased sense of pride in Métis identity among performers and attendees. Yet this chapter also raises three key concerns. First, these categories have failed to bring about meaningful relationships with Métis people and peoples, at best simply drawing some attention to the presence of Indigenous fiddlers who have long participated in old-time contests; here, though, it is worth noting that attendees may not always be sure whether or not they are listening to a Métis "voice." Second, they may function to contain Métis fiddling, insisting that it be positioned through sounded/visual difference and "traditionality" (meaning the use of certain tunes seen as particularly traditional and clogging); certainly, they are unable to realize the ways in which Métis music exceeds the boundaries of style. And third, they may be used and understood as part of a larger process of instrumentalizing Métis identity for the creation or sustenance of Manitoban/Canadian identity, similar to Saul's description of Métis identity as something that is "deep within us" (that is, all Canadians). In offering these critiques, I am not arguing that Métis-style categories, or old-time fiddle contests more generally, could never be places of good relationship or Métis musical vitality and creativity. Rather, I believe that they have, so far, failed to be these kinds of spaces. In the next chapter, I consider in more detail the vitality of Métis musical practice, while, in the final chapter, I draw on two case studies to better understand what it might mean to listen and build real relationship.

6

Cultural Festivals as Recognition and Resurgence

> The forty-ninth parallel divides two countries … it divided the Métis nation for many years, but now we're back together here [at Metisfest …]. It's not just the music … you'll see people smiling and laughing, and shaking hands, and hugging, and you know you'll see even crying, but it'll be more tears of joy, you know, I found a relative and I never seen you for the last fifty years. We've made this connection here and you'll see people they will come back, and they'll just continue coming back.
>
> – Dan Goodon, interview with author (30 August 2012)

Métis cultural festivals are vibrant gathering spaces for Métis living across and beyond the Métis Homeland. These Métis-led gatherings centre on music and dance and embrace both the unity of the Métis peoples and the distinct communities and histories of the regions where the festivals take place. Sometimes conceived of as a "Pemmican Trail" of festivals (borrowing from the concept of the Powwow Trail, and referencing pemmican, a vital traditional source of food and economic sustenance for Métis), they are separate yet interconnected events. At the larger festivals, attendees can witness fiddler after fiddler performing in a wide range of tunes and styles, while experiencing the thundering rhythms (or their gentler footwork, if wearing moccasins) of jiggers and square dance troupes. These fiddle and dance performances are interspersed with vocalists singing folk, gospel, rock, and classic country hits, as well as original songs in French and English and, occasionally, songs in one of the Michif dialects (Métis languages). Just as importantly, attendees can become active participants by grabbing a partner and dancing on the always-open dance floor; competing in the fiddling, jigging, and talent competitions; attending a church service (often, but not always, Catholic); or by joining a jam session.

This chapter surveys three of these Métis festivals,[1] addressing their local and broader national significance pertaining to the Métis Nation beyond provincial and state boundaries. Although they may appear to be apolitical spaces for the celebration of culture, I suggest that, in practice, they are complex political spaces – that is, opportunities to influence political processes and outcomes – where issues of recognition and resurgence intersect. As described in the opening epigraph, for some, Métis cultural festivals function as family reunions, placing them within a framework of contemporary kinship and alliance.[2] They also function as pilgrimages that facilitate reconnection with ancestors and reclaiming of place in the context of dispersal and disconnection from land; as spaces to (re)learn cultural practices under the guidance of Elders and community; and as opportunities to engage with the settler state in order to be recognized as Métis, or alternatively, to publicly enact a nation-to-nation relationship with the settler state. The Pemmican Trail serves as an example of the ways in which music- and dance-centred cultural events can enact, sometime simultaneously, engagement with and turning away from the settler state. More succinctly, they are spaces for Métis to regain their spirit as peoples (as expressed in an oft-quoted statement attributed to Louis Riel).

I begin with Back to Batoche Days, in Batoche, Saskatchewan. Held at a site that is deeply meaningful to Métis, Back to Batoche is the oldest continuously running Métis festival, with connections that date back to the late 1800s. For these reasons, it has developed iconic status as *the* cultural festival to attend at least once in a lifetime, though some people attend annually. Next, I consider Oshawa Métis Heritage Festival, a unique event because it takes place outside of the Métis Homeland. Because of its location in southern Ontario, key issues addressed through the festival include lack of recognition and understanding of Métis identity, history, and presence. This is similarly the case in Choteau, Montana, where the Mitchif[3] Heritage Keepers hold the Métis Music and Art Festival. However, the lack of recognition in Choteau is distinct because it extends to a lack of *government* recognition: that is, American government policy does not recognize Métis as a distinct people as is the case in Canada, only accepting non-Indigenous or "American Indian" identities.[4] These examples – three of many, many Métis cultural festivals that have been held since the 1970s – tease out some of the ways that festivals work both within and beyond the expectations of settler states. More generally, they point to the multifaceted approaches to festivity within the Métis Nation.

This chapter includes a mix of fieldnotes, interview excerpts, descriptive prose, and images. I have also posted supplementary materials (videos, images, and descriptive blogposts) drawn from my fieldwork at these and similar events, on my website. Though I do include some analysis (such as my argument above that these festivals do political work, specifically that they engage with both recognition and resurgence), the chapter is largely descriptive in nature. In approaching this chapter in this way, I aim, as an outsider, to describe some of the complexity and richness of Métis festivals, reveal my process and thinking, and make room for readers to come to their own, possibly alternative, interpretations. I furthermore want to be able to show readers how Métis music and musicking, in the twenty-first century, is so much more than a singular style or approach; it is a process embedded in a series of rich and shifting relationships with kin and place. Of course, writing and field documentation do not replace the rich face-to-face relationships at the heart of these festivals. Specifically, I am conscious of how the very thing that makes Métis cultural festivals so important and meaningful to many – namely the visiting and personal connection in community (as Goodon notes in the interview referenced above) – cannot be translated to the page. However, perhaps the descriptions that follow will encourage those who have not yet attended a Métis festival to join the Pemmican Trail.

A Pilgrimage Back to Batoche

Back to Batoche Days – known for its first fifteen years as Métis Heritage Days – is the oldest, continuously running Métis cultural festival.[5] While the modern, or vitalized, festival began in 1970, Métis have been gathering in, and returning to, Batoche for celebrations since the 1880s, connecting it to a much longer history of cultural celebration. As Michif historian Diane Payment notes, the first National Métis celebration was held in 1884, with 24 July becoming the official day of celebration in 1886, though it seemed to go dormant in the 1930s (1990, 56–7). Held next to the historic Batoche town site where the Canadian government defeated the Métis in 1885, the festival site and surrounding area have a layered history of Métis community and kin; of trauma, devastation, defeat, and sorrow; and of strength, resistance, and resilience in the face of extreme hardship and suffering. Since the 1970s, the Back to Batoche Festival has become a vital place for bringing together the community, attracting as many as 10,000 attendees (though there is an ebb and flow of audience size from year to year and decade to decade). The festival serves numerous functions. It is a celebration of Métis culture, as well as an opportunity for reconnection to land and kin; it makes a powerful statement about continuing presence at a site that, for many years, was understood as the moment when Canada defeated the Métis. In this way, it is a statement about still being here after everything. As noted by Sylvia Johnson, former Minister of Health and Region Six President (Métis Nation of Alberta), "Batoche brings us back to our traditions, to our culture, to our roots. It really cements in firmly here in the ground who we are as Métis" (2018).

Back to Batoche Days began as a collaboration between a Saskatchewan-based Métis political and cultural organization, then known as the Métis Society of Saskatchewan, and the Saskatchewan and Canadian governments who were starting to transition toward policies of multiculturalism. Though the collaboration was valuable from the perspective of funding and perhaps also public-facing visibility, the settler government collaborators placed parameters on the gathering. As noted Métis activist Duke Redbird said, "federal and provincial governments agreed to fund the event provided it was not used as a political rally" (1980, 50). However, Redbird and others knew that cultural events could do important work, even if they were often seen as "non-threatening" to the mainstream (48). Indeed, attendees of the vitalized gathering have explicitly connected, on many occasions, the modern celebration to the struggles and the rights that Métis fought for in the 1885 Resistance. In a 1983 radio interview during Back to Batoche Days, respected Elder Maria Campbell described, for example, her deep-rooted familial connection to Batoche through the generations. She emphasized the connection between the Resistance of 1885 and late twentieth-century Métis struggles. As she expressed after discussing the Resistance,

> For me, coming back here, it's a combination of all those things. It's my great-grandmother and her feeling [that] the struggle never stopped, and it will go on for many, many years. For me to come here as a little girl, and to remember that, to come here as a young woman, to come back here as a mother with my children, and now to be back here with my grandchildren, and, you know when Winston [Wuttunee]

> was talking this morning and he says that if there's one of us standing on this ground there are thousands of people that stand with us, I really believe that. (Campbell 1983)

Renowned Cree/Métis entertainer and Elder, Winston Wuttunee, was featured in the same radio interview. As referenced by Campbell, he spoke about the connection with the past and with ancestors, stating,

> Those people down at that mass graveyard this morning, they never died. Because even as I looked around there, I could see all those people, and the people that were living, the spirits of them. The people that are living are the manifestations of those people. And those old people that died in that battle, I'm sure sometimes their last prayers was, "Father take me to be with you," and also was, "don't let what we're fighting for, don't let that die, right here. Let it continue on." Now when I hear this music over here like this, there's [this] fellow over there playing fiddle. He's over there playing and people are jigging. Those people over there playing and those people over there jigging, that one man that cried out to the father, father take me to be with you, don't let what we're fighting for, don't let that die here. His prayers are answered. That music that you hear over there, and that jigging that you hear over there, those are the answers to that, to that soldier's prayer. (Wuttunee 1983)

His comment is striking for the way in which he emphasizes music and dance as a statement about continued presence on the very land where Métis ancestors fought for freedom.

Métis history exudes from every corner of the land around where the festival takes place; there are reminders of the deep connection at every turn. As I wrote in my fieldnotes,

> This morning, before going to the festival site, I travelled to Duck Lake. The town is worn and unkempt. Many of the buildings seem to have fallen into disuse. But this isn't necessarily true: the pub (with a Louis Riel sign) is – according to the locals I spoke with – still open [see figures 6.1 and 6.2] … The murals for which modern Duck Lake is known (most painted in the 1990s) are peeling, their dulled colours hazy with dust [see figure 6.3] … From Duck Lake, I headed to St. Laurent shrine.

6.1
Three buildings in Duck Lake

> There was a grotto (erected in the late 1800s), a church (built relatively recently), and an outdoor church area, including confessionals. A graveyard is also on the site [see figure 6.4]. Blanketed with small grasshoppers, it is here that the Métis killed at Duck Lake were buried. (fieldnotes, 19 July 2018)

Visiting Duck Lake and the cemetery is a powerful experience. To be in the town where the Northwest Resistance began, and to stand by the graves of the Métis men killed, brings to life that history in a way that books cannot. To feel the same wind blowing across your face that these Métis ancestors felt, to experience the dust and heat of the July sun and see the endless prairie grass blanketing the ground creates an embodied understanding of this history and an embodied connection to the people who came before.

My stop at Tourand's Coulee (also known as Fish Creek) was equally powerful, though the power of that place, admittedly, was lost on me until later, as I learned more about its significance. My fieldnote entry for Tourand's Coulee is short:

> The Fish Creek site has a monument, as well as several plaques in a fenced-off area (barbed wire), describing the significance of the site.

6.2
Duck Lake Hotel

6.3
MacDonald, Riel, and Dumont, Duck Lake mural

6.4
Cemetery

> Plaques line a pathway that borders around a coulee. What from afar looks like metal outlines of soldiers are a main feature (showing the battle with General Middleton). (fieldnotes, 20 July 2018)

Tourand's Coulee is a celebrated site of a Métis victory. Specifically, it was at Tourand's Coulee that Métis were temporarily able to halt General Middleton's advance toward Batoche. After visiting, I learned about Josephte Tourand (1831–1928). Josephte and her husband Joseph had moved from Saint-François Xavier (in Manitoba) to the Saint-Antoine-de-Padoue Parish in Batoche just a few years before the Northwest Resistance. Though the historical documents about the Tourand family do not address why they moved to the Batoche area, the discrimination and violence Métis faced in Manitoba – and of course the land loss – undoubtedly played a role in their decision. Furthermore, Métis had been moving through Batoche for a hundred years; it was part of the Homeland. So, they moved with eighty head of cattle, and much equipment, ready to start anew. Just a year after arriving in Batoche, in 1884, Josephte's husband passed away. Nonetheless, Josephte, with the help of her children, was able to build a farmhouse with all the necessary buildings to run a successful farm.

When Middleton's troops arrived in 1885, Josephte was forced to flee her new home. The troops burned her farm, killing and scattering her animals, and taking her horses and wagon. Furious, she went to Middletown's encampment and took back her horse and wagon, a small moment of victory following an act of resistance. Just weeks later, two of her sons were killed at the Battle of Batoche. She lost another son two months later, and a fourth and fifth son in 1886 and 1887. Four years later, she lost a daughter, then only twenty-five years of age, and she lost another child in 1898. All of this death on top of the loss of a child in 1870 at the age of three. Josephte lived with this immense loss until 1928, when she died just a few years short of her hundredth birthday. I now think of this woman, whose name is carried on in this place, when I think back to the beauty of Tourand's Coulee. Beauty, pain, loss, resistance, and resilience all come together in the coulee.

This is, perhaps, a long introduction to a Festival that is ultimately about music and dance – to borrow an overused but apt cliché, a festival that is about "fiddling" around. But setting the scene is vital, a reminder of where people are travelling to when they go "Back to Batoche," and a reminder that the music and dance, though key to bringing people together in celebration, is just one part of the Batoche experience. The setting of the festival – the worn-out nearby towns and historic sites, and the memories of loss – is in many ways a stark contrast to the joy and celebration at the heart of Back to Batoche Days. There is, perhaps, no better way to explain this than to describe the opening ceremony. My own notes on the 2018 opening ceremony do not do it justice, though snippets from a recording come closer. Listening back to it nearly six years later, I marvel at the energy and pure joy expressed by the emcee and the crowd:

> Emcee: Good morning, Elders, veterans, honoured guests, ladies and gentlemen, boys and girls. It is my pleasure to be the emcee for the Back to Batoche 2018 opening ceremonies. On behalf of the Métis Nation – Saskatchewan and Batoche festival committee members, I would like to extend a warm welcome to you all. We have quite an agenda lined up for you today, so let's get started! Cue the music!
> [Recording of "Red River Jig" begins and continues through the hour-long ceremony.]
> Emcee: Dignitaries are making their way to the stage, everybody. Flag bearers, veterans, Dumont scouts.
> [A few people begin clapping to the music.]
> Emcee: You guys can clap if you want to start clapping. You can clap your hands!
> [Cheers from the crowd as more people join in the clapping.]
> Emcee: It's a celebration!
> We have Mr. Tom Isaac. We have our Métis Nation – Saskatchewan president …
> […]
> Big round of applause for … Mr. and Mrs. Back to Batoche 2018.
> [Cheers, clapping, and whistling reach new heights as the "Red River Jig" continues to play.]
> […]
> Emcee: Alright, a big round of applause everybody for all the special guests who are here today!
> [Cheers and clapping]
> […]
> [Elder Norman Fleury leads a prayer in Michif, while the "Red River Jig" continues. He ends in French noting that we do not want to forget our languages. The crowd claps loudly in response.]

While the crowd is loud and appreciative throughout the opening ceremony, the excitement of this first official event is easily topped by the cheering and energy of the jigging competition. This is the event that seems to draw everyone to the mainstage. (There is a smaller stage area and an area for horseracing, which means that the main stage only ever attracts some of the Back to Batoche attendees.) As I wrote in my fieldnotes the day of the 2018 jigging competition, "This is the most important event in terms of audience turnout." The main stage was indeed buzzing with excitement as the six and under class took to the dance floor, followed by eight additional age categories (6–12, 13–18, men 19–34, women 19–34, men 35–60, women 35–60, senior men, and finally senior women) for a total of nearly fifty competitors across all ages. The joy is contagious, ringing through the main stage area, energizing the crowd, pulling them to their feet, cheering, clapping, feeling the beat, revelling in the fancy steps, celebrating the dance, the music, the people.

A flag party procession is a common way to begin Métis cultural festivals, honouring Elders, veterans, and special guests; in 2018, the opening ceremony and flag procession was a particularly important moment that marked a melding of culture and political processes. The dignitaries included Clément Chartier (then-President of the Métis National Council), and the presidents of all the associated provincial Métis political organizations.[6] There were also non-Métis dignitaries, most notably the local MP and MLA, and Carolyn Bennett, then Minister of Crown-Indigenous Relations. These dignitaries were present because the Back to Batoche opening ceremony was used as an opportunity to sign two Memoranda of Understanding (MOUs) and a "framework agreement." One MOU was between MN-S and the Saskatchewan School Boards Association (aimed at strengthening educational commitments to Métis student success), and the other was between the MN-S and the Saskatchewan Health Authority (aimed at improving health outcomes for Métis). The Framework Agreement, signed by the Minister of Crown-Indigenous Relations, centred on "reconciliation negotiations" and included a commitment to significant funding for Métis from the federal government. The insistence on melding culture with political processes is a clear example of refusing how things are done within a "multicultural" framework of recognition, where too often cultures are reduced to music, dance, and food, to the exclusion of political processes (see, e.g., Greenhill 1999). The opening ceremony was, ultimately, both an aural and visual reminder of Métis peoplehood and self-determination.

Unfortunately, I was unable to make it to the 2022 Back to Batoche celebration – the first July celebration held since 2019 due to the ongoing COVID-19 pandemic. However, the news of what happened at the opening ceremony reached me quickly, in fact, just a few hours after the ceremony ended. I was sitting in a hotel room in Lisbon, Portugal, preparing to present a paper on Back to Batoche Days, when the news came across my social media feed: during the Back to Batoche opening ceremony, Métis MP Dan Vandal took to the podium and announced that, after five years of negotiations, and 137 years of Métis insisting that they are still here, the federal government had agreed to return 690 hectares of land at the Batoche National Historic Site back to Métis Nation – Saskatchewan. Though the announcement, in the moment, felt unprecedented (and certainly it was unprecedented in some ways), the 2022 transfer agreement was preceded in 1996 by a smaller land transfer. Namely, the federal government returned a much smaller parcel of land, specifically the Back to Batoche Festival grounds two kilometres north of the Batoche town site, to Métis ownership. In other words, the return of land began with the festival site – a detail that, it seems, is a significant comment on the importance of the event for processes of real, not metaphorical, decolonization. Later, I listened to the short clip of the announcement available online. Hearing the excitement in the air and remembering the feeling of the 2018 opening ceremony, how I wished I could have been there to feel and hear the community come together in joy.

Back to Batoche is not, however, primarily about political relationships with the various levels of Canadian government, even if this relationship was centred during both the 2018 and 2022 opening ceremonies. Rather, it is about gathering *as Métis*. As one regular attendee told me when I asked why he keeps coming back, "These are my people." Reflecting on her first experience at Batoche, fiddler Brianna Lizotte similarly spoke to the idea of community ties, both present and past:

> BL: I feel really connected here. And it's really nice having a bunch of people that have the same culture as you and common interests … my great uncles and my great grandparents, they all used to play the fiddle. And we all had kitchen parties when I was growing up, so it was always a part of my life having instruments or music in my life, and by the time I was around the age ten, they all passed away, and so I decided to keep our family tradition of fiddling going, so that's why I started playing.

> […]
> MG: Do you play some of the old tunes?
> BL: Oh, yeah. That's what I mostly, mainly play, because kind of having … the old stuff being played, like, yeah, some of the new stuff is really cool but having that old music around is really grounding as well … so that some songs don't die off. (B. Lizotte, interview, 2018)

Lizotte's use of the word "grounding" is important here, tying her understanding of music as a way to connect to people and place.

Riel Aubicon, also a fiddler, similarly emphasized that his reason for coming was to connect to his culture, noting that his culture has always been part of his lived experience:

> MG: How long have you been coming to Batoche?
> RA: I've only been here three times. I came here for the anniversary. I think that was 1985 … and I was here last year. I played again last year. So, this is my second time, really, for a long time …
> MG: What does it mean to you to come here?
> RA: Well, this is my culture. I mean, I live the culture, because I go back a long ways because of my age. I won't tell you how old I am, but I remember coming to Meadow Lake in a horse-drawn wagon, from the farm, so that's a long ways. And they had two livery stables in Meadow Lake, two blacksmith shops, wooden boardwalk, a place to tie your horses up on main street … I'm not a hundred, but I'm working on it. (R. Aubicon, interview, 2018)

Melissa St Goddard addressed similar themes, while emphasizing that the music is what keeps her coming back:

> For me, I don't always come just to play. I come to enjoy, because myself, I love the music, I love dancing, and, of course I do come to play sometimes which I also love performing and all that. And I think it's just so nice coming to this community. Everyone's so nice, and you get to know people, right. This is the only time you get to see some people, cause people from all over come here. You know what I mean? So you meet new people and its just, I just love the music. That's why I come back all the time. I just grew up with it and I've always loved it. And

> the best of the best come here, so it's a great place to come. (M. St Goddard, interview, 2018)

St Goddard's message here is that music and dance are key aspects of the event for her, but it is also about connecting with individuals and community, some of whom only come together at events such as Back to Batoche. Music and dance, then, facilitate building of relationships.

While the opening ceremony emphasized a coming together of representatives of Canada and representatives of the Métis Nation, Back to Batoche ends with a pilgrimage to the Batoche town site. Unlike the opening ceremony, this pilgrimage does not explicitly include settlers or centre on settler recognition; rather, it is a time for the community to gather and visit with the ancestors. The pilgrimage begins immediately after a mass held on the mainstage. Attendees gather at the Métis veteran's monument (which includes all of the names of the Métis veterans who fought in the 1885 Resistance, World War I, World War II, and Korea) and then take to the highway to make the two-kilometre journey to the Batoche town site. A fiddler and the flag bearers lead the procession (figure 6.5). While most people walk down the highway, Elders and others with reduced mobility travel in golf carts. The solemn procession slows and stops traffic – though typically minimal in this area – as attendees move from the festival site, to the Batoche town site, and then to the cemetery that Wuttunee referenced in the above quoted interview.

The pilgrimage to the cemetery is an apt reminder, as the event closes, of how music and community come together at Back to Batoche in a powerful (re)claiming of place. (It is worth pointing out here that a fiddler, playing a mix of up tempo and slower tunes, is at the head of the procession.) While the procession to the Batoche town site is an explicit pilgrimage, the event as a whole functions as a kind of pilgrimage (as anthropologist Sarah Quick points out [2009, 125]), a coming home – either literally to the place where attendees' ancestors once lived, or a spiritual return to a place that resonates with Métis strength, resilience, and joy. As Métis Nation – Saskatchewan President Glen McCallum noted, "Batoche is the heart and soul of the Métis Nation and is an enduring symbol of everything Louis Riel and our people stand for: freedom, equality, and self-determination" (Parks Canada 2020). And so, although Back to Batoche includes important moments of engagement with the province and with Canada, it also includes, and in fact centres,

6.5
Back to Batoche procession

connection with kin and with place – turning attention away from Canada to Métis peoplehood.

"Those Métis Are Doing It Again" at the Métis Music and Art Festival

I arrived in Choteau, Montana, at 10:00 am (having left Lethbridge at 7:00 am). The mountains were a beautiful backdrop to the drive. It's cattle country – wide open roads, some deer (or possibly pronghorns) casually snacking in the fields.

[I had no trouble at the border, although the border guards didn't know what I meant by "Métis" when, after being asked where I was headed, I told them that I was going to a Métis festival in Choteau, Montana. "Oh, Native American," is what they said when I explained.]

Immediately upon my arrival, Kathy Moran greeted me with a warm welcome. She quickly introduced me to Fred "Jiggs" Charette. He was equally welcoming.

> Shortly after 10:00, Al Wiseman began a presentation based on items he had collected over the years. He spoke for about one hour [about Red River Carts, the use of oxen, willow and horsehair bird catchers, use of chokecherries, and more].
>
> A jam session began immediately after Elder Wiseman's presentation … Elder Charette asked me to play a few tunes, and Kathy Moran accompanied me … Kathy and Julie Moran were the main musicians the first day. Kathy played guitar and sang, and Julie played fiddle, occasionally singing (sometimes in harmony with her sister). They sang (among other songs) Tammy Wynette's "Apartment No. 9" and Hank William's "Your Cheatin' Heart." They also played "Faded Love," "Arkansas Traveller," "Redwing," and the "Red River Jig."
>
> – Fieldnotes (8 June 2018)

> Some of the highlights from Julie and Kathy's playing: Kathy sang "Seven Métis Angels" and a Métis version of "Coat of Many Colours."
>
> Kathy and Julie also sang some short, Michif songs that their mom used to sing. (She passed away a year ago in February.) They were songs in Michif (e.g., a lullaby) and songs that were adaptations with a Michif word (e.g., "Crawfish Pie"). Their version of the "Heel Toe Polka" ("Kispin") was fun. They explained that it meant, "If you love me come and kiss me."
>
> – Fieldnotes (14 June 2019)

Situating Métis music and culture within the history of Montana is fundamental to the work done at the Métis Music and Art Festival (MMAF) in Choteau. MMAF is a newcomer on the festival scene. It began after a conversation among Fred "Jiggs" Charette, Kathy Moran, and Linda Beaudry during a festival in Lewistown, Montana (the site of a much longer-standing Métis festival that began in 1979). Charette told me that they felt that they were not getting enough time to play music. Music, as Charette noted, "brings us together, makes us happy … we just need it" (interview with Charette 2018). With this goal in mind, they decided to start their own festival. In 2017, three years after the original conversation, the festival became a reality. While MMAF therefore emerged from the idea of having an extended jam session, it developed into much more. As Charette explained, it became a festival about Métis history, language, and music, with of course a focus on the Montana Métis experience. As he told me,

> JC: The original intent of this was, like I said, to start off, was a jam session. Then, someone said, "well … why don't you talk about history?" And I said, yeah, we could do that. Said, you know, I said, Al Wiseman's really good at that. If we get Al to come, I said, I'll ask him. Of course, he said sure right away. And he's gotten awards, the highest awards in Montana from historical societies.
> MG: Right.
> JC: And he's really good at it. So, then we decided, yeah well let's go some more with this. My daughter Reno said, what about food, Dad. What did you eat? Oh, I said, we ate rabbit, we ate wild game, whatever we could get. Galette, our bread. Bannock, as some people call it. And, she said, you know, I could do that. And I said, good, you can do that. And it kind of went like that, working on people that would come and do this for nothing. So, we've gotten it started, and we've developed it. Now this is our second year, and we're coming up with other ideas of things to do. One of them is a family reunion. They could come and have them with us. We'll have the food, the entertainment, right here for them. And, they can come and join us.

While Charette hoped to develop the "family reunion" aspect of the event as explained above, in many ways it already functions as a kind of family reunion for extended kin. In fact, at the 2022 event, Charette shared the following stories with me over supper (both documented afterwards in my fieldnotes with permission granted to publish the stories):

> Recently, Charette met a woman who had been adopted out and was now looking for her biological family. She had found out that she was a Charette, but she knew little else about her family. In any case, she decided to attend the Métis Music and Art Festival, and, when she arrived, the first person she met when she walked into the hall was Jiggs. Her husband introduced himself, and then Jiggs said who he was (Jiggs Charette) and then turned to the woman who had tears running down her face. The first person she met was a Charette! (fieldnotes, 3 June 2022)

Charette's second story similarly centred family connection:

> At MMAF one year, someone came up to Jiggs and said that he wanted help finding family. He had a big binder and opened it to the middle.

> Jiggs saw the photo and said, "That's my great-grandfather." Someone nearby saw the photo and said, "Oh, that's Jean-Baptiste Charette, my great-grandfather." None of these men had met before the festival. (fieldnotes, 3 June 2022)

Music, then, is at the heart of the event, but Charette also understands music and the festival as an opportunity to (re)connect kin.

While it is fair to say that Métis history was, for more than a century, ignored in Canada, certain events – in particular, the Métis Resistances – have always been referenced in Canadian history books, though usually from the point of view of the Canadian state as rebellions. In 1982, Métis were recognized as a distinct Aboriginal people in the patriated Canadian Constitution. In this way, Canada and Canadians have always recognized Métis, at the very least, as people who used to live on the plains (i.e., often not acknowledging contemporary presence), and more recently as people who are Indigenous to the plains. In contrast, there is no long-time history of recognition of Métis in Montana, or in the United States more broadly; it is only recently that non-Métis (and even many Métis) have begun to acknowledge the Métis history of the state, though the American government does not recognize Métis as a distinct, Indigenous people. Even though some elements of the festival are similar to Back to Batoche Days (especially related to pilgrimage, as discussed later), these issues of recognition create a very different backdrop for the festival and its attendees. Indeed, in 2019, I shared a bit of background about Canadian recognition of Métis with the Choteau mayor (who is not Métis but was attending MMAF to represent Choteau) during a casual dinner conversation. Learning about this difference inspired him to refer to it in his speech to attendees later that evening, using it as an example of the possibilities for Métis and of the need for further work in Montana to recognize Métis contributions and presence.

Montanans, then, are generally unfamiliar with who the Métis are, often understanding only the category "American Indian." As a side note to make this point, I have found that US border guards have needed clarification when I tell them I am travelling to attend a Métis festival (as detailed above). Interestingly, when I travelled to Choteau for the 2022 event, the border guard was familiar with the event because his daughter planned to compete at the fiddle contest, making this the first time crossing that I did not have to explain the term "Métis." Nonrecognition is significant because it seems to have affected how Métis position themselves vis-à-vis the state. A case in point is the aforementioned festival in Lewistown, Montana, which features some of the fiddle music heard at Métis events in Canada, but that centres, indeed prioritizes, a two-day long powwow, organized by the Métis in the region. I refer to this difference not to disparage the Lewistown event in any way, but rather to show how government categories shape how people conceive of their identities. In this case, people that the Canadian government would likely consider "Métis" align themselves with "American Indians" and with practices that, in Canada, might be considered First Nations practices. (Of course, kinship networks connect Métis and First Nations in Canada. However, my point here is that, in Montana, there is little recognition of a core Métis culture that is distinct from First Nations cultures.) Making Métis history more evident is, then, one of the main goals the festival in Choteau.

The work done by Al Wiseman during and beyond MMAF, and Vrooman as well prior to his passing in 2022, is particularly important for making Métis presence – named as such – known and recognized in the Choteau area. Vrooman was one of the main historians working with the Little Shell Tribe of Chippewa Indians in Montana and is the author of *"The Whole Country Was … 'One Robe'": The Little Shell Tribe's America* (2012). As part of the 2019 gathering, Vrooman provided attendees with a fascinating overview of the Little Shell Tribe, tracing their kinship connections to Métis in Canada, thereby challenging the border, highlighting familial relationships with people who do identify as Métis, and establishing the long presence and history of Métis in Montana. (This long presence was something that Rosalyn LaPier also spoke about during her 2022 talk for MMAF.) While Vrooman's presentation was modelled on academic talks (that is, it was a lecture and PowerPoint presentation), Wiseman's contribution to the festival brought tangible items that attendees could see and touch, as well as storytelling, to the forefront. In particular, he used an extensive display of Métis belongings combined with his own family stories connected to the belongings[7] to tell a place-based Métis history. For example, he told the story of his grandmother catching small birds with a net like the one in his display and showed attendees a stone mortar and pestle for grinding chokecherries. After his presentation, he invited attendees to visit the belongings to learn more about them and experience them up close (figure 6.6.).

The opportunity to see and learn Métis history "up close" was a key aspect of Wiseman's willingness to take attendees, in 2018, to a Métis cemetery, located about a twenty-minute drive outside of Choteau, as part of the weekend events. Standing at the cold and windy base of the Rocky Mountains,

6.6
Item from Al Wiseman's display

Wiseman pointed out the wild onions that were growing all around us and other features of the landscape, including an old root cellar (the nearby Métis home long gone) and the stone that marked the Old North Trail. Métis established the cemetery in 1890 with the burial of Marguerite La Rance (1817–1890).[8] It is the final resting place of many Métis (in fact Wiseman told me that there is only one non-Métis person buried in the cemetery). Many of the grave markers have worn away with time. Those that remain bear the names St Germain, Bruno, and Bettsy, among others. While Wiseman keeps up the cemetery himself, rather than acres of lush grass as one might expect in a modern or city cemetery, he allows the natural plants and grasses to flourish (though he keeps them trimmed down). Wild strawberries abound alongside the native grasses. This space is a powerful one, providing an opportunity to connect with the ancestors that rest here and to understand how they lived. As Wiseman told me, when he goes to the cemetery, he gets a feeling – like the spirit of his ancestors – but this only happens when he is alone (otherwise he thinks everyone gets some of the spirit and it becomes more diffused). The location of the cemetery also tells the story of Métis being forced to retreat into the Rocky Mountain Front, as settlers encroached, and discrimination became more rampant.

While the cemetery quite literally marks Métis presence in the Choteau area, this same spirit of connection – a connection to place and to ancestors – flows through the music that fiddlers and singers perform at the festival. In fact, Wiseman shared his comment about the spirit he senses in the cemetery not when we were at the cemetery, but rather when we were in Choteau, at the community centre where MMAF takes place. Furthermore, he shared the story as a way to explain that an attendee had gotten that same feeling of spirit and connection when I played "Snow Deer," noting that her father used to play that very same tune. (Because there are so few fiddlers in the area, Charette always asks me to bring my fiddle and to contribute what I can to the event. In being asked, even expected, to play, I am reminded of Peter Erasmus's description of a dance during the fur trade, referred to in chapter two, and his remark that pointed to a sense of responsibility to play, given his skill as a fiddler. Charette does pay musicians who play, making sure that he both acknowledges their contributions and takes care of them through financial support.[9]) The attendee that Wiseman was referring to shared this same story with me afterwards, confirming that her father used to play the tune and that she felt that spirit of connection when she heard the tune echoing through the hall, quickly leaving the kitchen (where she was preparing food for attendees) to stop for a moment and listen.

While the pilgrimage to the cemetery was the most memorable part of the weekend for me personally when I attended in 2018, the most meaningful moment of the 2019 event was when Kathy and Julie Moran shared their Michif songs. The first was a song that Kathy referred to as a "ditty" about the buffalo hunt – that is, a short song that explained a Michif way of life. The second was one that her great-great-grandmother used to sing. In an interview after I heard her sing, Kathy shared the following details about the song:

> The song is about how the Métis lived many years ago, and probably are still living. They have a lot of trials to go through, just like today. But it tells about how poor they were, and sometimes they didn't … even have food to eat. And … it compares them to poor little birds. But then the creator, or Jesus, takes care of them just like he'll take care of the Métis people … My mom sang that song, but I got it from my great, great grandmother. Her name was Marie Swain, and she married … Josue Bercier, and they were up in the Turtle Mountain area, but when they were married they probably just now [were] recognizing the 49th parallel … so they'd go back. They had family on either side of the border. (K. Moran, interview, 2019)

Kathy noted that she has never heard this song anywhere except in her family: "It's something that was passed down in my family, and who knows how old it is." (Given that her great-great-grandmother passed away in her nineties in 1967, it must be at least 100 years old, and probably older.) This song, then, is her family history, and the history of her people.[10]

The elements of pilgrimage to the cemetery and the singing of these old songs connect attendees to the past. However, Charette is also thinking about the future. As he noted, he wants to leave a cultural legacy for his descendants:

> JC: It's my dream that if I live long enough, that we can pass all those songs to our children, and that's my biggest, biggest, dream in this, is to teach the youth how to enjoy themselves and have something that they can pass on, a legacy if you will of our people, the history, the

> music, the food, the comradery, the love we share. And we have no alcohol, and no drugs. We can do it without that. And we enjoy each very, very much, and that's just the way we want it. And we don't need last names or anything. When we see people that we know, we can wave across the room, just glad to see each other.
>
> […]
>
> MG: So, it's really about family and connection …
>
> JC: Yup.
>
> MG: … and passing down what you know.
>
> JC: And then the kids, bring the kids in. Teach them that they can have a lot of fun without drugs and alcohol. It's just enjoyable. (J. Charette, interview, 2019)

The festival thus combines aspects of looking back with looking forward, building contemporary kinship relations while honouring past and future kin.

Like all events of this type, a great deal of organizational work happens behind the scenes. A successful event takes hard work, dedication, money, and an interested public. The efforts of Charette and the Michif Heritage Keepers has already paid off with increased recognition and strengthened connections among Métis kin, and – though it has not been without challenges – it will continue for the foreseeable future (though Charette had to step away from the work in 2023). As Charette told me at the end of our interview,

> JC: My wife and I were talking about [planning the event] after breakfast one morning and she said well how much money do we have? And I said we have enough to do it. She said, what's holding you back [laughs]? So, I just called everybody else, and said we're going to do it. Where's the money coming from? I said, I got it. I'll do it, this time. So, they said, OK, if we make any money then we'll, we'll reimburse you. So, OK if you can pay me for the rent, I'll pay for the rest of it. So, that's the way we planned it. And we done it! And we're doing it again! And that's what the ad says in the local paper here. Those Metis are doing it again! (J. Charette, interview, 2019)

Though Wiseman and Vrooman had done work in the Choteau area for many years prior to the start of the festival to bring about awareness of Métis presence and culture (as evident in a town museum that now includes some Métis history), MMAF brings that culture to life for a broader public and marks this *continuing, contemporary presence*. It is therefore both outward looking, reaching the non-Métis public through the event itself and the reporting on the event (referenced by Charette, above), and inward looking, connecting kin across the generations.

Recognition and Connection at Métis Heritage Celebration

> In conversation with [a Métis Nation of Ontario Senator], he told me that he believes that the Métis local in Oshawa was the first [in southern Ontario] to hold a cultural event like Métis Heritage Celebration. His view was that it was a way for them [local Métis] to prove to themselves that they are Métis – a kind of manifestation of their Métis-ness.
> – Fieldnotes (2 February 2017)

> Politically the festival [a large-scale public presentation of Romani culture in Austria] had offered public proof of the existence of "ethnic traditions" of Romani culture, something very necessary in the process of political recognition.
> – Ursula Hemetek (2006, 47)

In 2007, the Oshawa and Durham Region Métis Council (ODRMC) – one of the political districts within the larger umbrella of Métis Nation Ontario – started Métis Heritage Celebration. ODRMC held the first event as a one-day gathering at the Brooklin Community Centre in Whitby, Ontario, east of Toronto. The following year, organizers were able to secure space at a park in central Oshawa (just east of Whitby), and the event was extended to two days. Although organizers cancelled Métis Heritage Celebration in 2019, it returned in 2022 as a one-day event, held at an Oshawa arena. Unlike the other events described in this chapter, Métis Heritage Celebration takes place outside of the Métis Homeland. Métis people moved to the city after it was established, coming from Georgian Bay (Penetanguishene, Waubaushene, Port McNicoll, and Victoria Harbour, among other towns and hamlets) and from across the Métis Homeland, often in search of work in the automotive industry.[11] Although there is now a significant presence of Métis people in the area, the general public has little knowledge of Métis history and culture (though, they may be able to recite the common Canadian incantation of "First Nations, Métis, and Inuit"). Furthermore, many Métis people have become disconnected from their own culture. Perhaps because of this history, Métis Heritage Celebration, like MMAF, centres issues of recognition and reconnection; it is a teaching tool for both Métis and non-Métis people in the area, and an opportunity to mark contemporary pride and presence.

While the theme of loss and disconnection is common across the Métis Homeland, the particular circumstances of Métis in the Oshawa area – as people who are living at such a distance from home communities – bring this issue to the forefront. As one of the founders of the event, Robert Pilon, told me, "When I first went to meetings of the [ODRMC] … they were always talking about getting together and everything, and I always asked [attendees] questions about it. I knew the answers already, but I asked them why do you meet? What's the purpose of meeting for? You can't meet just for the sake of meeting. So, the first thing we talked to them about, I told them what keeps us together is culture … If we don't preserve the culture and everything, how do you know we were a people?" (R. Pilon, interview, 2017). Pilon's comment emphasized the importance of culture to peoplehood. At the same time, he acknowledged the loss and disconnection experienced by so many Métis in the area. As he explained, "I had [fiddler] Darren Lavallee here [in Oshawa], and the first thing he asked me was "How come they don't dance here?" And, ah, I think it's because they lost their culture and everything … when we gather [out west …] we dance at all the weddings, and we do the traditional dances plus, you know, the modern dances, mix it all together. Country music, fiddle music, and the modern music. Yeah, but everybody dances" (R. Pilon, interview, 2017). Connecting to Métis culture was, then, important for Pilon, and he encouraged ODRMC to centre Métis practices as they planned a Métis cultural event. Describing the early days of organizing, he shared,

> Well, we were having a board meeting there at, I don't know how many years ago now, when I first started, I guess, and we had a successful potluck and they wanted to do something in the summer time, and they were talking about having a celebration for our heritage, and everything. I was probably part of the board, but I was president for only about a year, maybe, and they … wanted to do a heritage celebration. We were talking, and "Oh, yeah, that's a good idea." Celebrate our heri-

> tage and celebrate everything. But then they started talking about what they needed to get … Well, one of the elders said, well my grandson plays in a rock band, and maybe we should get them to play the music and everything. And they started talking about all these things, and after about ten minutes of discussion I asked them to answer the question, "What does a rock band have to do with Metis?" It's not our heritage. Well, we had a discussion, "What is our heritage?" (R. Pilon, interview, 2017)

One of the ways that Pilon and early organizers worked to address this disconnect was by bringing in Métis performers from western Canada. These included JJ Lavallee, Brad Moggie, the Gaudry Brothers, Jason Appleyard, Brendan Chartrand, Ramsey Rae, and Yvonne Chartrand, among others. The first year, renowned Ojibwe fiddler Laurence "Teddy Boy" Houle (from Manitoba) also performed, though his presence was coincidental since he happened to be in Toronto at the time.

The presence of dancers and fiddlers from the West during the early years of the event helped to establish both a fiddle and dance group in the Oshawa region. In fact, organizers announced the creation of the Olivine Bousquet Métis Dancers during the first Celebration (interview with Pilon 2017), directly influenced by the presence and teaching of celebrated Métis jigger and choreographer, Yvonne Chartrand. The Gravel Road Fiddlers began not as a direct result of the Celebration but through the connections made with JJ Lavallee during the event. ODRMC invited Lavallee back to Oshawa in 2010 after the ODRMC received funding for a short-term fiddle program. The Gravel Road Fiddlers continued practicing together for many years after Lavallee left and performed annually at the Celebration at least until recently, while dancer Auriele Diotte (who began with the Olivine Bousquet dancers) continues to perform at events in southern Ontario today. By the time I was attending the Celebration (2015, 2016, and 2017), the connection with performers from the Prairies had largely ceased. An organizer told me that this was in part because Robert Pilon was no longer involved; he had facilitated these connections. However, the organizers also wanted to create a stronger local community of Métis performers. Cecile Wagar noted that the organizers "really wanted to get more performers from Ontario" and had featured several local groups over the past few years. In a sense, the connection with the West helped local performers and organizers establish a Métis presence, which they have been able to carry on in recent years.

Since its earliest years, then, the Celebration has brought Métis people together in community to learn and connect with their Métis culture. During my time at the Celebration, I was especially struck by the connections made among the youth workers in attendance. As they explained to me, the Métis Nation of Ontario (MNO) pays their wage, and after receiving training, they put on workshops for schools, daycares, seniors' residences, museums, and more, for no charge. While Métis Heritage Celebration is thus just one event in a network of events that these youth workers attend, it is unique because it is a large-scale, Métis-focused event. (In contrast, the youth workers are often part of a line up at other events, or else the event is relatively short.) At Métis Heritage Celebration, they spend the day sharing music, dance, and stories with the broader community through workshops, while building friendships through their cultural work. As one youth worker in her third summer of the program told me, "I love doing it because I learn a lot about my culture through certain activities like beading, and finger weaving, and I also learn through my colleagues. I've honestly made the best friends through this program. And why I come back is to reconnect with all my friends, make new friends, and it's the best job in the world, to be honest ... we learn from each other" (MNO youth workers, interview, 2016). Another youth worker, in this case in her first year of the program, similarly indicated the importance of the connections she's made, emphasizing how she has shared her learning with her family:

> I love the opportunities that I have to ... meet amazing people. I've made so many friends, learned so much, like being a part of this program. I think this is, I don't know how many events we've done so far, quite a few events. And every time I feel like I'm learning something new, either from the other facilitators, or from other people we meet in the community. So, it's just a great opportunity to meet other people in the community. I know growing up I didn't know a lot of Métis people, so, yeah, it's just a great way to connect ... I grew up in Toronto, but my family, we, like a lot of Métis families, we just didn't know a lot about our culture and our heritage, and so it's been over the past few years that, once I turned sixteen, that I really started to get to know more about what it meant to be Métis. (MNO youth workers, interview, 2016)

A third youth worker stressed the desire to learn within the community. As she told me, "I enjoy it because I feel like the community wants to learn, and they want education on the Métis people, but they don't necessarily have the resources and the funding to have it. So, this program, thanks to the MNO, provides that. It gives them the opportunity to have that resource as opposed to them trying to find the funding to bring people in since we do these workshops for free" (MNO youth workers, interview, 25 June 2016). It was clear in my conversations that they had become colleagues and friends through their summer work. Although this work would continue with or without Métis Heritage Celebration, the Celebration is part of the nexus of alliance among Métis living in southern Ontario and beyond. It is one of the spaces for building community among young Métis citizens (see figures 6.7 and 6.8). And this is a key goal of the Celebration. As one organizer told me, she hoped that cultural events such as these could bring Métis people back together (personal communication, 28 June 2015).

While (re)connection is such an important part of this event, so too are the formal and informal moments of teaching – including teaching the local Métis and the broader non-Métis communities in Oshawa. Some of my favourite moments were those informal moments where the youth and other participants were clearly learning from each other and sharing, exchanging dance steps or taking part in a jam session. However, more formal teaching moments are also important to the event. For example, the Summer Youth Cultural Group demonstrated the "Red River Jig" and the "Butterfly," and then gave a workshop on how to do the seven-step and heel toe polka. Several people came up to learn the dances, while others watched from their seats. The MC similarly added to the teaching/learning aspect of the event, providing historical notes, such as telling attendees about the Red River cart and the sash.

Although the event is a gathering of Métis people, the music (at least when it was held as an outdoor event from year two to year twelve) echoed across the park and through the city. This, along with the vendors selling their wares as part of the event, attracted many local, non-Métis residents, some of whom were encountering Métis culture for the first time. Though some attendees told me that they were supporting performers (and were often relatives of performers), pointing to the event as a gathering of the Métis community, others just happened to see the event advertised and decided to drop by – having no knowledge of Métis history and culture prior to attending. One first-time local told me, "I actually forget how I heard about the event, but I knew it was here, so away we came." Another local told me that they come every year, but forgot about it, and they "just spotted

6.7
Youth dancers

6.8
Jam session

it [i.e., noticed the signs] by mistake, that it was here, so [they] just came over again" (personal communication, 25 June 2016). Others noted that they come every year just because they enjoy the music. Because it is a free event held at a central park for much of its history, many people passed through without necessarily staying for the entire festival or even for the day. This allows for degrees of engagement with the Celebration, from observing to participating in many or all of the youth-led workshops (see figure 6.9 for event signage).

Performers and workshop leaders clearly understood that part of their job was educating and helping attendees build understanding of Métis culture. For example, when I asked dancer Auriele Diotte about her choice to wear hard-soled shoes with metal plates, she said,

> I wear tap shoes because the beat is very important for Métis culture in general because [Métis people] had to accompany themselves. The use of the drum and the fiddle works too, but [Métis people] also liked their feet because it emulates the horses … Also, it just sounds good! … I think it also adds something even more exciting to [the dance] because then the audience can hear what you're doing. It's like the Irish hard shoe dancing. It's all about the feet and the rhythm that you can emulate with your feet. You can do it with the drums, [but] you can also do it with your feet. So, I think that [tap shoes] helps audiences connect it better, especially since not that many people know about Métis culture in general, so to have those things, like the belt dance, oh, that's like the Scottish highland dance, and having the shoes, oh, that's like Irish dance … [It's] a way in for other people outside of the Métis community to understand it. (A. Diotte, interview, 2016)

For Métis youth worker Simone Blais, teaching culture is important, but it is ultimately a way to teach about deeper issues. As she pointed out, "I always say that we're educating people about Indigenous issues through culture. We're not just teaching culture. We're actually getting to a bigger cause, but through culture. Because I think that's the best way to learn. When you can actually physically do it, I mean, you can dance and you can finger weave, people understand it because they're doing it. You know, you're not just telling them words" (S. Blais, interview, 2015). Certainly, Métis history and culture is brought to life through hands on experiences at Métis Heritage Celebration: attendees can look at and feel sashes, moccasins, and other leather and fabric products created by Métis artisans; and they can see examples of the intricate beading and tufting that adorn these items. Attendees can learn about Métis history through these cultural displays as well as through a historical timeline displayed near the stage. They can also talk to one of the many knowledgeable Elders at the event. Children and adults alike can learn how to finger weave or try out some dot art (a modern art form inspired by traditional Métis beadwork). Attendees can stand beside a canoe – so important to the fur trade and to Métis people – and fully appreciate their size and the incredible craftsmanship of their makers. They can likewise have a picture taken with the iconic Red River Cart, the preferred mode of transportation for nineteenth century Métis hunters and traders in the plains.

Part of the reason and need for this teaching is to help Métis gain recognition as Indigenous people within the local community. The impact of the event toward this goal was evident in my interview with Métis Heritage Celebration founding organizer, Cecile Wagar:

> MG: There was a sense then that the first Celebration blossomed into other things.

6.9
Métis Heritage Celebration signs

> CW: Oh, it did, right away. One day wasn't enough. We thought we needed two.
> MG: When did it move over here [from Brookland to Oshawa]?
> CW: It moved here the second year. We got funding from Celebrate Canada right away the first year, and got more after that for the second year, and we've had funding ever since through them. It was really great, and the city just was really great as well. The mayor at the time gave us his council office for our meetings ... We applied for in-kind services from [the city], and we got it. I had to work at it for the first four years or five years, and then we were put on the list as partnership people. Anytime we've had events the mayor's always there to bring greetings ... He would always mention us and our celebration, every time he did. It was really great to see. And then we've kind of blossomed with us doing our celebration and then the city [began] asking us to do different events for them. And then I got in with the Ministry of Education, coming on board with Aboriginal education, then I was part of the Aboriginal Education Advisory circle, the Public Board, the Catholic Board, Durham College, and [Ontario Tech University]. (C. Wagar, interview, 2016)

The kinds of relationships that the Celebration helped start led to much greater visibility and recognition of Métis in the area. As Wagar continues,

> CW: You can see the progress there as to how First Nations stuff was coming out first, but then I was always there, what about the Métis? And so all three [places of education] have really gotten on board, always remembering the Métis, giving them a special day on certain events that they were doing ... They started to have Métis day every year, and we went, we brought our stuff and talked a little about it. ... We got in really good with the city and then we were in with Ontario Power Generation [OPG], and so we asked for funding from them. So, we had funding from the City, funding from Celebrate Canada, funding from OPG, which really helped, and, so that's really blossomed out too. And so now we have good corporate partnerships I guess, because we do things with the city now, and we do things with OPG.
> MG: So, you're saying that Heritage Celebration has helped open up those partnerships?

CW: It has, it has. It opened up the awareness, and cooperation with everyone in the area. (C. Wagar, interview, 2016)

In addition to bringing out the mayor, the local member of provincial parliament typically attends Métis Heritage Celebration, creating an additional point of contact with the settler-state's political system – an enactment of that relationship through a cultural event. Local dignitaries such as the Mayor of Oshawa, the region's member of provincial parliament (MPP), and the MNO president are an important presence during the opening ceremony, taking the opportunity to address the crowd. MNO senators (i.e., specially appointed Elders) are also a visible presence, as are Métis veterans and Métis youth. By working within a model of recognition, this event has given Métis in the area opportunities to do educational work both during and beyond the Celebration. In a sense, the event offers Métis and non-Métis sensory evidence of Métis presence and peoplehood.

The Multifaceted Work of Métis Festivals

The sound of the Métis fiddle
And the familiar strains of the "Orange Blossom Special"
The excitement of the crowd, rising, rising
The dancers' red crinolines bouncing gently
As their feet quicken with the speeding fiddle
A blur of intricate movement
As they each take a turn to show off their best fancy step
The crowd rising, rising, standing
The energy reaching to the rafters
Reaching into my body, vibrating my body
Feeling my body
Making me feel
A resurgence
Propelled by the fiddle, by the dancers' feet, by the rising crowd
(International Peace Garden, USA/Canada, video recording in personal archive, 2011)

✦✦✦

When I first wrote the above description of the Norman Chief Memorial Dancers' performance at Metisfest in 2011, I was expressing my sense of the failures of field recording technology, or at least the failures of the handheld devices that I (and many other ethnographers) use.[12] Though our ability to record sound and moving images has come such a long way since the days of crackling, fragile, and limited-length wax cylinders, as I listened back to my video recording of these dancers, I realized that I was still missing so much. I could use the recording to remember the sensations of that joyous moment; to remember my excitement and the excitement of the crowd; to remember how the whole room vibrated, and how these vibrations seeped into the outdoors; and to remember how my body vibrated because of the music, the thundering steps, and the cheering crowd. Yet listening and watching the recording did not replicate the affective power of being there or the affective power of Métis music festivals more generally. Since then, I have come to think of this short description as my "you had to be there" poem. You had to be there to feel and understand the depth of that moment – a moment that I remember as one of the best fieldwork moments of my career, a moment that was so much more than the recording and so much more than sound and movement.

Following from this understanding, the above descriptions of three Métis cultural festivals are just a small peek into the Pemmican Trail. I nonetheless hope that they demonstrate the multifaceted work accomplished through cultural gathering, showing how spaces of festivity can use recognition to build resurgence. This is in part because they are public facing (and often actively engage with city/provincial/federal representatives), while centring the needs and desires of Métis attendees (i.e., they assume a largely Métis audience, even though they include and are open to non-Métis). Work toward recognition is perhaps most notable in the elements of the festivals that focus on teaching, and in the explicit engagement with provincial, city, and federal governments and representatives. At the same time, they are not limited to or by a multicultural frame, nor do they cater to an audience of non-Métis: each of the festivals described moves beyond settler expectations to show or display Métis-ness in a particular way and to separate the cultural from the political. Though music and dance are at the centre of the festivals, returning year after year in celebration, music, dance, and song, and in an expression of "still being here," is a foundational part of the work that these festivals accomplish. Batoche and Choteau in particular centre the "reclaiming, restoring, and regenerat[ion of] homeland relationships" (Corntassel and Bryce 2012, 153), while Métis Heritage Celebration emphasizes recognition even as it contributes to stronger relationships with kin. Ultimately, and perhaps most importantly, these events point to the efficacy of Métis cultural festivals. The final chapter of this book builds on the theme of efficacy in music-centred spaces to examine the work that has been and can be done through musicking, in this case, within contexts that have been explicitly positioned as cross-cultural productions.

7

On Moving from Louis Riel *to* Li Keur

Chapter 1 began with Handscomb's 1906 review of a classical music performance in Winnipeg. In it, he suggested that Wagner's music was becoming the city's "classic" music and that it was replacing melodies "scraped by the Metis fiddler," thereby framing Métis music as incompatible with modern "metropolitan" music and indeed incompatible with classical music (1906, 8). Now, this statement seems laughable, as the *Globe and Mail*, for example, reports on a "new wave" of Indigenous opera in Canada (Simeonov 2023), and as the Winnipeg-based Manitoba Opera Company premieres the new opera, *Li Keur: Riel's Heart of the North* by Métis librettist and "opera architect"[1] Dr Suzanne Steele, Métis fiddler and composer Alex Kusturok (who is indeed bringing Métis fiddling to the opera stage), and non-Indigenous composer Neil Weisensel. Though Indigenous opera has a long history, this is an exciting time as it moves into the public eye in new ways.

However, challenges remain – challenges that, in this chapter, I frame using the concept of "ethical responsiveness." Developed by Dreher and Mondal, ethical responsiveness attends to the issue of voice, and to whose voices are heard and valued. Though Dreher and Mondal tie their interest in voice to the rise of social media, it has taken on new resonances post-TRC, as Canadians begin to show greater interest in Indigenous stories and to understand the need to consult and engage with Indigenous peoples on all issues that affect Indigenous lives. This has led to a growing number of Indigenous-specific positions in major arts institutions; more consultation with Indigenous people and communities; and more "Indigenous content" in programming. It is an exciting and necessary shift. Yet Dreher and Mondal's work is a reminder that the efficacy of voice needs to be examined; voices may be heard (that is, our bodies receive the sounds), but not really *listened to or acted on*. Ethical responsiveness thus turns attention to what is done with knowledge that is shared, or "voiced."

This chapter examines many of the same issues discussed throughout this book, namely erasure, (mis)recognition, (mis)representation, appropriation, and resurgence, but through the frame of listening and responsiveness. Specifically, it uses two case studies that, on the surface, may seem similar insofar as topic and genre. The first is Mavor Moore, Jacques Languirand, and Harry Somers's opera *Louis Riel*, written in 1967 as part of Canada's centennial celebrations. I focus in particular on a 2017 restaging that attempted to update the opera to address concerns raised by Indigenous people around lack of consultation in the creation of the opera, lack of Indigenous representation in staging, and the appropriation of a Nisga'a song by Somers. In addition to appointing Estelle Shook (Métis) as assistant director, updates included a new role, namely the Folksinger, played by Jani Lauzon (Métis); the creation of a "Land Assembly," a silent chorus of Indigenous performers who bear witness; new Cree translations; a dialogue in Michif, with translation by Elder Norman Fleury (Métis); and the casting of two Indigenous performers in secondary roles, namely Joanna Burt (Métis/Saugeen Ojibway) as Riel's sister and Everett Morrison (Cree) as Wandering Spirit. These changes opened vital dialogue about the ways that arts institutions engage with, or do not engage with, Indigenous peoples, especially when telling Indigenous stories; yet the 2017 restaging remained a failure from the point of view of Métis representation and engagement – a band aid solution. Though I have argued elsewhere (see Giroux 2018b) that the 2017 restaging led to the death of the opera (i.e., the realization that it should no longer be staged), some of the discourse that followed the production suggests that some opera aficionados still want to rescue the opera, pointing to a lack of responsiveness, in some cases at least, to Métis concerns.

The second case study is the creation and staging of *Li Keur: Riel's Heart of the North*, an opera with spoken metanarrative that was conceived of in 2017 and premiered fall 2023 – just as I was finishing this book. *Li Keur* demonstrates some of the ways in which a production can and has pushed back against erasure, appropriation, and misrepresentation, while caring for the "seeds of resurgence" planted by past generations (Simpson 2011, 66). *Li Keur* insists that Métis people must be lead creators of productions that centre Métis stories, and as such all the lead roles are played by Indigenous singers and actors, as are most of the smaller roles. And all the design work (from flyers advertising the production to costume design) was done by Indigenous creatives – most Métis or close kin. Just as importantly, *Li Keur* centres creation practices that emerge in and through relation with land and kin; engages with past, present, and future through archival and story work; centres (re)connection of Indigenous peoples in the heart of the continent, including through language revitalization; foregrounds a rich and nuanced representation of Métis life with both its sorrows and its joys; centres Indigenous women; re-places the Métis people at the heart of a polycultural, multilingual continent; and ultimately, values process over product. This case study nonetheless points to some of the challenges Indigenous creators face when working with primarily white legacy institutions. These challenges include the continued erasure of Indigenous creatives; the policing of what is allowable (a chorus of "no"s that Steele has experienced); and more generally, insufficient care for why a seemingly small detail, to a non-Indigenous institution, might be essential to authentic representation. This case study therefore draws attention to the limits of voice.

"The God-Damn [Opera] Is Dead": *Louis Riel* as (Sesqui)Centennial Celebration

> For make no mistake about it, Louis Riel is the first great Canadian opera. It is not the first opera by a Canadian composer, but it is the first to combine the qualities of being entirely Canadian-created, of being based on an entirely Canadian theme, and above all of being a stirring success … This is no time for quibbling. We now have the first Canadian opera that should be encouraged to stay around.
>
> –Richard Purser (1967, 29)

When the Canadian Opera Company restaged *Louis Riel*, in Toronto, Ottawa, and Quebec City in 2017, the production was met with a great deal of excitement, anticipation, and controversy. A seemingly endless number of newspaper and magazine articles, blog posts, and podcasts discussed the opera, including many that addressed director Peter Hinton's attempt to redress the colonial biases embedded in the work, in particular the complete exclusion of Indigenous perspectives and the appropriation of a Nisga'a song in the original.[2] Two University of Toronto graduate students, Taryn Jackson and Sarah Koval, created an eight-episode podcast in the year leading up to the production of the opera (hosted on SoundCloud but promoted by and linked to the Institute for Music in Canada), featuring discussions and interviews with academics, members of the cast, and Métis poet Gregory Scofield.[3] Immediately following the premiere, the University of Toronto held a day-long symposium, titled *Hearing Riel*, with well-known Canadians such as Adrienne Clarkson, Beverley McLachlin, and John Ralston Saul contributing talks.[4] Renowned Métis lawyer, Jean Teillet, was also in attendance, presenting on Métis history and activism during "le grand silence" (the period from the 1880s–1960s), as were Métis sociologist Adam Gaudry, Métis playwright Marie Clements, and then-President of the Métis National Council Clément Chartier. Other speakers included faculty and graduate students from the University of Toronto, and several members of the opera production team, including Peter Hinton, Estelle Shook, and Joanna Burt. Emerging from the symposium, the humanities-focused journal, *University of Toronto Quarterly*, published a special issue focused on *Louis Riel*, with editors Caryl Clark, Linda Hutcheon, Sherry D. Lee, Tegan Niziol, and Carolyne Sumner (2018).

In addressing *Louis Riel*, I want to elaborate on three themes: first, the curious obsession with the life and death of Riel; second, the related issue of the erasure of *Métis*, the very people whose story was being told through the production; and third, the attempt, in my view, to *rescue* the opera and its creators from shame or oblivion.[5] The obsession with the life and death of Riel is curious because, over at least the past seventy years, representations of his life and death have been so numerous, and because they have been moulded and shaped to mean many things – perhaps whatever Canadians have needed at a particular moment in time. Though this moulding has been accomplished in many ways, creative, artistic practice has led the way, starting perhaps most notably with the sympathetic work of John Coulter who, in 1950, wrote a play about Riel, simply titled *Riel* (published in 1962), followed by two additional plays on Riel in 1968, namely *The Crime of Louis Riel* and *The Trial of Louis Riel*.[6] Since then, Riel has been the subject of numerous additional plays, including at least one theatrical production inspired by Chester Brown's graphic novel, *Riel: A Comic-Strip Biography* (2003).[7] There have been many popular songs, classical compositions, and fiddle tunes written about Riel, and, in 1979, the CBC produced a film, titled *Riel*, that was broadcast across the country.[8] Though most of these creative works have been authored by non-Métis, more recently, Métis women have taken up the story of Riel, focusing less on Riel and more on the Métis women around him. In addition to the work by Steele discussed later in this chapter, Métis composer, Karen Sunabacka, wrote a quartet, titled *Mama's Painting: Louis Riel's Dream* (2015), that continued a visual art project that her late Métis grandmother, Lenore Clouston, had started years earlier; and Yvonne Chartrand, in a collaboration with Ania Storoszczuk-Smeets, created a dance production, titled *Marguerite* (2000), based on the life of Marguerite Monet dit Belhumeur, Riel's wife.

The opera *Louis Riel* is, then, part of a seventy-year history of representing Riel through the arts, and, like many of the artistic creations and productions on Riel, it embodies a kind of love/hate relationship with the eponymous character, as traitor, martyr, and hero, sometimes all at the same time. As librettist Mavor Moore suggested in an interview published in the *Winnipeg Free Press*, it was these very tensions that drew him to Riel. As he noted,

> [Riel] is an immensely colorful personification of some of the great liturgical themes of mankind. One is that of the idealist driven mad by continued betrayal of ruthless realists in whom he mistakenly trusts. Another is that of the thinker paralyzed by his thinking, the Hamlet syndrome. Another is that of the half-breed, the schizophrenic outsider who belongs to no people. Still another is that of the leader of a small nation standing in the way of 'progress': is he hero or fool? All these themes are timeless as is the theme of revolution, which was Riel's way of life. (*Winnipeg Free Press* 1969, 15)

Though *Louis Riel* portrays Riel as bordering on, or perhaps simply, insane, depending on audience interpretation, he is represented as a sympathetic character whom the audience is supposed to root for, perhaps even empathize with (Koval and Dubois 2018, 60). Koval and Dubois's interpretation of the character is similar to the interpretation journalist Richard Purser provided fifty years earlier suggesting that the opera's "creators take sides. They are obvious devotees of historian Joseph Kinsey Howard's pro-Riel approach to the subject" (1969, 29). Quoting a review of Howard's book *Strange Empire*, Purser further describes the opera as "'impassioned in its pleas for the defenceless' … [and] equally scathing in its treatment of Orange bigotry in Ontario and of Sir John A. Macdonald" (29). However, as perhaps indicated by Purser's review, Moore and Languirand arguably succeeded in positioning Riel as the hero not because he is a complex, nuanced, or especially likeable character; rather, the audience is compelled (somewhat) to overlook Riel's flaws because the other characters are not just flawed but morally corrupt: there is the drunken, lying, and manipulative John A. Macdonald, the childish and impulsive Thomas Scott, and the Orangemen filled with glee as they sing, "We'll hang him up the river and he'll roast in hell forever." The opera is, in a sense, a conglomeration of conflicting and conflicted characters, and Riel is not the worst of the characters.

The opera, however, ends with Riel's death. Indeed, it closes with the words "the goddamn son of a bitch is dead." This final pronouncement is intoned by John Christian Schultz, founder of the Canada First Party, which in the late 1800s functioned as a forum for Protestant agitators in Red River.[9] Schultz, Macdonald, and the Orangemen live on as the opera ends; but Riel is no more. This ending is the most important and the most complex of the conflicting messages of the opera, because how the moment is interpreted is foundational to the opera's meaning. The audience has just watched the death of a man with whom, through the nearly three-hour opera, they have come to sympathize. Perhaps, as the opera closes and the horror of the moment hangs in the air, the audience can come closer to understanding and feeling the horror of what happened. Or perhaps they can use that moment to exonerate themselves, that is, allow themselves to believe that *of course they would have supported Riel and his cause, of course they would not have hanged Riel*. Or perhaps that moment simply marks a moment that many did (and still) view as inevitable: Canada gaining control of the Northwest. Whatever the case, with Schultz's final words and the closing of the curtain, the audience is compelled to applaud (after all, the opera has ended). Is this applause a celebration of Riel's death, a celebration of the production, or a celebration of Canada's victory over Riel? As musicologist Sherry Lee points out, the audience is left with no solace and with the opera's "dissonances unresolved" (2018, 27). *Louis Riel*, then, encapsulates the complicated and conflicted relationship between Canada and Riel, and the ambiguities that Riel represents.

The success of *Louis Riel* might have to do with the flexibilities allowed through these ambiguities; it can be, and has been, interpreted through the narratives contemporaneous to each of the productions. As noted earlier, *Louis Riel* was written to mark Canada's centennial, tying it to nationalistic discourse. According to literary and cultural theorists Linda Hutcheon and Michael Hutcheon, librettist Mavor Moore intended to "use the conventions and traditions of Grand Opera as a form of nation-building, a platform for discovering who we are" (2016, 18). The opera is an unexpected medium for

Canadian nationalism, but Hutcheon and Hutcheon speculate that Riel's story, "the story of a man who resisted, even defied, the newly founded nation of Canada," served as "ironic, subversive cultural commentary: a warning about the dangers of defining any single national Canadian identity that erases manifest diversity" (18). In this way, they interpret it as prefiguring multiculturalism as Canada's unifying value. However, in the late 1960s and '70s, it was interpreted from the framework of managing the complicated relationship between French and English. Purser noted, for example, that "It is the right opera at the right time in the right place … And it is thoroughly bilingual and bicultural; the libretto by Mavor Moore and Jacques Languirand has the characters sing in English or French as appropriate to the moment" (1967, 29). This emphasis on French/English relations was also evident in a press release for a 1975 revival of the opera by the Canadian Opera Company (COC) which positioned the drama as a "provocative foray into Canadian political mythology" that captured "the tragedy and high drama of an episode that almost tore the country asunder, an episode which has had important and lasting effects on the relationship between French- and English-speaking Canada" (quoted in Hutcheon and Hutcheon 2016, 24). Hutcheon and Hutcheon suggest that this interpretation is reflective of the conflict-ridden years of the Quiet Revolution, the October Crisis, and Quebec separatism (24). *Louis Riel* was therefore flexible enough to fit both the bicultural/bilingual and the multicultural narrative.

As the above outlines, Canada has a curious obsession with the life and death of Riel. Though perhaps unintentional, one of the most problematic results of this obsession is that it has centred *Canada* and *Canadians* to the exclusion of Métis people as a *living peoples*; as historian Albert Braz notes, Riel has typically been "situated not in a Métis context but in a Canadian one" (2003, 3). The most obvious aspect of this exclusion is the complete lack of engagement with Métis until the 2017 production. When Moore and Languirand created the libretto, they did not consult Métis people (Teillet 2018, 30), and in 1967, 1968, and 1975, Métis and other Indigenous peoples were not included in any aspect of the production. Though Jean Teillet notes that Louis Riel's grandnephew was invited to a performance in Montreal in 1967 (2018, 30), Métis have been largely absent from the audience, even in the most recent production. Indeed, it has been difficult or even impossible for most Métis to attend the opera because it has never been staged in the Métis Homeland, where the majority of Métis continue to live,[10] and because the cost of tickets is prohibitively high. In an anonymous interview, a Métis woman who attended the opera in Toronto in 2017 told me that she attended in part to honour her mother, who wanted to attend the 1967 premiere, but could not afford a ticket. In its early years, then, the production ignored Métis perspectives, failing to engage with contemporary Métis communities and the Métis Nation – the very people that Riel fought for. (Though much has been said about Riel fighting for everyone as a visionary advocate of social welfare and multiculturalism [Hutcheon and Hutcheon 2016, 20], it is important not to elide the reality that Riel's impetus to push back against Canadian nationalism was his strong sense of Métis peoplehood.) The opera and discourse around the opera, like many other representations of Riel, has in this way continued a long history of erasing Métis as a living peoples.

The problematic lack of engagement with Indigenous peoples in the creation and staging of *Louis Riel* was at the centre of discourse around the 2017 production. As dramaturg Paula Danckert observed in the forementioned journal issue that followed the *Hearing Riel* symposium,

> In 1967, there were no Indigenous people in the opera. It was a non-issue at the time because, after all, it was an opera and Native opera singers did not exist – at least as far as anyone knew.[11] Added to this is the assumption that Aboriginal people do not go to the opera, so any consideration of inclusion was moot.[12] It was clear who the audience was or, more specifically, who they were not. By 2017, to do anything about Louis Riel without the involvement of the Métis was an anathema – grotesque racism and a further act of colonization. (2018, 45).

While Danckert then points to Hinton accepting the responsibility of addressing this omission while still "respect[ing] the original intent of the libretto and the score" (45), like many instances when settler governments and institutions do the right thing, it is important to back up and examine the impetus for change.[13] As Cole Alvis told me, in her capacity as Executive Director of the Indigenous Performing Arts Alliance she was given the opportunity to address a group of arts leaders, many of whom were interested in doing some "TRC-inspired programming."[14] She "wanted to encourage them to be partnering or engaging with Indigenous communities or Indigenous artists … making sure there were Indigenous people in leadership roles" (C. Alvis, interview, 2017). Alexander Neef, then general director of the COC, was present and subsequently met with Alvis who was able to guide

Neef in the COC's attempt to address the problems inherent in *Louis Riel*. Though Alvis is in no way claiming that she was responsible for ensuring that the COC engaged with Indigenous peoples (and she also mentioned Jani Lauzon's work), the point here is that Indigenous artists *pushed* the COC to do the right thing. They needed to be told that, to do otherwise, was anathema. In fact, Alvis further noted that the COC had already cast the main roles and "was very proud of having an all-Canadian cast for the show" but that they had "not quite extended their analysis to seeking out racially appropri ate casting" (2017).

By the time the opera opened, the COC was engaging with Indigenous people in significant ways. Michif speaker, Norman Fleury, was brought in to translate text into Michif, resulting in some sung Michif and surtitles in Michif, a first for an opera. Hinton also added a silent "Land Assembly" made up of twenty-five to forty-five Indigenous people (depending on the city it was performed in) who were on the stage from curtain to curtain. This Land Assembly was intended as "a way of keeping the otherwise absent bodies present in the performance and a way of hearing their silenced voices" (Danckert 2018, 46). Hinton furthermore cast Joanna Burt (Métis/ Saugeen Ojibwe) in the role of Sara Riel (Louis's sister); created a role for Cole Alvis ("the activist"); had Jani Lauzon (Métis) sing a formerly pre-recorded introduction; and commissioned Santee Smith (Mohawk) to choreograph a new dance for a buffalo hunt scene,[15] performed by Justin Many Fingers (Blackfoot). COC leaders were moreover meeting with Dylan Robinson, who had contacted them a month before opening night, and representatives from the Nisga'a nation (namely Wal'aks Keane Tait, G̱oothl Ts'imilx Mike Dangeli, and Sm Łoodm 'Nüüsm- Mique'l Dangeli) to discuss the "Kuyas" aria, a song that Somers took from a recording of Nisga'a music made by anthropologist Marius Barbeau.[16] The COC was also a co-host of the symposium held the day after the opera opened, which, as mentioned earlier, included several Métis speakers who were able to put the opera in context, emphasizing the history of the Métis Nation, and the continued presence of Métis as a living peoples. While these inclusions were important, it is vital to note that there was no in-depth conversation about how Métis *culture* was represented in the opera (or perhaps more accurately, how it was not represented), something rather surprising given that it was a major *cultural* production. Nor were there substantive discussions of appropriation beyond the "Kuyas" aria. This is in no way meant to diminish the importance of discussions about the aria. Instead, it points to how the analysis of appropriation stopped at this particularly egregious example, failing to consider the more nuanced ways in which the opera might be understood as appropriation.

In my conversations with Métis attendees, I was struck by their desire to see Métis culture meaningfully and authentically represented on stage. As one Métis attendee, Marcel Larouche, told me, "When the woman was singing to her baby in Michif, that was a very powerful moment. I think that's what really changed the production because I'd never heard Michif in operatic form. And I just, it was magical as I said … just a wonderful experience. So that was a true … Métis experience for me" (2017). Larouche also referred to a duet between Sara and Julie (Riel's mother), noting that, "The mother and the [sister] of Louis Riel did a wonderful job, and at some point … when they had that duet … that was incredible, the two of them on stage." Another Métis attendee similarly found the lullaby to be the opera's most beautiful moment, a moment where Riel was a father and a husband, not just a rebel, and where Marguerite (Riel's wife) was a loving mother.[17] In the Ottawa production, this scene was changed – the cradle and baby were taken out – because that beautiful lullaby was, in fact, the stolen Nisga'a song, and the Ottawa performance a small attempt at redress, one that, as an unfortunate side effect, removed some of the humanity from the opera. The way that these Métis attendees spoke about the representation of Métis culture and family life reveals a profound desire to see beautiful expressions of Métis culture in a "high art" space. As Larouche shared,

> I did wear my Métis sash with my suit. I like to dress up at the opera. And I had a lot of people come up to me and ask me about it, and talk to me, which was touching … and I think that's what was important about this very unique experience of mixing opera with Métis culture, is that it brings an awareness in venues that wouldn't be traditionally exposed to Métis culture. So, I think it gives the public, especially the operatic public a different exposure, a different experience. And I would welcome seeing more of this. (M. Larouche, interview, 2017)

Later in our interview he reiterated that he was "so proud of [the opera] happening," and that was why he wore his sash. It was clear that he wished and hoped for more space on large, mainstream stages for Métis people and culture.

However, these attempts to find beautiful moments of Métis-ness in the production highlight how Métis culture was largely forgotten. Larouche followed up his comment about Julie and Sara Riel's duet by noting that "[the creators] could have used those roles more and introduced more cultural elements in the opera" (2017). While Larouche therefore viewed the opera as a small step, others were not so positive. For example, one attendee (who wished to remain anonymous) repeatedly told me that she thought the opera was terrible, referring to the music but also to the way in which Riel was portrayed. As she told me,

> There were certain aspects that I don't agree with, that they ... really played up in the opera, and that was the bit about Riel being, he was a visionary, but he certainly wasn't, how can I put this mildly ... I don't think he was insane and seeing the archangel or anything like that. He was a visionary, and he was able to see that, you know, people had to come together and the opera itself was really kind of pushing the, I thought it was kind of pushing the fact that he was possibly having mental health problems, and I don't think that was the case. I think he was frustrated because he could see what was happening around him, and he had some ideas of how to fix it, but he was not being given an opportunity to make any of those things happen. (anonymous, interview, 2017c)

Later in the interview she reiterated,

> He was a visionary, absolutely, and he was able to see, and try to pull people together ... and you know people do that today and they're not called insane ... so that piece of it, I did not like ... he was a bright guy. He went to university. They didn't portray any of that very well ... a lot that was missing. They didn't really show him in university and the rejection he got from the people around him in Montreal, and you know his heart was broken because he fell in love with a woman and her father wouldn't let him marry her because he was a half-breed ... I would never recommend [the opera] to anybody, and I would never go and see it again. (anonymous, interview, 2017c)

What came through so clearly in this attendee's comments was her feeling that Riel was more than just his participation in the Resistances, and that his leadership was not madness. Perhaps even more poignantly, she remarked that Métis were and are more than the horror portrayed. As she emphasized, "It wasn't all just doom and gloom ... There was lots of happiness ... and dancing and jigging and ... people bringing out the guitars, or the violins. There was a lot of happiness happening, and ... the camaraderie of ... sitting and playing cards, and just all that type of stuff ... [the opera's depiction of Métis life] seemed like a very sad existence, when I know that my family was not sad. There was a lot of happiness and lot of wonderful things going on" (anonymous, interview, 2017c). Though some of the Métis attendees did their best to find small, beautiful representations of their peoplehood, contemporary Métis peoplehood and presence were hard to find in much of the discourse around the production, and critical analyses of the opera tended to overlook the very peoples whose story the opera tells.

As noted earlier, the appropriation of a Nisga'a song became a significant part of the discourse around the opera. This was, and continues to be, a vital conversation that may have lasting reverberations through the classical music world, as arts organizations, patrons, performers, composers, and directors finally become more aware of appropriation within classical music, or perhaps more accurately, begin to show that they are willing to listen and act on this appropriation.[18] Significantly, following the 2017 production, Somers's estate commissioned Métis composer Ian Cusson to write a new aria to replace the aria that appropriated the Nisga'a song. Titled "Dodo, Mon Tout Petit," it is an example of concrete action taken to address one of the most blatantly problematic aspects of the opera. However, the Nisga'a song was not the only moment of appropriation in the opera. Indeed, there were two (supposedly) Métis songs in *Louis Riel*, "Le Roi malheureux," and "Buffalo Hunt." While there was almost no discussion of these songs in any of the discourse around the opera, musicologist Colette Simonot-Maiello, does include a footnote in her article published in the special issue of the *University of Toronto Quarterly*. This footnote follows an absolutely correct statement that Somers "incorporated very little music of the Métis people into his opera" (Simonot-Maiello 2018, 76). Yet the genealogy of "The Buffalo Hunt" that she includes in the footnote is incorrect. She writes,

> Two folk songs included in Somers's opera are directly connected to Métis cultures: "Buffalo Hunt" and "Le Roi malheureux," both attributed to Métis songwriter Pierre Falcon (1793–1876). Both of these

> songs appear in Margaret Arnett MacLeod's collection of *Songs of Old Manitoba*. Falcon set his own French lyrics for "Buffalo Hunt" to a tune called "Cécilia," but his original French lyrics have not survived. (The text in MacLeod's collection is probably an English translation of Falcon's text that was published in Agnes Laut's fiction book, *Lords of the North*, in 1900). Somers altered the music of this song so that it might sound more "primitive"; he made the metre more irregular and altered the accent patterns in order to give an impression of heightened ex citement before a hunt. Furthermore, the entire first verse is accompanied by hand clapping and foot stomping." (76)

That the only detailed information about the use of Métis music in the opera is relegated to a footnote is significant, as are the omissions and key mistake in the note. There is, in fact, no evidence that "The Buffalo Hunt" was written by Falcon. Rather, it comes, word for word, from Ontario-born author Agnes Laut's racist and dehumanizing book; the lyrics of the song are Laut's, not Falcon's. *Lords of the North* is a typical "Indian" novel of its time, telling the story of a white woman and her child who have been stolen away by an "Indian." The main character, Rufus Gillespie, eventually takes part in a buffalo hunt, where he is introduced to Pierre, a character described as a "half-breed rhymester," obviously based on Pierre Falcon. This is the context in which we find the first publication of a song titled "The Buffalo Hunt." MacLeod included it in *Songs of Old Manitoba* after a prolonged search for a buffalo hunt song to be part of her book. Though she had heard that Falcon had written one, his song was lost. She therefore used *Lords of the North* as her source, attributing it to Falcon. Because it was not accompanied by music, MacLeod spent a great deal of time searching for a melody, eventually settling on "Cécilia" by little-known Canadian composer Jean Klinck (Giroux 2015b, 48–51).

The buffalo hunt song used in the opera was, then, an adoption of one written by settler Canadians who were trying to represent Métis people: an appropriation of an appropriation. Considered alongside the appropriation of the Nisga'a song, Moore, Languirand, and Somers's attempt to add a little bit of Indigeneity belies a lack of attention to the source (e.g., being a nation-specific song, or being written by a Métis composer) and context (e.g., being an actual lullaby) of the quoted or appropriated music; these little bits of Indigeneity are used to colour the opera – give it a flavour of "Indianness" – but do not constitute meaningful engagement with Indigenous musics or cultures. Though the 2017 production did attempt to engage with Indigenous people more substantially than any of the previous stagings, many of the same issues emerged, in particular, a lack of attention to nation-specificity (also pointed to by Simonot-Maiello 2018, 77) and lack of critical engagement with the impact of the opera on Métis (though the symposium's engagement with Teillet and Gaudry are important). It is significant to once again note that the opera has never been performed on the Prairies where there would be greater community accountability, and that the inclusion of Métis in the 2017 production remained limited to the assistant director, Estelle Shook, and to Jani Lauzon and Cole Alvis, alongside an unknown number of Métis people in the silent chorus. (*Louis Riel* has a cast of sixty people.) Furthermore, one of the articles published in the special issue of *University of Toronto Quarterly* does not even mention the word Métis, and one of the interviews on the abovementioned podcast does not as well: it is all too easy for Canadians, it seems, to forget the Métis (especially as a people and not just as individuals) even as their story is being told.

While the explicitly appropriated materials in the opera were few, limited to three songs, Alvis told me that the opera as a whole – given its lack of engagement with Métis people and communities – can be considered appropriation. As she noted,

> The entire production is appropriation to me in that 2,000 people a show, over seven shows, 14,000 people came and thought they saw Métis culture, or think now they understand the Métis story, and beyond Jani getting to sing in Michif, and some Indigenous, some Métis and otherwise Indigenous people being on stage silent, I don't feel as though … Métis culture has been represented here. And so my concern then falls in people's perceptions of Indigeneity, and in this case Métis culture, specifically being further misled as they are by the educational system, and the media, and the government. And so I think that's maybe what I meant by the band aid solution that Peter Hinton was able to bring, in no way was this the Indigenous production that I want for the COC. And yet I chose to participate because I could see the potential for learning, and slight structural shifts that may lead to an Indigenous opera on their stage (C. Alvis, interview, 2017).

Alvis also commented that a Métis person had seen the opera in Vancouver in 2010 and had been appalled by the way in which Métis were shown acting violently against Scott, tackling him and engaging in a brawl; in reality, that act of violence did not occur but instead emerged from stereotypes. For Alvis, then, this is where harm can occur: when non-Indigenous people tell Indigenous stories, they don't have "the same kind of level of accountability to community" (C. Alvis, interview, 2017). During our conversation, Alvis and I considered the omission of Métis culture: would it have been better to include Métis culture, even if this might be understood as appropriation? Or was it better that Métis culture is omitted from the opera? We could not come up with an answer because both situations (appropriation or continued erasure of Métis voices and communities) are, of course, far from ideal.

When I first wrote about *Louis Riel* for the online edition of *Canadian Notes and Queries*, adding my own voice to the cacophony of conversation about the opera, I interpreted the opera's failures as a moment of reckoning. This was a constant theme in my interview with Alvis: she was interested in what could come from this, about using it to have a "critical discussion about what can come next" (2017). As I wrote in my original analysis of the opera, "In the midst of all the mistakes – the missteps, the appropriation, the forgetting of the very people whose story was being told – an important shift happened within the collective consciousness of a major Canadian arts organization [or perhaps, I would now add, of major Canadian arts organizations], a shift that ultimately marks the death of the opera *Louis Riel*" (Giroux 2018). In other words, I suggested that there was no (ethical) way to ever produce this opera again. Thus, drawing on the final words of the opera, I stated that the "goddamn opera was dead." That is, it should remain only a score, a relic of the past that is studied for what it can teach us about unethical relationships, but that never leaves the page. I still believe that this is true: that it should not and likely will not ever be restaged. Certainly, there is a newfound consciousness within many settler institutions about the importance of Indigenous peoples telling their own stories (see, e.g., Derksen et al. 2019). And to reiterate, this was the result of the hard work of Indigenous artists, creators, academics, and community members before, during, and after the production. Yet after publishing the article, I was struck by attempts to *rescue* the opera, and a lack of *listening* to the very Métis who were asked to join the conversation – a problem that came through prominently in the special issue of *University of Toronto Quarterly*.

The special issue did, importantly, include an article by Jean Teillet, who was very critical of the opera. As she noted in no uncertain terms in her article, the opera is "a deeply troubling piece of art" (2018, 30). Then, in her concluding statement, Teillet extended her critique to the COC:

> Despite Hinton's efforts and the fine performances, the central message from the remounting of the opera has now become a sermon. If a story is repeated on important occasions, it acquires a religious, ceremonial aspect. This sermon is the story of how Canada executed Riel, justified the necessity of its action, and exonerated itself. Choosing to tell this story in an opera in 1967 to celebrate the centennial of Confederation sent a powerful message about the triumph of English Canada in 1885 and how it intended to march forward as a country over the dead bodies of Indigenous people and francophones. With all the current attention to inappropriate terminology with respect to Indigenous peoples, offensive mascots in sport, famous authors who turn out to be of questionable Indigenous authenticity, and tensions in the artistic community about cultural appropriation and naming, one would have thought the Canadian Opera Company would be more sensitive to the messages in the sermon it was remounting in the *Louis Riel* opera in 2017. (Teillet 2018, 35)

The editors' decision to include Teillet was a significant one, demonstrating at least some attempt to value Métis voices. However, it is also important to note that the COC came to the realization that the opera could not be staged without Métis leadership (and therefore hired a Métis assistant director to work with Hinton), but the journal did not reach the same conclusion: not only were none of the editors Métis, but there is no evidence that any specialize in Métis history or culture. The editors of the special issue all have impressive track records as academics, as do the contributors; and as such, this critique is not intended as a personal critique of anyone involved, but rather a critique of an ongoing and persistent structure where the value of the opera is seen as greater than the stories Métis tell about Riel, or Métis responses to the opera. This lack of Métis oversight likely contributed to the more surface level examples of not listening, such as referring to Rebellions rather than Resistances in two of the articles,[19] the misspelling of the name for the Métis language, and the use of the phrase "Métis and Indigenous" in several of the articles (as if Métis are not Indigenous). It may have also contributed to subtly problematic language in the introductory essay, including the statement that "Riel in death, as in life, managed to reawaken hostilities between

Ontario and Quebec, Orangemen and Catholics, English and French" (Clark et al. 2018, 2), as if he were to blame.

Again, it was an important decision to include Teillet and Gaudry in the symposium and Teillet in the special journal issue. And certainly, some of the articles in the journal are critical of the opera (in particular, Collette Simonot-Maiello's which points to the need for Indigenous-led and -created stories). Yet Teillet's critique and Simonot-Maiello's contributions were presented alongside those that attempted to rescue the opera (and in fact the entire 2017 production might be understood as attempted rescuing). By "rescue" I mean articles or approaches that suggest that the opera can be ethically staged, or that its problems were staging problems rather than integral to the work. For example, one author wrote,

> as critics in 1968 were quick to point out, each component part of *Louis Riel* suffers from significant problems. And yet somehow the opera succeeds in spite of these limitations; the whole is greater than the sum of its parts. It seems that Somers and Moore left *Louis Riel* as an essentially incomplete work of art that invites – indeed, demands – substantial creative input, engagement, and imagination from the large team of artists required to mount a production of it. When that team brings as much creative insight, inspiration, and brilliance to the task as did Peter Hinton, his Métis and Indigenous collaborators, and the entire COC team that brought *Louis Riel* to life in 2017, the results make for a memorable evening of music theatre. (Elliot 2018, 18)

The striking conclusion that Elliot comes to is that Somers and Moore intentionally left space for the creative work of a production team, and that past failures might be blamed on the team involved in staging. Renihan similarly notes that "What Hinton achieved in this production is a realization of the element of haunting that is missing form all previous productions of the opera, despite its prominence in the original play," here referencing John Coulter's play that Moore drew inspiration from (2018, 56). Like Elliot, the suggestion (in my reading) is that the failures of the past were production and staging issues, rather than integral or structural issues within the opera. Staging it in an appropriate way, then, can save it. And perhaps the further implication is that we *should* save it. Reading the clear and pointed critique of a prominent and respected Métis woman (Teillet) alongside articles that attempt to rescue the opera points to the hard work that still needs to be done to address the erasure of Métis peoples. It also tells me that the perceived inherent value of the opera – and perhaps of *opera* – continues to take precedence (for some) over telling authentic Métis stories.

In closing this reflection on *Louis Riel,* I want to share an excerpt from my fieldnotes, written after attending the opera in 2017 in Toronto.

> I sat next to a woman who grew up not far from where Adam Gaudry grew up. [She shared this detail with me because she had recently heard him speak.] I asked her after the first intermission if she was enjoying [the opera]. She said she really *wanted* to. She told me she had been to many operas (and even had binoculars). She then told me about a symposium she went to the previous Friday, with University of Toronto professors, John Ralston Saul, Adam Gaudry, Jean Teillet – all live streamed because the room was at capacity. (It held about 200.) She noted that she wanted to enjoy [the opera] because at the symposium they talked about how the stories of First Peoples were not told in Canada. (fieldnotes, 23 April 2017)

As I was writing this chapter, I re-read my fieldnotes and came across my entry about this conversation – one that struck me as vital after five years of thinking about the opera. Though I did not understand the implications fully when I originally wrote the fieldnote, I was struck in my more recent reading that someone could come from this day-long (and very well attended) symposium with the idea that they should really try to like *Louis Riel.* That the opera – *Louis Riel* – should be rescued from its own datedness and hard-to-like aesthetic. And I was struck by how difficult it seems to be for many to listen to (critical) Métis voices.

Li Keur: Putting the Heart Back into Métis Stories

> Here's the crux of it. This isn't about a performance. This is about four years of relationships.
> – Suzanne Steele, interview with Giroux (2021)

To the outside observer, *Louis Riel* and *Li Keur: Riel's Heart of the North* might seem similar: both are about Métis leader, Louis Riel, and both fall somewhat uncomfortably in the opera genre. (Many have suggested that

Louis Riel is not quite an opera, perhaps a musical drama. Suzanne Steele[20] has similarly noted that *Li Keur* does not quite fit into the category of opera.) However, their stories are dramatically different, as were their processes of creation. The idea for *Li Keur* began to crystalize in 2017 after poet, librettist, and researcher Suzanne Steele's agent put her in contact with another one of his clients, newcomer composer Neil Weisensel, who was interested in writing an opera about Louis Riel. (Here I use newcomer rather than settler because it is Steele's preferred term.) They successfully applied for funding through a Canada 150 New Chapter Award, a funding opportunity created as part of Canada's sesquicentennial celebrations. For Steele, receiving this grant was an opportunity to "tell the story [she] need[ed] to tell about Riel," while also making sure that Métis women were central to the narrative (2021). In this way, she aimed to address a problematic omission in many versions of Métis history. To find this story, Steele (from the Gaudry/Fayant families) embarked on a 10,000-kilometre trip across the Métis Homeland, leaving from her home in Vancouver, British Columbia, and travelling to Montana, the Dakotas, Wyoming, Manitoba, Saskatchewan, and Alberta. Though she was aware of the *Louis Riel* opera, she purposefully did not read the score beyond the first few pages, so she did not, and does not, know the plot or structure. She furthermore did not read any contemporary creative writing about Riel, though she did create a substantial bibliography of primary and secondary sources that she consulted, including Riel's complete writings.

When asked about this rather unusual way (from a Western perspective) to start writing an opera, Steele noted that she "had to listen to the land" (2021). As she shared with me,

> I wanted to go and be as much off grid as possible. I wasn't really looking for Riel as much as I was looking for the story I needed to tell about Riel, and in particular I knew, women, our women needed to be a big part of that. But in order to do any of this, I had to listen to the land. That was so important to me … and in fact, the whole thing opens with a becoming story. I don't call it a creation story. It's a becoming story. And it's very much about the land, about the Milky Way, about the natural world, or the great universe, and the ancestors that are still there, amongst us, and so … I wanted to hear what I needed to tell, and I just trusted that. So, I went off with my husband, who's a guitarist, my daughter, who's [a traditional Métis] fiddler, and her partner who

> is a naturalist … we camped off grid for a couple of weeks … he [her daughter's partner] really opened my eyes to the flora and fauna. It was amazing actually having him there. And then Jeff, my husband, and Ella, my daughter, they were playing music. That opened a whole other world … at one point, we drifted down the Missouri river, and one of the arias, "Baptize Me in My Galilee," that came from camping … at Pelican Point and, in fact, Riel sings that, and that just came to me, but I had to sit there on the side of the river and just listen to the river. (S. Steele, interview, 2021)

While the plants, animals, and landscapes were important, so too were the people she met along the way. She shared with me how, in a moment of pure happenstance, she ran into Nicholas Vrooman, a well-known folklorist who worked closely with Métis in Montana and North Dakota as well as north of the border (and whom I mention in chapters two and six). She purchased a copy of his book (which is by far the most comprehensive look at life for Métis in Montana), and he told her that she was on the right track. Steele also spoke about meeting an Indigenous family in Montana, and though they did not identify as Métis, she was able to piece together their connection to Métis kin through their family names, the fiddlers in their families, and so on.

During our interview, Steele explained to me that her family story is "a classic Métis family story of diaspora" (2021). Her many times great-grandfather, Louis Gaudry, was a translator for Sitting Bull, and as a navigator, businessman, and rancher, the family had some capital and wealth. Yet within a generation or two, that was lost, replaced by extreme poverty. Just as painfully, this loss resulted in disconnection from musical and cultural life; and this is a source of regret for Steele. As she told me,

> For me, everything I do in this is a project of recovery. Because I witnessed firsthand the shame and the loss … and it really makes me sad because I'll go back to the homeland and see the Arcand family, for example … and they're this huge wonderful musical family, and I think, "Wow, I wish that the Gaudrys had been able to do that." But for some reason, we lost everything through diaspora … the Gaudrys were in Red River Settlement and the land they owned was next to the Riels … and at one point Louis [Gaudry] was a secretary to Riel … just during the provisional government time. (2021)

Steele's grandmother attended residential school,[21] and then married a wealthy white American. From that point on, her grandmother never spoke Michif-French. The family knew that she was French, and thought that they must be part First Nations, but "it was never spoken of" (S. Steele, interview, 2021). Steele began her own process of recovery after meeting a Métis scholar who asked her, "You're Métis, aren't you?" This scholar put her in touch with a genealogist who was able to trace fourteen generations of her family lineage to France. But, as she noted, after a certain point in her family tree, it was "Métis marrying Métis ... mostly because [they] shared a common culture, this beautiful Métis culture" (2021). Steele has worked since then to recover these family connections building Métis community in Vancouver and more widely in the Homeland, while bringing music back into her family through her daughter who is, as noted above, a traditional Métis fiddler who studied with renowned Métis fiddler, John Arcand, at his fiddle camp. In one of our many informal conversations about *Li Keur* and Métis music and dance, Steele referred to the opera storyline as "piecing together Riel's missing years" and how that might be understood as a metaphor for what Métis are now doing: reconnecting with the knowledge, worldviews, ways of life, and more, of their ancestors.

While Steele was travelling across the Homeland, she visited the North Dakota State Archives in Bismarck, where she was able to access a diary written in 1870 by an unknown Englishman. In it, she read the story of Baptiste Robideau, a man on the run from Canadian authorities who had agreed to act as a guide for the Englishman. Though Robideau's identity remains shrouded in mystery and speculation, the timeline, along with other details such as Robideau's poetry, led historian Heather Devine, who first identified the diary, to speculate that Robideau was, in fact, Louis Riel, living under an assumed name. In addition to Robideau, the diary described Josette, a beautiful, sharpshooting Métis woman. These real figures became part of the central storyline in Steele's libretto; and though Devine identified the diary, it was Steele who found the love story that became integral to the opera. Though Steele used a historical document as the spark for her opera "comb[ing] through it for details" (Steele 2020a), in the context of writing the opera, she told me, "We are artists, not historians" (2021). I understand her statement as an acknowledgment that the heart or spirit of the story is what mattered to her in writing the libretto. Robideau may or may not have been Riel – and that is indeed a central question to be considered through this opera; yet the strength of Métis women and the richness of Métis culture within an Indigenous polycultural, multilingual society was the thread that she was able to take from the story. It is the true Métis story, and it matters more than uncovering the *fact* of who Robideau might have been. And so, it was this beautiful culture and the complex social relations of Métis society that she placed at the heart of the opera. Though Riel is an important part of the story, *Li Keur* is much more than the story of one man; and notably, *Li Keur* does not centre on the Resistances or on Riel's death but rather his life, relationships, and people. After reading a draft of this chapter, Steele noted that she is "appalled at the thought of Riel being murdered again and again and again" through the staging of *Louis Riel;* and she is, "far more interested in his life than his death." Steele's focus on life, relationships, and women (and in fact there is no "star" role, but rather an ensemble of main characters) makes *Li Keur* fundamentally different from so much of the artistic mythologizing of Riel referenced earlier.

The creation process for this opera therefore began by engaging in relationship with family, community, land, and culture, as Steele travelled the homeland of her ancestors. Weisensel similarly travelled across the Métis Homeland in preparation for his work as a composer. Yet, as Steele and Weisensel began writing the opera, the process took on a more standard approach, with Steele writing the libretto, and Weisensel writing the music. Before long, Steele was not satisfied with the approach. As Weisensel told me,

> What happened is, we were about three-quarters of the way through the opera in English and with Suzanne kind of throwing some French in there, and then she was like, "This needs to be Indigenous languages." And I was like "OK" [spoken with an air of wonder or gravity]. So, then, we found the translators, and so then I basically, the stuff that I had written already in English and French had to be rewritten, and so, you know, if I had an English word that was like that long [visually indicating length], and then I had a heritage Michif word that was that long [indicating length], ten syllables. So … everything had to be kind of recalculated and redone. But what it actually did, is it made the music much more interesting … that was the really fascinating part. (2021)

Though Steele disputes the sequence of events, noting in particular that she knew that she had to write with Indigenous languages from the beginning, this comment – and of course the falling back into a more standard approach to writing an opera after the 10,000 kilometre journey – speaks to the constant pull of the status quo, and foreshadows the push back Steele has faced (what she refers to as always being told "no") as she tries to do things in ways that are different from business as usual. Nonetheless, through her persistence, she was able to ensure that this vital aspect of her vision for the opera became reality.

In her introductory essay about the opera, Steele writes about the process and protocol of visiting with the translators in St Laurent, Brandon, and Winnipeg, as well as the hard emotional labour of the work and of the process of being "vetted" by the community (2020c). This was not a process of simply having the libretto translated; it began with relationship and continued through relationship. Building on a first visit in St Laurent, Steele and Weisensel began working with seven language specialists and two research assistants (one Indigenous and the other a newcomer) to translate the libretto into Anishinaabemowin (the Ojibwe language) and two Michifs; as a result, about seventy per cent of the opera is now in an Indigenous language.[22] The language aspect of the opera was, for Steele, an important way to place the *soundscape* of the late 1800s at the centre of the opera. As she writes,

> Language, story, and visit are central to all cultures, as indeed to Indigenous cultural identity. Story and language is thus central to the body of this new work on Louis Riel … it has been my intention, as storyteller, to flip the expectations of a 21st century opera-going audience from a Eurocentric to an Indigen-a-centric narrative, one that reimagines our world of 150+ years ago. I thus saw that my most creative, and powerful tool would be through language. My goal has always been to try and emulate the linguistic aesthetic that potentially echoes the linguistic landscape of Riel's world (1840 – 85) – and indeed, the peoples at the heart of this continent for centuries, and millennia – peoples such as my French, my Michif, and my Anishinaabe ancestors. (Steele 2020c, 2)

Thus, in working with the translators, Steele creates space for the languages, and the people who speak the languages, on the stage (both literally and metaphorically). As Steele writes,

> A further goal of mine is to weave the languages in a manner *similar* to my understanding of the languages of the prairie kinship webs of my mother's people at the heart of the continent. Indeed, this cross-cultural and linguistic weaving was a lifeblood of the times. Many of us have ancestors who were translators and navigators, specifically because they not only spoke five to seven languages, but also because their kinship webs crossed the heart of the continent. Ultimately I wanted an Indigenous audience to see and hear *us* once again rightfully placed centre stage at the heart of the continent. (Steele 2020c, 2)

The translators were key to this process, becoming co-creators of the libretto. (Though the words are Steele's, the translators provided *aesthetic translations* as described below, thus contributing to the artistry of the work.) Both Steele and Weisensel cherish the relationships they have built with the translators. In fact, for Steele, this work has become the heart of the project. One of the most important outcomes was a digital database of the translations completed for this opera. Partnering with Canadian Mennonite University where Weisensel works, Steele completed this work with utmost attention to ethics, drafting an "Indigenous Memorandum of Understanding" that was shared and agreed upon by all project participants. It explicitly stated that "all intellectual property that [the translators] contributed belonged to them and their estate in perpetuity, and that any time they wished to have it withdrawn they could" (Steele 2020c, 3). The database is currently freely available online for use by those singing music from the opera, or those who wish to learn the languages.

Beyond serving as a resource for language learning, Steele's aim with this database is to better understand the poetic elements of the Indigenous languages that are part of the database. As she explains,

> What is different about this project is what I call aesthetic translation … Translation is very often literal translation. But … you don't understand a language if you just do literal translations … what we're going to look at is how our translators … look at my words. My text is being used as a foundation. What I'm asking the translators to do and what we'll be examining is, how does a translator get around this concept, especially because I'm a poet, and I write a poetic concept … for example, there's an aria called "Mending the Violence of Men" … Marie Serpente is called in to literally sew together some men's wounds.

> They've got in a boxing match, they got too violent, and so she's called in to mend them, to sew their skin together, and to repair them … My original words were … "What strange mending is this of the violence of men." So that's quite a complex concept. So how the Anishinaabemowin translators … Debra Beach Ducharme and Donna Beach, how they approached it … if you look at their Anishinaabemowin, they go "How strange is it that I sew a man's skin just like I sew a dress." … So that to me is really insightful, how … they would use an object like a dress rather than do a literal translation. (Steele 2020a, 15:00–17:03)

She further points to the importance of ensuring that the Indigenous languages remain poetic through the translations. As she noted, "you don't want it to be too prosaic, too plain" (Steele 2020c, 17:30–18:05). For Steele, then, the database is an essential component of supporting language revitalization for future generations and provides an opening into the beauty and artistry of Indigenous languages.

While the libretto was being created with a team of Indigenous people, this was not enough for Steele. As Weisensel told me, "Suzanne sees her work as a collaboration between her and the seven Indigenous translators. And she thought … it would be really great for you to have an Indigenous person on your team, and … I had never thought about that because composers are such lone wolves. We don't collaborate with other composers, as a rule" (2021). For Steele, it was important to have an Indigenous composer working on the project. (It is vital to note, however, that Steele is a trained vocalist with a degree in music, and she did not and does not shy away from providing feedback and suggestions on the music itself.) As she told me, "I worked so closely with our translators. I said to Neil … we really need to have an Indigenous voice in the music … because I don't think, he wasn't grasping, he did beautiful work, beautiful [spoken with an emphasis on beautiful]. But our story isn't beautiful. Our story is … beautiful, but there's a big dark thread in it" (2021). Weisensel and Steele had seen Métis fiddler Alex Kusturok at an event in Winnipeg a few years earlier and had both been impressed with his work, but it was not the right time for Kusturok to join the project. In the meantime, there were fiddlers involved in the project, but none were part of the creative team. Three years into the project, in 2020, just as COVID-19 was shutting down the world, Kusturok was brought on board to compose about a dozen tunes for the opera. Speaking specifically about bringing Kusturok into the project, Steele shared, "I just needed his energy. He has an understanding of the depth and suffering of our peoples … but also how unbelievably joyous we are as well … especially in adversity" (2021). The addition of Kusturok's compositions is, possibly, one of the most exciting and innovative musical aspects of this work. As Kusturok told me, Steele's "vision of this is to have the fiddle almost in a, like a war with the orchestra, right, to kind of show … the Western culture and the Métis culture kind of going like this, right [hitting his fists together to indicate a clash]" (Kusturok 2021). Steele explains it this way:

> He's one of the four black geese of fate, who is the disrupter who's going to literally disrupt the orchestra … It opens with this becoming story … it's about li Grande Shasews [the Great Female Hunter] hunting our universe … she hunts for centuries. She hunts li Gran Buffalo, and he's got this rumbling in his stomach, and it's the music, it's our music rumbling in his stomach. And, anyway, she finally hunts him down … So, she slits open, she kills li Gran Buffalo, the great buffalo, our universe, slits open his belly, and out comes all our music and that's when Alex is going to rise in the middle of the orchestra and just be totally disruptive in like just the best, most awesome way. He's going to torment the conductor, the first desk violin, you name it … he's there to disrupt all together musically. You know, and … so in the beginning, we're very newcomer sounding, and by the end it'll be just him. At the very end. (2021)

While the opera does include some traditional Métis tunes, Kusturok, as noted above, wrote original compositions. In other words, musically, the opera connects the fiddling of the past with the fiddling and Métis music-creation of today. Steele's storytelling about music emerging from li Gran Buffalo is also fascinating to me because, like the stories shared in chapter two, Métis music is described as emerging with the Métis peoples.

As evident in the creation process, *Li Keur* began as a collaborative project between a Métis creative and a newcomer composer. However, under Steele's direction, it became a creative work embedded in ever-deepening community relationships – as she noted, "This isn't about a performance. This is about four years of relationships" (interview, 2021). Like the opening story of the opera, this opera is a story of emergence (or reemergence), of becoming and reanimation through relationships – something that is so evident in the ongoing layering of relationship-building at the heart to the work. As Steele shared, "a lot of people who call themselves allies really haven't a clue what that [allyship] means, and they don't realize that it takes a lot of hard work to make good relationship" (S. Steele, interview, 2021). Later, she reiterated the importance of relationship in the following exchange:

> SS: I'm very proud of … what I've given. I'm very proud. I'm very proud that a dozen Indigenous translators are revitalizing their language, and they tell me that this has really exercised their brains and made them even more interested in their work as translators … So, that's what I'm proud of … so here's the crux of it. This isn't about a performance. This is about four years of relationships. And that's what I think a newcomer culture doesn't understand too well.
> MG: Right, yeah. We get so hung up on the product that we forget about the process.
> SS: Yeah, the process, the relationships we've formed along the way. You know, those two young research assistants have formed wonderful relationships with these translators. These wonderous Elders. You know, so that's great, and I think Neil has too … I'm sure he has … I think they're quite fond of him, and so that's great. (2021)

Though it is yet to be seen how or if this process-centred approach will impact Weisensel's future work, Steele's insistence on centring relationships certainly has impacted his business-as-usual approach. As he told me, "for Suzanne, the process [of relationship] is more important than the product … And I've really started to come around to that way of thinking too" (2021). *Li Keur* is not, however, only about those relationships of the now, but rather about building connections with the past for future generations. This is at the heart of how Steele wrote the libretto, which is narrated by a young woman living in the twenty-first century, while moving between the mystic present and past and the late nineteenth century. This connection among past-present-future is central to how Steele envisions herself as an artist. As she stated in a podcast interview with her research assistants, Hannah Connelly and Bryna Link, "I think when an artist does their job well, they get the heck out of the way, and someone tells them the story. And I think that these young women [in the diary] told me the story when I read that diary, and that my great grandmothers are telling me the story, and that my daughter is telling me the story. So, the connection is very real, and that's an Indigenous point of view, that they're with us still, and not just on paper. They're not just on paper" (Steele 2020a, 12:17–12:38).

The work done through *Li Keur* resonates strongly with Indigenous thinking on resurgence: it connects past-present-future, articulates and envisions what a contemporary Métis creative practice does and might look like; centres the work and process of relationships (including by rejecting the typical format of "star" roles); creates and connects through land and kin; and refuses past representations of Riel and the Métis people by centring women and balancing both the joys and sorrows of life (indeed, the opera will make the audience laugh, cry, and want to dance). To borrow from the work of Jarrett Martineau, it might be understood as an example of the resurgent "visioning and anticolonial work accomplished through Indigenous creative practices" (2015, 5). Steele has, however, referred to *Li Keur* as a work of reconciliation (which in some interpretations might set it slightly apart from resurgent practices that turn away from the settler state [Simpson 2014, 2; Corntassel 2012, 89]), and as such she has purposefully engaged with cross-cultural collaboration, and with colonial institutions – including an opera company, a symphony orchestra (the Regina Symphony, which did a "sneak peek" in oratorio format in 2019, and the Winnipeg Symphony for the 2023 premiere), a university (Canadian Mennonite University), and the most challenging institution of all, the classical music hierarchy. Steele shared that despite being a classically trained singer (University of British Columbia) with experience in composition, arranging, and orchestration, working within the classical music hierarchy, she is assigned the label, "Librettist," a subordinate role to "Composer," even though the work is story, and positioned as "Indigenous led" (by Steele and other Indigenous talent in the production and in news stories), and despite it being situated within an Indigenous worldview of storytelling, collaboration, and relationship (S. Steele, personal communication, 4 November 2023). She comments that she has also faced numerous (racial and gendered) microaggressions throughout the six-year timespan of creating this work.[23]

As the Indigenous lead, and in consultation with community, Steele has spent countless hours advising organizations on protocol, advising or drafting memoranda of understanding for institutions; providing material for grant applications; editing copy for grants and publicity; sharing her community relationships and knowledges; and participating actively in nearly every aspect of creation and production (including casting, hiring of production staff, imagery for advertising, contracts, costumes/clothing design, and more), frequently without formal recognition, paid or otherwise. And even though this opera would not and could not exist without her – it was her creative vision after all – she has faced having her name literally erased from references to the opera, or has had her role (and Kusturok's as well) represented as secondary to that of Weisensel's (and in fact the *Globe and Mail* story noted at the start of this chapter contributed to exactly this erasure through the imagery used to accompany the story). In her work as lead academic on a Social Sciences and Humanities Research Council (SSHRC) grant through the Canadian Mennonite University (CMU) – specifically the innovative Li Keur Riel's Heart of the North Indigenous Language Database mentioned earlier – she is not named as a Principal Investigator because she is not affiliated with a university, though she is the only PhD in the project. Drawing on her Master of Library and Information Science degree, and working with CMU's head librarian, Vic Froese, Steele and Weisensel, with their two teaching assistants, Bryna Link (Peguis First Nation), and Hannah Connelly, created a model for language revitalization and community engagement. And yet Weisensel remains named as the Principal Investigator, an illustration of the structural inequities at work in not only artistic but academic collaborations as related to *Li Keur*.

Despite the many roles she has played in the creation and production of *Li Keur*, Steele has been absent from (i.e., left out of) major decisions around the work or has not been informed about key aspects of the production process because of the institutional silo-ing of roles, while at other times her ideas have been shut down (e.g., her vision for the fiddler and orchestra "clashing" did not come to fruition at the Winnipeg premiere). Although undoubtedly all creatives face some push back and end up having to compromise, the "no, that's not possible" resonates differently when your people have been misrepresented for a century and a half. Furthermore, some of the "no"s she has faced highlight a lack of care about what is important from a Métis perspective (i.e., decisions that were made illustrated that the collaborators did not understand what was being cancelled, that they were not just a small, inconsequential details) and a seeming unwillingness to listen to what and why a "small detail" might in fact matter to Steele and to her Indigenous collaborators. It reflects a lack of understanding or care about *how* communications happen, and how these communications shape relationships. Steele is a seasoned professional, having spent her entire life on stage in one form or another, producing, performing, presenting, and more.

She understands the production arc, and that negotiation and compromise are involved; during a workshop for the opera that I attended at the end of August 2023, I saw firsthand this compromise and negotiation. But some things are nonnegotiable. For example, Steele shared with me a story about a thoughtless interaction with Elders by a member of the production team during one of their gatherings (despite Steele teaching and leading by example vis-à-vis building relationships and communicating to non-Indigenous production members the idea that work with Elders is "non-transactional nor extractive" [personal communication, 4 November 2023]) which I will not share here, but reference as a way to point to the incessant nature of these kinds of interactions, and the extent of the gaps of cultural knowledges with some non-Indigenous partners.

Nonetheless, as described in this chapter, the production has had many high points. In recognition of positive relationships through the process, Steele wished to make the following statement about *Li Keur* and the Winnipeg production:

> Despite all the challenges of this project, I am careful to acknowledge what I observe to be real efforts being made towards reconciliation, especially in the context of the Manitoba Opera production, particularly by Larry Desrochers, the CEO, and Darlene Ronald, the head of marketing, and many members of their teams. Both have worked very hard to learn, be consultative, and inclusive, as well as responsive to the Indigenous creatives and cast and to me. Larry and I have had many frank and intense talks, and he has shown me great respect and a huge willingness to understand and to learn and has become proactive with problem-solving. Larry "gets it." Further, the Manitoba Opera, through the recommendation of my agent, Ian Arnold of Catalyst TC, made a really wise decision to hire Nicole Stonyk, a classically trained pianist, a Métis-Cree-Ukrainian woman, now researching a PhD on "the white possessive" of Indigenous classical music. Stonyk works alongside me as a "cultural attaché" and represents me when I cannot be present in public events as well as during the production weeks when I cannot be present. An interesting outcome is that not only does Stonyk provide a "safe" presence for the Indigenous creatives and myself in this production, she provides the same for non-Indigenous creatives who are able to approach her and ask advice or about protocols, or even just to chat – and that, in my mind, is a great outcome of this work couched

> as an act towards "reconciliation." I always think of Maria Campbell's 2019 CBC interview with Carol Off, following the republication of *Halfbreed* in which she says, and I paraphrase, that change comes through storytelling, singing songs, and visiting and talking. I have always envisioned *Li Keur* as a series of visits that began a long time before the stage production, and that will carry on long afterwards. (personal communication, 5 November 2023)

This is the hard work of intercultural relationship. And Steele has been honest and open about the good, the bad, and the messy parts of this work. She has been clear with me about the huge growth in understanding that she has witnessed, just as she has been clear about the challenges. Like the Indigenous collaborators for *Louis Riel*, Steele is generous and collaborative, and willing to teach and lead by example. But it has not been easy. As Steele adds:

> The one thing I suppose nobody could fully have anticipated, is the heightened emotion of bringing this work to the big stage, and what it means for the performers as well as the audience. In some ways, and for some of us, this production feels like a coming together of kinship networks after a century plus of separation. The extent of community engagement is unusual for a work of this size and venue, including the choruses on stage which in some cases will be actual descendants of the peoples depicted in the opera itself. Because of this, my Indigenous collaborators and I recognize the need for a grounding of the production with prayer given by one of the Elders in the cast, or a visiting Elder, or a cast member, or sometimes I will give "good words." Cultural safety, as well as physical and mental safety have always been a priority for me, [and] I believe Larry Desrochers and Manitoba Opera concur. (personal communication, 5 November 2023)

This statement points to Steele's humility and her understanding that this is in fact a learning process for all, herself included. In our more than a year and a half of conversations, it has been clear to me that she has no ego in this and is doing this work for her people.

As an outside observer who has had some inside access to the creation of this work, I have witnessed the weight of emotional labour on Steele's shoulders. I have witnessed the condescension that is, too often, the response to legitimate concerns. (I experienced firsthand this attitude when I contacted a Toronto-based blogger about an article that he had posted about a performance of arias from *Li Keur* at the Toronto Harbourfront Centre that did not mention Steele's name – only mentioning the white composer. Not only was his email response to me snarky and defensive, but his updated blog post was equally belittling of the need to properly attribute Steele and Kusturok.) I have witnessed the ways in which this "work of reconciliation" has quite literally made Steele sick. And I have seen how the emotional labour has robbed Steele of some of the joy and excitement that such a production might bring to other creatives who do not have this heavy labour. (She has, however, expressed how wonderful it has been to see so much Indigenous talent come together on a major stage. And in our 2021 interview, she noted – referencing the Regina sneak peek – that "it's so gratifying to look out at the audience and see all the Indigenous people there, just loving it." It is clear for whom she wrote the opera.) As noted above, bringing Nicole Stonyk into the process and production as a "cultural attaché" has been vital, and in fact, Steele suggested that every intercultural production such as this should hire someone in that role, to create a sense of safety for the whole ensemble. But the need for a "cultural attaché" highlights how difficult it continues to be for one Métis woman to have her voice *listened to*, respected, and responded to with action. This intersection, of being both a woman and Indigenous, cannot be ignored. Steele told me that she sometimes wonders, had she been a male Métis creative, if she would have experienced half of the difficulties she has faced for so long. She believes that in some minds she is portrayed as "a difficult woman" rather than a "visionary." As a witness, I am quite certain that she is correct.

On Moving From *Louis Riel* to *Li Keur*

> Truth and reconciliation: first of all, the truth begins with listening and making space.
>
> – Suzanne Steele (2020b, 32:12–32:16)

As I pointed out at the start of this chapter, the subject and form of *Louis Riel* and *Li Keur* may, on the surface, appear similar, both featuring the story of Louis Riel in operatic, or quasi-operatic form. However, they represent radically different approaches to creation and production. *Louis Riel* began without Indigenous engagement, following a "lone composer" model (i.e., with the composer and librettist working in relative isolation) and any engagement with Indigenous peoples has remained "additive," dependent on Indigenous people insisting on change and the good will of those staging the production. In contrast, *Li Keur* began through relationship with land and Indigenous kin, and has continued deepening relationships through the process of creation and staging. This does not mean that *Li Keur* has solved the problem of intercultural music creation. In fact, as described above, one theme that has frequently come up in my conversations with Steele is the continued erasure of Métis people and peoples, even as Steele provides clear guidance on respectful relations. When I shared my plans for this book with Steele, and how a key theme would be the erasure of Métis fiddlers and music, she immediately connected this historic erasure to her own, ongoing experiences. As addressed earlier regarding the work that Indigenous people have done to hold the COC accountable in creating *Louis Riel*, the change that *Li Keur* requires and insists on is the result of Steele's – and other Indigenous collaborators' – hard work and persistence in spaces that remain unfriendly and unwelcoming to Indigenous ways of creating, and as Steele notes, to women. Though *Li Keur* remains a rich and meaningful example of intercultural and Indigenous-centred work, it also highlights how much still needs to be done so that legacy institutions do not remain primarily white institutions; so that productions do not tokenize Métis or other Indigenous peoples; and so that, more generally, they become spaces Indigenous peoples wish to be part of.

Given the generous teachings of Indigenous people involved in the restaging of *Louis Riel* in 2017, Steele's exemplary work, and the teachings and knowledge shared by Indigenous scholars, creatives, and activists more generally both through these productions and through many other venues (e.g., see Derksen et al. 2019, and of course the considerable work done by Indigenous creatives via X, formerly Twitter), the issue is not that newcomers do not know what needs to be done; Indigenous people have used every platform available to make their voices heard; what non-Indigenous people need to know has been repeatedly shared and emphasized by Indigenous people. The question becomes: what will newcomers do with that knowledge, so generously shared? As suggested by attempts to rescue *Louis Riel*, will settlers/newcomers continue to find ways to hold on to works and ways of creating and producing that harm Indigenous peoples, perhaps simply finding ways to tweak them, add a bit more Indigenous content or a few Indigenous individuals, or otherwise attempt to justify the continued relevance of these harmful creative works in the twenty-first century? Or, with a commitment to justice and foundational change, will institutions and individuals *listen* to Indigenous voices first and foremost, even if this means letting go of repertoire (for example, including but in no way limited to *Louis Riel*) or approaches to creation and (lack of) engagement to which they are attached? That is, will non-Indigenous people listen to Indigenous creatives with an intention to act on the learning gained?

POSTLUDE

Métis Music

This book has been "in the works" for ten years, slowly taking shape since I finished my dissertation in 2013; a long time to be working on a book that, in the end, feels small though I hope not insignificant. I could lay the blame for the time it has taken on family life, birthing and raising three children, the stresses of moving multiple times (in fact, my children were each born in a different province), or COVID-19, which has hit many, perhaps most, of us physically, mentally, and emotionally. Yet, as I struggle to make the final edits, to get each word just right, it strikes me that it has taken ten years for a very different reason: namely, the second I felt like I had "pinned something down in words," gotten it "just right," my sense of "just right" changed. (It is not lost on me how this framing resonates with Dylan Robinson's critique of the zoological aspects of collecting practices, a pinning down with words [2020, 149].) Furthermore, if I were starting again, I would take a different approach – one more deeply embedded in community co-creation and rematriation, although it seems to me that universities and granting agencies have a long way to go before being able to create programs that support this kind of work.[1] What has allowed me to finish the book is embracing the value of providing a perspective, embedded in place and time, and I invite readers to view it as such and to use it to think toward the future. Some of my shifting perspectives over time are likely evident to readers in the differences among chapters, some of which provide more definitive analyses, and others that are more open to ambiguities and readers' own interpretations. Finishing this book has meant being vulnerable, and accepting and valuing my changing relationship with knowledge and methodological approaches – a perspective that I learned, as a PhD student, when I first read Shawn Wilson's *Research Is Ceremony* (2008).

This book, then, reveals some of my thinking about and with Métis music over the past decade. Rather than being a definitive account of Métis music, I position it as a series of stories that emerged from my own relationship with Métis music and musicking within particular places and moments in time. I have nonetheless made several observations about the telling of histories; multicultural containment; erasure; (re)connection; relationship-building; and, of course, how these issues intersect with recognition and resurgence. I suggest that Métis music is, too often, separated from Métis peoples and communities, treated as merely sound. A genealogical approach to writing fiddle dance history, for example, looks to origins outside of Métis communities, to practices that may share some common DNA but that are not necessarily from or of Métis communities; and it looks to moments of sounded emergence (i.e., when the music began to sound *different to outsiders*), instead of emergence within Métis stories and oral history. I further suggest that current ways of understanding fiddle styles, influenced by a process of what might be called multicultural containment, have positioned *sounded difference* as more important than Métis relational networks. As a result, Métis fiddling (or what is positioned as Métis fiddling) has become (to some people) something that anyone can play (*merely* a style), even if they have no connection to, or engagement with, Métis communities or people. Both genealogical and multicultural approaches have thus de-emphasized the social relationships, responsibilities, and connections to the land that are integral to Métis musical practice, and that are more strongly emphasized within Métis storytelling about music.

Issues of sounded difference and multicultural containment are intricately tied to a politics of recognition. As I observe, in the late nineteenth and early twentieth centuries, Métis music was used as fodder to create a thrilling past for settlers who were new to the Prairies and thus unrooted in the land. Newspaper accounts of Métis music give some insight into this early recognition, showing that Métis music was often mentioned, but if it was named as such, it was positioned at a temporal or spatial distance from settlers, or otherwise clearly positioned as a fictional account (which also functioned to distance Métis music, and people, from settlers). During this period, recognition might be understood as serving the needs of settlers (creating a thrilling past) while avoiding what some might have understood as the danger of proximity. However, recognition, as this example indicates, is fickle; as Métis fiddlers and fiddling grew in popularity within mainstream spaces in Manitoba – at dance halls and in posh ballrooms, at community events such as picnics, and on the radio – the Métis-ness of Métis music was increasingly erased. Closely linked to Métis people and identities being pushed into hiding, this erasure signaled the supposed inevitability of the disappearance of the Métis. In the late twentieth century, Métis fiddling was once again recognized in mainstream Manitoba as *Métis fiddling*. This was during a time of Métis political and social reemergence, as well as a period when non-white, non-Anglo people were beginning to be positioned as a core part of Canadian culture and identity, one centred on multiculturalism rather than assimilation. Though seemingly less problematic, this new recognition, like a hundred years earlier, might be understood as continuing to serve the needs of the settler public, highlighting the importance of understanding the *who, what, and why* of recognition.

Despite the attempted erasure of Métis music and strategies of distancing used to create separation between Métis peoples and the white settler population, Métis have always been here (i.e., in the spaces that the non-Indigenous public has claimed for itself). Though evident when reading between the lines of newspaper articles (the very articles that often erased Métis), Métis past and on-going presence is especially clear when considering Métis-created and -led festivals. Back to Batoche Days, for example, is part of a long history of Métis gathering in celebration as a peoples, away from the expectations and the gaze of the non-Indigenous public; though developed in its current form in the 1970s, it dates back to just after the Battle of Batoche. In recent years, these large-scale cultural festivals have become key spaces for Métis – many of whom live outside of their own communities or in diaspora – to come together, to visit, to music, and to dance; these festivals help to (re)connect Métis music to community; to Métis people and peoplehood; to kinship networks; and to place. Métis festivals are therefore vital spaces of resurgence. Although Métis people run these festivals for their own community, they are also spaces to enact political relationships between the Métis Nation and the settler state, inextricably entwining culture and politics. Musicking in the context of festivity is therefore much more than sound (though sound is integral to coming together and establishing presence): music and musicking are used to sound presence (toward recognition), but are just as importantly an expression of peoplehood that, as was evident in 2022, supports the decolonization (i.e., the taking/giving back) of Métis land. In this way, festivals point to the complicated and sometimes entangled nature of recognition and resurgence.

The positioning of music as community is a foundational part of the practice of many Métis creators, as evident in Dr Suzanne Steele's vision for *Li Keur*. This opera centres Métis community in a genre (opera, with a spoken metanarrative) and within what have previously been spaces (primarily white, legacy institutions) that, at best, excluded and erased Métis peoples and musics, and at worst, appropriated and misrepresented Métis culture and stories (e.g., as is the case of the opera *Louis Riel*). While *Louis Riel* did not engage with Métis culture or people and ended with Riel's death (which could be read as standing in for the supposed death of the Métis Nation), Steele's work reanimates the polycultural and multilingual society of the nineteenth century through the protocols of visiting and relationship building. *Li Keur* insists that Métis people must be lead creators of musical productions that centre Métis stories, and provides a model for a production that is more than a product, more than a script, and more than a score. Indeed, for Steele, *Li Keur* is about relationships. The creation and staging of this work has, however, not been easy, placing a heavy burden of labour (whether paid or unpaid) on Steele who has been required to teach protocol and respectful relations (with the support of Indigenous creatives and collaborators) to non-Indigenous collaborators from the beginning stages right through to staging (and likely beyond). She has nonetheless maintained her vision of supporting the flourishment of Métis peoples past, present and future. And because of this, *Li Keur* is one example of how the political, cultural, social, spiritual, and relational power of Métis music can be re-placed within the lived networks of Métis musical practice.

✦✦✦

I began this book with my own words and family story, followed by the words of Handscomb and Lederman, both of whom recognized Métis music vis-à-vis its purpose within, or in supposed relationship to, Canada. I end with the words of Métis creator, Dr Suzanne Steele, specifically the final words of *Li Keur*. Spoken by the young (twenty-first century) Métis heroine, Joséphine-Marie, Steele's words are not an ending; rather they speak to the future – a future where Métis live the life their ancestors wanted for them,[2] a life where Métis tell their own stories:

Maarsi, Pépère, the story now, is mine to live, maarsi, maarsi
nous sommes les entrailles, li keur, d'Nord …
[thank you, grandfather … thank you … we are the guts, the heart of the North]
(she picks up Riel's cane)
Maarsi Pépère, Ben, s't'istwaire, si pour mwai d'la conti …
[Thank you, Grandfather, Well, now this story, it is mine to tell …]

Notes

PREFACE

1 Kovach similarly writes: "A prologue … encompasses essential information for the reader to make sense of the story to follow" (2009, 3).

2 Here, and throughout this book, I use the term *settler* to refer to "the non-Indigenous peoples living in Canada who form the European-descended sociopolitical majority" (Vowel 2016, 14). Though I recognize that the term is seen by some as divisive (though I might suggest that this is in part a reaction by settlers to being named as anything other than "neutral"), I use it to emphasize and name relationships of power and privilege. Certainly, the ancestors of many settler Canadians did not have a great deal of power when they arrived in what was, to them, a "new world." Yet they were nonetheless part of the ongoing process of settler colonialism, that is "the deliberate physical occupation of land as a method of ownership over land and resources" (Vowel 2016, 16). Though many would like to place settler colonialism in the past, the term settler is a reminder that the relationship of occupation and ownership of land and resources remains fundamental to the relationship between Indigenous peoples and European-descendant peoples in Canada.

3 Also see Cindy Gaudet's article, "Re-matriating Territorial Acknowledgement" (2023). This first section was originally published in *The Routledge Companion to Ethics and Research in Ethnomusicology* (Giroux 2022).

4 The story that follows is adapted from my article "Metis Music and the Settler Imagination" (2015a). See Kovach (2009, 3) for discussion on incorporating personal stories.

5 Andersen and Adese note that "Métis studies has taken a distinctive turn toward research by and for the Métis people" (2021, 3). This is not yet the case

with Métis music. I suspect that this has to do, at least in part, with the structures of music programs and departments, which to this day create barriers for anyone trained outside of the Western art music paradigm.

CHAPTER ONE

1 C.W. Handscomb (1867–1906) was an English immigrant who came to Winnipeg via Ontario when he was fourteen. He was a well-known critic for the *Free Press* until his untimely death from diphtheria in 1906 (Arrell 1999, 114).

2 This "destiny" did not become reality, as 1912 marked the end of Winnipeg's first "boom" (Blanchard 2005, 5).

3 While John Christian Schultz's conflicts with Louis Riel make him the most known of the founders named by Blanchard, all the men noted were heavily involved in political activities, military duties, or business practices that dispossessed Métis people of their lands, or that capitalized on eastern Canada's negative sentiments towards Métis. Of Norwegian and Irish ancestry, John Christian Schultz arrived in the Red River Settlement (what became Winnipeg) from Upper Canada in 1861, setting up a practice as a physician and surgeon. In 1865, he became the sole proprietor of the *Nor-Wester*, a newspaper that appealed to eastern Canada's views of the west, and was a leader of the Canadian Party, a group that vociferously demanded annexation of the Red River Settlement to Canada.

James Ashdown moved to Winnipeg from London, England (via Ontario) in 1868, becoming an important, and very rich, businessman. Ashdown's first job in the Red River Settlement was with John Stoughton Dennis's survey crew, sent by William McDougall in preparation for the arrival of Canadian settlers. His many business activities included real estate speculation, a practice that, in the 1870s and 1880s, dispossessed many Métis peoples of their lands.

Irish-born Charles Valentine Alloway arrived in the new province of Manitoba in 1871 as part of the second Red River Expeditionary Force (sent by Canada to ensure peace, although many of the men harassed Métis, leading to what has been termed the "reign of terror"). Alloway soon became involved in scrip speculation (a form of theft described later in this chapter).

Edward, Frederick, and George Drewry moved to Winnipeg in the late 1870s from St Paul, Minnesota, where their parents had settled in 1860 (from England). While they are best-known for their brewery (Drewry Brewery), they were important members of Winnipeg's elite class at the turn of the century.

4 The "hiding in plain sight" trope has been criticized for the way it absolves people from their disavowal of their Indigenous relations and the opening it provides for some to claim a Métis identity with little to no connection to a Métis community. These criticisms are valid and important. However, there are countless stories about parents encouraging their children to blend in because they did not want them to face the discrimination they had endured (see Oster 2021, 6). These stories are important to acknowledge.

5 For comparison, see George Upton's note about "half breed" music in Chicago in the nineteenth century (cited in Quick 2009, 12–13).

6 I was unable to immediately write down what was being said. However, I believe that my own wording is very close to the words used, and certainly captures the spirit of the statement.

7 My understanding, based on personal communication with a member of the committee, is that Manitobans were asked to submit suggestions for an appropriate name for a new February holiday, and a committee decided on the name from those submitted.

8 In addition to fiddling, Métis peoples developed a large song repertoire. These songs were often adaptations of old songs from France, though others were newly composed on the Prairies. Most famously, Pierre Falcon (1793–1876) wrote songs that told the history of his people. Louis Riel also wrote songs, often adapting new lyrics to older melodies, to document events or express his emotions. In one such song, he sings of the joy he feels to see his sister after a long time apart, pointing to the close ties within Métis families and the importance of song in self-expression. Though the known composers of these songs were men, the song repertoire was very important for women, with many, such as Johanna Carrière (Andy Dejarlis's sister), having large song repertoires.

9 Though rarely adopted outside of music studies, the term "musicking" has been widely used by musicologists, ethnomusicologists, music educators, and others working with music since first coined by music educator Christopher Small. As a verb, it is intended to emphasize the ways in which music is a process, involving far more complex networks than simply the musicians and composers, rather than a product (1998). This is a conceptualization of music that resonates strongly with many Indigenous nations' understanding of music that position it as more than object.

10 Though the use of the singular "Métis people" is somewhat more common in current literature, in this book, I use the plural "peoples" to emphasize the diversity within the Métis Nation. It is not intended to suggest that the term

"Métis" can, or should, be used for all "mixed-race" people, or for people with no connection to the historic Métis communities within the Homeland.

11 Thank you to Dr Suzanne Steele for sharing how these events impacted her own family and providing me with a nuanced and personal view of the aftermath of the Resistances.

12 The genocide of Indigenous peoples in what is now Canada is well-documented in the Truth and Reconciliation Commission's final report (2015b), and the final report on Missing and Murdered Indigenous Women and Girls (National Inquiry 2019).

13 In 2019, the Little Shell Tribe gained federal recognition.

14 While a "white paper" is simply a policy paper, in this case it was understood ironically to refer to the *whiteness* of the policy, that is, how it was an expression of white Canada's approach to the "Indian problem."

15 Since this recognition, many groups with no connection to the Métis peoples of the Northwest have tried to claim Aboriginal rights as Métis. This includes the Labrador Métis Nation, which eventually changed its name to NunatuKavut Community Council, and various so-called "Eastern Métis" groups, as documented in Daryl Leroux's research (2019).

16 The term "land back" refers to a grassroots, Indigenous-led movement centring self-determination of Indigenous peoples and Indigenous control over, and access to, territories and resources (Wente 2021).

17 Taylor used a word here that is considered ableist. I have replaced it with a synonym.

18 Hearing is something that we largely cannot control, that is, it is a passive process whereby soundwaves come into our ears. Listening, however, suggests an intentionality and a desire to engage with and process the soundwaves to understand their meaning.

19 Many of these scholars are mentioned in this book. Others, however, are not directly cited, though they have all shaped my worldview and scholarship. To them, I am grateful.

20 Many scholars and Indigenous activists have pointed to the problem of good intentions, namely that good intentions do not eliminate the possibility of causing harm (see, e.g., de Leeuw, Greenwood, and Lindsay 2013).

21 Kofi Agawu provided important, turn of the century, critiques of ethnomusicology (2003, 1995), as did the influential book *Shadows in the Field* (Barz and Cooley 1997, 14–15). Nettl also provides an overview of these changes/critiques (2010, 64–6).

CHAPTER TWO

1 Quick similarly notes that many of the early sources on fiddle dance performances "provide only generalized and often judgmental descriptions" and "suffer from the nostalgic over-generalizations of which historians are wary" (2009, 135). Her forthcoming article "Hungry Narratives Turned on Their Head (or Danced on Their Toes?): Towards Decolonial Listening in Ethnohistorical Practice" deals with similar issues of "what we are able to learn about the performers and what they perform through such (largely outsider) narratives" (Forthcoming, 150).

2 One of the anonymous peer reviewers rightly pointed out that similar descriptors (sawed, shrieked, screamed) were used by Francis Kilvert in his diary to describe another Englishman's playing (1964, 151–2). This description might emerge from elitism on the part of Kilvert (and certainly issues of elitism and race intersect), but it is also important to note that Kilvert was describing someone who was a beginner, and that there is no evidence that this beginner was accepted by his community as a fiddler of choice at events. Furthermore, elsewhere in the diary, Kilvert speaks positively of fiddles/fiddlers, though perhaps the events that he described positively were higher class – more elite – events (1964, 206). In contrast, the descriptions of Indigenous fiddlers that I refer to in this chapter are aimed at people who were fiddlers for their community.

3 Here I wish to acknowledge Dr Suzanne Steele's positioning of her opera *Li Keur* as re-placing Indigenous languages centre stage, where they belong.

4 Referencing the "historical myths and colonial mindsets" that continue today, Regan notes that "it is instructive to explore how colonial violence is woven into the fabric of Canadian history in an unbroken thread from past to present, which we must now unravel, upsetting our comfortable assumptions about the past. At the same time, we must work as Indigenous allies to 'restory' the dominant-culture version of history; that is, we must make decolonizing space for Indigenous history – counter-narratives of diplomacy, law, and peacemaking practices – as told by Indigenous peoples themselves" (2010, 6).

5 It is possible that this marks a time when ethnomusicologists are turning more toward stories, what they mean, and how they can become a more significant and valued part of our ethnographies. I was particularly struck by the powerful stories shared during the 2023 annual meeting of the Society for Ethnomusicology as part of a President's Round Table titled "Tell Me a Story – Translating Experience into Ethnography."

6 In the same document, Ballantyne describes a fiddler in Red River playing "upon a violin of his own construction" (1848, 97). However, in this instance he is telling a story about the rivalry between the HBC and NWC (which would have been prior to 1821) and therefore it is difficult to know if this detail was handed down accurately.

7 The HBC established York Factory on Hudson Bay in 1684, and the inland Fort Dauphin, located near Winnipegosis, Manitoba, in 1741.

8 He has just described reading as an activity that some employees use to fill time, noting that employees at smaller forts could borrow books from the larger forts with more extensive libraries.

9 Mishler provides Gwich'in names for many dances, including the Red River Jig ("Jig Ahtsii Ch'aadzaa"), Duck Dance ("Dats'an Ch'aadzaa"), and Rabbit Dance ("Geh Ch'aadzaa") (1993, 50).

10 Prior to this, there was limited interest in *collecting* Métis music, but no academic research, perhaps a reflection of biases towards traditions that were viewed as not pure.

11 Since completing her thesis, Lederman has published other "tracing of origins" articles such as "Aboriginal Fiddling: The Scottish Connection" (2013) and "Metis Fiddling: Lost or Found" (2009).

12 Anthropologist Sarah Quick's dissertation includes a chapter titled "Emerging as Heritage: Towards a Genealogy of Métis Fiddle Music and Dance in Alberta" (2009, 134). Though my conceptualization of a "genealogical" approach did not directly emerge from her use of the term, she suggests that "previous studies tend to focus primarily on the origins" (what I would term a genealogical approach) whereas she partially adopts this approach while demonstrating "more critical awareness of the shifts in circumstances for … performative contexts over time" (134). In other words, I would consider her chapter more of a genealogy of the heritagization of Métis fiddle dance than a genealogy of the tunes/styles, though a clear distinction between the two is not possible. However, her later chapter ("Métis Fiddling Heritage: Repertoires, Aesthetic, Affect, and Models") does pay considerable attention to origins, and in my opinion is therefore more "genealogical" (2009, 231–6, 265–6).

13 Métis people do not accept colonial notions of blood quantum. It is not lost on me how similar the tracing of "mixed" origins of tunes is to the tracing of the "purity" of bloodlines.

14 I make this assertion based on having heard the story many times at events, or in conversations with community members. However, there is one addi-

tional version, Oliver Boulette's version, available in written form (Boulette 2006, 162).

15 This interview was transcribed by David Morin and has been lightly edited to remove repeated words and to add some additional punctuation. Pelletier's stories are included with her permission.

16 See Andersen (2014) for a critique of this tendency vis-à-vis the Métis.

CHAPTER THREE

1 The number of First Nations people living in Manitoba during this era is never indicated in history books, and I have not been able to find any statistics that would fill in this significant gap. Also of note are the boundary extensions of 1881 and 1912, which saw settlers claiming a larger and larger area of what had been the Northwest Territories.

2 On 8 March 2013, the Supreme Court ruled that the Crown failed to provide the land promised to the Métis in the Manitoba Act. It is yet to be seen whether this ruling will have an impact on Manitoba Metis.

3 The population also included Mennonites, Ukrainians, Poles, Germans, and French Canadians.

4 This distancing is tied to the "pervasive, pernicious, [and] self-serving" myth of the disappearing Indian (Dunbar-Ortiz and Gilio-Whitaker 2016, 9), that is, the belief that Indigenous people will inevitably disappear with the coming of civilization. Reaching its peak at the turn of the twentieth century, the myth, as described by Roxanne Dunbar-Ortiz and Dina Gilio-Whitaker (Colville Confederated Tribes member), "was used to advance dubious – even nefarious – political agendas aimed at the continual seizure of Indian lands and resources. It was used by both the 'friends' and foes of Indians to justify policies of forced assimilation, which would mean the final solution to the 'Indian problem,' the ultimate disappearance of Indians to facilitate the transfer of Indian treaty lands to settler ownership" (2016, 9). Indigenous peoples needed to disappear – and therefore were imagined to be disappearing – in order to address the land issue. This myth intersects with stereotypes of the noble and ignoble savage, which places Indigenous peoples into an impossible binary – never able to overcome their supposed inherent brutality (which had no place within so-called civilization) or embodying an innate innocence or childlike closeness to nature that, inevitably, would be corrupted by the coming of civilization. These myths, along with other harmful stereotypes about Indigenous peoples, were one strategy of erasure used to make room for the settler present and future.

5 Though the author is unnamed, he makes a number of references that indicate that he is a man.

6 This is a reference to the carts (known as Red River carts) used by nineteenth century Métis traders.

7 The "Potlatch laws" would have been in effect during this period, making it illegal for Indigenous peoples to dance and take part in their traditional ceremonies (see Joseph [2018, 47–9] for further information).

8 This is likely referring to a "grand chain," where dancers start by facing their partner and then move up or down through the line or circle by alternately taking the right and left hands of other dancers.

9 This is a reference to the popular fiddle tune titled "The Girl I Left Behind Me."

10 A similar, though more brief, description is found in an article in the *Winnipeg Daily Tribune* about St Peter's treaty days in 1893 (*The Winnipeg Daily Tribune* 1893, 2).

11 For similar articles published in newspapers during this time see *The Winnipeg Daily Tribune* (1894, 1); and *Manitoba Free Press* (1908, 15).

12 In 2008, Peguis First Nation accepted a land-claim settlement of $126 million, as compensation for their illegal removal from St Peter's Reserve.

13 These include the *Stonewall Argus*, the *Baldur Gazette*, the *Roblin Review*, the *Miniota Herald*, the *Rapid City Reporter*, the *Shoal Lake Start*, and the *Hamiota Echo*.

14 Representations of a "thrilling" past were not unusual at this time, nor were they limited to articles describing music (see *The Gazette* 1924, 7; *The Gazette* 1906, 3; *Manitoba Morning Free Press* 1899, 14; *Manitoba Morning Free Press* 1899, 14).

15 The Métis, French Canadians, and "Indians" are all named as such, but Mary's ethnicity is not mentioned. In this way, "A Daughter of the Ranch" creates a white, unmarked, Anglophone centre.

16 Here it is important to acknowledge that this term is racist and extraordinarily hurtful to Indigenous women.

17 As horrifying as this description should seem to readers, the sexism is even more overt in other parts of the story, for example in a description of "squaws [who] kept time, tune and step with their lords and masters [the braves]" (McLeod 1924, 6).

18 I believe that readers are supposed to "read" the fiddler as white given that his ethnicity is never mentioned. However, the story is somewhat contradictory in that the same fiddler plays throughout the evening, even when the

French/Metis men are demonstrating dances that were described as unusual to the white guests. Did they dance to "white" fiddle music? Did the fiddler know Métis tunes? While these are interesting questions, as a piece of fiction, the issue of accuracy is less important than the way in which the story constructs Métis/settler relations and what this tells us about white attitudes towards Métis people when the story was written/published.

19 *Richeau* (or *rechaud*) is fried pemmican. Pemmican was also eaten "raw" (without cooking or heating), and as part of a stew referred to as rubbaboo.

20 St Paul de Métis was founded in 1876 as a Métis colony. In 1909, settlement was opened to non-Métis. In 1936, it became the Town of St Paul. It is located in east-central Alberta.

21 For a discussion of Old Timers' associations in Alberta, see Quick (Forthcoming 157–65; 2009, 146).

22 Troy Bannerman, Métis genealogist, was able to confirm this for me.

23 Métis fiddler Bob (Léon-Robert) Goulet had recorded the "Red River Jig" about a decade earlier.

24 In September of 1949, about 3,000 people were in the audience (*The Manitoba Leader* 1949, 7). This is a significant number given that the population of Portage la Prairie where the event was held would have been only about 8,500. The general trend was a decreased audience in the years that followed, in some cases, perhaps due to late harvest (*Manitoba Leader* 1956a, 13). The contest had significant financial troubles in 1956 (*Manitoba Leader* 1956b, 13), but seems to have recovered for a few years afterwards, with, for example, about 1,100 people in attendance the following year (*Manitoba Leader* 1957, 8). In the 2010s, the Manitoba Championships drew about 150 audience members.

25 See *Swan Valley Star and Times* (1930, 4), *Winnipeg Free Press* (1934b, 3), *Winnipeg Free Press* (1934a, 18), *Winnipeg Evening Tribune* (1934, 5), *Stonewall Argus* (1936, 8), *Winnipeg Free Press* (1938b, 13), *Winnipeg Free Press* (1938a, 1), *Winnipeg Free Press* (1941, 7), *Winnipeg Free Press* (1942b, 7), *Winnipeg Free Press* (1943, 6), *Winnipeg Free Press* (1944, 10), *Winnipeg Free Press* (1946, 5), *Winnipeg Free Press* (1948, 23), *Winnipeg Free Press* (1949b, 7), *Winnipeg Free Press* (1949a, 3), *Stonewall Argus and Teulon Times* (1950, 5) *Winnipeg Free Press* (1950b, 14), *Winnipeg Free Press* (1950a, 3), *Manitoba Leader* (1951, 7), *Winnipeg Free Press* (1951, 3), *The Dauphin Herald* (1951, 9), *Winnipeg Free Press* (1952, 37), *Stonewall Argus and Teulon Times* (1953, 2), *Carillon News* (1953, 5), *Springfield Leader* (1954, 6), *Stonewall Argus* (1955, 8), *Springfield Leader* (1955, 1), *Winnipeg Free Press* (1955, 4), and *Steinbach Carillon* (1958,

14). This list of references to the "Red River Jig" is not exhaustive, nor does it necessarily point to the most important references. Rather, it is meant to provide examples of the wide variety of contexts in which the "Red River Jig" was performed (and reported on) from 1930–60, and how, in all these contexts, the Métis-ness of the tune was erased.

26 Though his family name was spelled Desjarlais, he used "Dejarlis" as his stage name, evidently because it was hard for non-Francophones to pronounce. However, his name is spelled in a variety of combinations between Desjarlais and Dejarlis. Toward the end of his career, it was usually spelled "Dejarlis," hence the spelling used in this book unless quoting a source that uses an alternative spelling.

27 For example, L'Union nationale métisse Saint-Joseph du Manitoba was formed in 1887, while precursors to the Métis Nation of Alberta and the Métis Nation – Saskatchewan formed in the 1930s and '40s.

28 The Manitoba Metis Federation received unprecedented attention from newspapers. A search of the phrase "Manitoba Metis Federation" in newspaperarchives.com gets eighty-one hits for the 1960s alone, more than 1,200 in each of the 1970s and 1980s, and more than 1,800 hits in the 1990s. In the 2000s, there were more than 1,500 hits, and in the 2010s, there were more than 1600 hits.

29 L'Union nationale metisse Saint-Joseph du Manitoba has been active since the end of the 1800s but received relatively little attention in the papers. When their activities were mentioned, music was not a focal point of the articles. Rather, the articles typically focused on events that commemorated the death of Louis Riel. However, one very short article, published in the *Winnipeg Free Press* in the mid-1950s, described a two-day annual event, then in its fiftieth year, that brought together 300 Métis people (as indicated in the article) for a celebration at Louis Riel's family home in St Vital, Winnipeg. Sunday afternoon events included "Red River Jig," square dance, and old-time fiddling competitions (*Winnipeg Free Press* 1955, 4). It is clear from this one article that events such as these had been taking place throughout the century but were not generally reported on in newspapers.

30 See *Stonewall Argus and Teulon Times* (1990); Richard (1994, 13B); Auch (1997, 7B); *Winnipeg Free Press* (1997); Clemens (1997, 7C); *Winnipeg Free Press* (2000); *Winnipeg Free Press* (2002); Jones (2002, B1); Vivian (2002, A3); Lemieux (2005); *Steinbach Carillon* (2005); *Stonewall Argus and Teulon Times* (2005, 10); Villeneuve (2006a, 7); Lachnit (2006, 11A); Jackman (2007, 2);

Dowd (2008, A3); Villeneuve (2008, 37); *Brandon Sun* (2008); and Austin (2009, A2).

31 Over one thousand people took part in St Laurent's Metis Day celebration in 1990 (*Stonewall Argus and Teulon Times* 1990, 23), and about one thousand people took part in the first day of Metisfest in 2009 (Austin 2009, A2).

32 In her ethnography of the Festival du Voyageur, Joanna Simoens provides an excellent overview of the pluralism within Francophone Manitoba and its relationship to the festival (2023).

33 The "Forty Fiddling Fanatics" was led by Cameron Baggins (then known as Cameron Dick), a fiddler who later became a leading figure in the Frontier School Division's fiddle program.

34 Two additional groups are listed as performing Métis music in the 2001 Festival du Voyageur program. The "Ka-Wanni-Beck Eagles" are listed as performing Métis-style fiddle music, and the "Coyote Fiddlers" are listed as Métis fiddlers ("Artistes/Performers" 2001b).

CHAPTER FOUR

1 In the United States, the term "old-time" is used as an umbrella term for many styles of music including "fiddling music, Victorian parlor songs, Anglo-American folk ballads and even sacred songs" (Trew 2000, 192). In Canada, it has tended to be more narrowly used, referring specifically to instrumental music, and, by the mid-twentieth century, often to one particular style of fiddling, as discussed in this chapter.

2 The long history of Blackface minstrelsy in Canada is documented in Le Camp (2005). Though American minstrel troupes often travelled north to Canada, Canada also had homegrown minstrel shows (256, 371–2). Furthermore, Cheryl Thompson points out that in 1879, a blackface minstrel show was one of the first cultural events held by the Northwest Mounted Police in their barracks near Battleford, Saskatchewan (2021, 73), indicating presence of this racist entertainment in the Prairies during the early years of Canadian settlement. It seems that Blackface minstrelsy continued well into the mid- to late twentieth century, given that, as noted musicologist Ellen Waterman writes, Blackface minstrel shows were still being organized by the Rotary Club in southern Manitoba when she was a teenager (Waterman in Robinson 2020, 241).

3 I have been unable to find Jimmy Gowler's birth and death dates. However, I found a congratulatory announcement for his fortieth wedding anniversary in 1975 (*Winnipeg Free Press* 1975, 38).

4 This assertion is based on newspaper advertisements (*The Winnipeg Evening Tribune* 1925, 1; *Manitoba Free Press* 1927, 17; and *Winnipeg Free Press* 1953, 4).

5 The *Manitoba Free Press* printed a short announcement indicating that Victor Records had recorded the "Red River Jig" (*Manitoba Free Press* 1930c, 25). Though the very brief article does not mention the name of the fiddler, additional evidence links this recording to Bob Goulet. Specifically, some of Léon-Robert (Robert Léon, "Bob") Goulet's recordings are available on the *Virtual Gramophone*, with RCA Victor as the label with release dates listed as 1930 and 1931. See Porter (2020) for more about Goulet, and *Winnipeg Free Press* (1933, 32), for reference to a radio performance.

6 Dolly was an exceptional musician in her own right. Her collection of songs, recorded by Henri Letourneau, are now housed at the Centre du Patrimoine in St Boniface (under the name Johanna Carrière).

7 The Second World War, of course, had a major impact on performers. Due to health problems, Dejarlis was unable to serve, but many of his bandmates did.

8 Mackintosh (2010, 149–56) provides a list of his recordings and sheet music books.

9 The available description of the show on the website *cinema cinematheque* indicates that he was on episodes 23–49, along with long-time Manitoba fiddle collaborator, Marcel Meilleur.

10 Messer was also influenced by Dixieland and swing bands of the time, integrating clarinet, trumpet, and trombone, and taking solo breaks (Johnson 2012, 17).

11 Thanks to Troy Bannerman for finding Jimmy Gowler's family connections.

12 On his father's side Frédéric Genthon (1856–1941) was the descendant of Pierre Jerome (c. 1740–1821) who married a Cree woman who is unnamed in the records. Their son, Martin Jerome dit St Mathe married Françoise (ancestry unknown). Martin and Françoise's daughter, Marie Louise Jerome dit St Mathe was Frédéric's grandmother. On his mother's side, Frédéric Genthon is descended from Francois Bouchard dit Richard dit Granbois, who married a Cree woman, also unnamed in the records. Their daughter, Marie Rosalie Bouchard dit Richard dit Grandbois (1811–1874) was Frédéric's grandmother. Thanks to Troy Bannerman for confirming Genthon's genealogy.

13 Johnson indicates that Messer made seventeen tours from 1949–67 (2012, 17), and at least a couple more before his death in 1973. Based on newspaper listings, I was able to confirm that he travelled to Manitoba in 1950, 1961, 1963, 1965, 1967, 1969, 1970, and 1971.

14 Rosenberg, however, suggested that the popularity of Don Messer and his national fiddle canon encouraged advocates of other fiddle canons to promote their local styles. In other words, he argued that increased attention to local styles was a reaction to the hegemony of the old-time style. Lederman and Smith's comment, then, is more about how Messer was perceived than it is a comment on the actual impact locally.

15 The term "regular fiddling" is directly quoting the words of a Manitoba fiddler.

16 More recently, fiddle camps have sometimes reinforced this compartmentalization (offering a sampling of styles) as has the internet (because styles can be easily sampled with the click of a few buttons).

17 Dueck offers reflections on "collectivity and individuation" that resonate strongly here (2013, 164; 113–19). A possibly promising area of further research might consider the interface between sonic (or sounded) kinship connections and individual style.

CHAPTER FIVE

1 An earlier version of this chapter was published in *Ethnomusicology* (Giroux 2018). It is republished with permission.

2 This coincides with the emergence of fiddle contests in other areas of the country, including Prince Edward Island (Hornby 1985) and Ontario (Johnson 2006, 106).

3 Although most of the people I spoke with agreed to have their names published, I have decided in most cases to maintain anonymity because of the critical nature of this chapter.

4 The Miami competition sought out MMF sponsorship after the category was created but were unsuccessful in this endeavor. It is also worth noting that the MMF is not the only way in which a contest could seek out community engagement, though it is perhaps the most obvious way (at least to non-Métis) to engage.

5 Although the representative noted that it is fine for non-Métis people to win – and in fact pointed out that a fiddler of Ukrainian heritage won the first year the event was held – her comment points to vigilance and perhaps some concern about the potential for racism.

6 An organizer told me that this was a compromise since the MMF wanted three Métis-style categories (anonymous, interview in Lorette, MB, 9 March 2016).

7 One prominent MFA organizer during the early years of the Métis-style

category at the Manitoba Open was a member of the MMF, and there were, likely, other MMF members at the event. I was told that LaPlante likely felt as if she had a hand in the competition because this particular organizer was in attendance (fieldnotes, 30 November 2009). However, the organizer was not representing the MMF at this event but, rather, was representing the MFA. Furthermore, there was no indication to the audience that this person was representing the MMF. When I attended the Brandon Winter Fair competition in 2022, the MMF representative was unable to make it due to illness.

8 Normally, this would be a great example of deferring to Métis when it comes to Métis music. However, in the context of the judges deciding a winner in the Métis-style category, it is problematic.

9 The contest held during the Royal Manitoba Winter Fair in Brandon, Manitoba, has similar requirements. The 2015 programme notes stated the following: "In Metis style a contestant must play two tunes of choice and sit on a chair keeping the timing and rhythm with their feet. Traditional style Metis fiddling is very entertaining." The rules outlined in 2022 were almost the same noting that Contestants were required to play two tunes of their choice, sit on a chair (provided), and keep time with their feet. The rules further indicated that they would be judged on timing, Métis-style, and danceability. The Festival du Voyageur has adopted similar rules requiring clogging, though contestants are only required to play one tune, a reel.

10 The Brandon Winter Fair contest hands out $625 in prize money for the Métis-style category (divided among three categories) and $1,375 for the old-time fiddle categories (split among five categories). The categories are equitable (e.g., first prize in both the Métis-style and old-time categories, adults, is $150), but the key difference is that there is no Métis-style Open category (i.e., a category open to all ages and considered the category for the top fiddlers), which pays out $300. This is certainly justified in terms of attendance (e.g., there were few Métis-style category competitors when I attended in 2022) but it does speak to how the category is valued vis-à-vis the old-time categories.

11 For example, one fiddler won second place using a tune that they learned from a recording of Ontario fiddler Shane Cook (fieldnotes, 26 February 2012).

12 This is not intended to suggest that engagement with the MMF is not meaningful, just that it needs to go beyond receiving funding.

13 In my dissertation, I provide a detailed overview of how fiddlers negotiated these boundaries of tradition, and sometimes make choices about which

tunes are appropriate to use for competition based on the judges. In particular, contestants make decisions based on how open the judges are believed to be to new tunes or tunes from various traditions (Giroux 2013, 172–7).

14 The ways in which intimacies shapes musical practices is a key argument in Byron Dueck's book *Musical Intimacies and Indigenous Imaginaries* (2013).

15 This search for a Canadian identity was marked by the adoption of new national symbols such as the Canadian flag in 1965, which replaced the Union Jack, and the national anthem, "O Canada," in 1980, which replaced "God Save the Queen." On the political front, Canada patriated its Constitution in 1982, largely severing the authority of the British Parliament, while policy makers flirted with ways of incorporating Canada's multicultural reality (Hage 2000, 133) into political policy, eventually settling on a policy of bilingualism and multiculturalism in 1971. Canadians were divided over these changes, with the debate even trickling down into the fiddle scene, as examined in chapter four.

16 Artistic works about Louis Riel include Coulter (1962), Roux (1967), Moore, Languirand, and Somers (1967), Polgar (1967), Coulter (1968a and 1968b), Lidov (1970), Wiebe (1977), Dorge (1980), and Bouchard (1981). Works that reference Pierre Falcon include Reaney (1975) and Wiebe (1977). Works that are about the Métis more broadly or that use or represent Métis music include Benjamin (c1947), Adaskin (1959), Cass-Beggs (1967), Lederman (n.d.), Forsyth (1976), Hiscott (1991), Loukinen (1991), Whidden (1993, 1995), Downing (2018), and Coyes (2002).

17 By the early 2000s, interest in Métis peoples was becoming more evident in mainstream public events, such as the Festival du Voyageur, a large winter festival held annually in St Boniface, Winnipeg's French and Métis quarter. Having grown up attending and performing at the event, I had always understood it as *un festival franco-manitobain,* with a particular emphasis – as the name suggests – on voyageur culture. This is not to say that there has not always been Métis involvement in the *festival.* Métis people have played an important part in the event from its very beginnings in 1969, just as Métis musicians and dancers have always been active participants (drawing parallels to how Métis fiddlers have always been active in, and creators of, the old-time scene). Georges Forest, a Métis man who became well-known in Manitoba for his French language advocacy, is in fact credited with suggesting that the event should use the voyageur as its unifying theme (Beaudry-Loiselle 2019, 10). My point, however, is that, in the 1990s when I was participating, Métis presence – and Indigenous presence more generally –

was peripheral to the main event, in some cases literally through the inclusion of an "Aboriginal village" at some distance from the rest of the festival; in my understanding at the time, this separated Métis and First Nations culture from the event's more properly French, but non-Indigenous, culture. An article by Debra Thompson (1986) provides an interesting peek into the dynamics of Le Festival in the mid-1980s. Specifically, some Métis artists were arguing that they needed to be better represented as "direct descendants of the voyageurs" (22). The event's production assistant, Kelley Fry, noted that the festival's policy is "to have a certain amount of cultural exchange between Quebec and Manitoba each year" (22). An article from 1990 provides a rather exoticized glimpse into the role of Indigenous peoples at the festival. Indeed, the report starts by stating "If being unique is a prerequisite for addition to the Festival du Voyageur, then the native and Metis tents at The Forks qualify with flying colors" (Ostick 1990, 15).

18 See Johnson (2006, 205) for information on novelty categories in Ontario. One Manitoba contest added an own choice category but discontinued it after a year (fieldnotes, 28 July 2012).

19 Drew Hayden Taylor's documentary *Searching for Winnetou* documents "powwows" in Germany, fueled by a longtime fascination with Karl May's books (2018).

CHAPTER SIX

1 I do not discuss the John Arcand Fiddle Festival. This is largely because I consider it to be a different type of event from the cultural festivals described in this chapter. It was, however, hugely important for the teaching of Métis fiddling. For more information on that event and on John Arcand, see Sarah Quick's work (2010, 2009). I also do not discuss Metisfest, an event that used to take place in Manitoba. I have chosen not to write about it because I have already published a journal article centred on the event (2016).

2 Dan Goodon was describing Metisfest, the festival that he organized, which I have written about elsewhere (Giroux 2016).

3 Mitchif is an alternative spelling for Michif. It refers to both the language and Métis peoples. Some people prefer it to Métis because it is less likely to be misused to mean simply "mixed."

4 This is not to suggest that people who perhaps personally identify as Métis are never recognized as Indigenous, but rather that there is no separate category for Métis. Further, I am not suggesting that the United States should

necessarily follow the Canadian "tripartite" system (First Nations, Métis, and Inuit). Rather, my point is that this difference in how Métis are understood in the United States has impacted Métis.

5 There was no in-person gathering in 2020, due to the COVID-19 pandemic. However, a fall festival (instead of the usual July festival) was held in September 2021. The event was back to its usual schedule in 2022. Numerous online videos provide an overview of Back to Batoche. Rather than offer a list here (that may be obsolete in a few years), search "Back to Batoche" on YouTube to see currently available videos.

6 These were Métis Nation Ontario (MNO), the Manitoba Metis Federation (MMF), Métis Nation – Saskatchewan (MN-S), Métis Nation of Alberta (MNA), and Métis Nation British Columbia (MN-BC).

7 Here I borrow Métis archaeologist Kisha Supernant's concept of "belonging" rather than "artifact" to emphasize relational responsibilities to the belonging (2021).

8 Wiseman explained to me that La Rance and Lawrence are the same family name.

9 In the spirit of openness and disclosure of any possible conflicts of interest, I always donate any payment back to the festival. I consider my participation part of my job (and therefore my salary pays for my participation, while research funding covers my travel costs).

10 I have since connected this song to one that Richard Johnston recorded in Lebret, Saskatchewan in 1957, though the language used is considerably different. That recording is currently housed in the Canadian Museum of History (JO-At-17).

11 Since completing my fieldwork in Oshawa (between 2015 and 2017), the conversations around Ontario Métis identity have drastically shifted, including ongoing, and often difficult, discussions around which communities are indeed historic, rights-bearing communities, and how Métis rights intersect with First Nations' rights. Because these were not topics that I covered with my interlocutors, I do not address them in this section. Had I done this research over the past year or two, they would undoubtedly have been issues raised by performers, organizers, and attendees. As I note in my postlude, the research in this book is one perspective embedded in time and place, and this section needs to be read as such.

12 I was inspired to use poetry after reading Métis author and scholar, Michelle Porter's book, *Approaching Fire* (2020).

CHAPTER SEVEN

1 Thank you to Dr Suzanne Steele for sharing this evocative and helpful description of her role in the creation of *Li Keur*.

2 See, e.g., Hutcheon and Hutcheon's (2016) article in *Opera Canada. Maclean's* also published an article (Doherty 2017), as did the major newspapers in Canada and the *New York Times* (Cooper 2017).

3 About half of the episodes are still available on Soundcloud (see https://soundcloud.com/user-64387520). However, I have not been able to access episodes one to four.

4 When the University of British Columbia's School of Music staged the opera in 2010, they also hosted a symposium with many prominent Canadian music researchers presenting. In *Hungry Listening*, Dylan Robinson briefly discusses his own presentation at that symposium (2020, 159–61).

5 For an analysis of *Louis Riel* and *Li Keur* from the perspective of white possession, see Nicole Stonyk's master's thesis, "The Embodiment and 'Refusal' of the White Possessive in Opera: A Comparative Analysis of *Louis Riel* and *Li Keur* (2023).

6 Irish-born playwright, John Coulter's work was particularly important for the emergence of "Riel-based" art. His trilogy on Riel is among his best-known and most performed work.

7 *Riel, A Comic Strip Stage Play*, produced by Théâtre La Chapelle, Infiniti Theatre, and Persephone Theatre, is an example of work in this medium (Fraser 2016). Ruby Wiebe's 1977 book *The Scorched Wood People* is another example of creative writing about Riel.

8 Songs about Riel include "Louis Riel" by British garage band, Thee Headcoats; "Song For Louis Riel" by southern Ontario-based folk group, Same Latitude As Rome; "Louis Riel" by Mi'kmaq singer/songwriter Willie Dunn; and "Louis Riel" by Tex-Mex musician Doug Sahm, among others. Classical compositions include Hungarian-born, naturalized Canadian, Tibor Polgar's work, *The Last Words of Louis Riel* (1967); American-born, Toronto-based composer David Lidov's work, *The Vision of Louis Riel* (1970); Canadian composer William McCauley's work, *Louis Riel Overture* (n.d., circa 1979); and Cree composer Andrew Balfour's oratorio *Empire Étrange: The Death of Louis Riel*. McCauley also composed the score for the 1979 CBC production, *Riel*. In 1967, the Royal Winnipeg Ballet premiered a narrative ballet titled *Riel*, to mark the country's centennial year. Andy Dejarlis also wrote a fiddle tune titled "Louis Riel Reel" and Rick Neufeld has an unrelated fiddle tune titled "Louis Riel" (from his 1978 LP).

9 In her talk for the *Hearing Riel* symposium, Jean Teillet noted that Schultz was also one of the most prolific land speculators after the Manitoba Act was signed (2017, 01:19:00).

10 Musicologist Robin Elliott notes that there were preliminary discussions about staging the opera in Saskatoon to mark the 1985 centennial of the Northwest Resistance and Riel's death, but it never came to fruition. Elliott also states that the Association of Métis and Non-Status Indians of Saskatchewan denounced the plans, and that Métis historian, Murray Dobbin, suggested that funding could be better spent on projects that would benefit Indigenous people. Dobbin also noted that, should the opera be staged, Indigenous participation should be prioritized (Elliott 2018, 18). Whether any of this push back factored in the decision not to stage it in Saskatchewan may never be known. However, it is significant that these conversations – conversations that would happen again in 2017 – were front and centre in 1980s Saskatchewan. It seems that Moore and Somers may not have been able to get away with the lack of Indigenous engagement in the Prairies the way they did in eastern Canada in the late 1960s and '70s.

11 Here it is important to ask, who does she mean by "anyone"? I suspect she means people who make casting decisions at primarily white institutions.

12 Danckert is, of course, speaking to *assumptions of settler creators rather than to the reality*. There is a long history of Indigenous engagement with opera. The issue is furthermore tied to opera's prohibitive cost, and structures and attitudes that create a sense of alienation for potential Indigenous patrons.

13 For example, I often think about how the inclusion of Indigenous peoples in the Canadian Constitution in 1982 is positioned as a change that the Canadian government made, rather than a change that Indigenous peoples fought for (and had to work very hard for).

14 The Truth and Reconciliation Commission (TRC) concluded its work in 2015, releasing ninety-four calls to action, including several related to the arts. Call number 83, for example, "call[ed] upon the Canada Council for the Arts to establish, as a funding priority, a strategy for Indigenous and non-Indigenous artists to undertake collaborative projects and produce works that contribute to the reconciliation process" (Truth and Reconciliation Commission of Canada 2015, 9).

15 This scene was originally a drunken brawl. The new scene emphasized the creativity and beauty of Indigenous cultures.

16 Notably, this aria has, since 1967, become a popular song, often sung on its own outside of the opera. However, as Dylan Robinson, Wal'aks Keane Tait,

and G̱oothl Ts'imilx (Mike Dangeli) wrote in the programme notes accompanying the 2017 restaging, not only do Nisga'a people consider it a legal offence to misuse the song, they believe that, if misused, it can have a negative spiritual impact on singers and listeners.

17 Critics similarly praised the aria. Though the human and musical aspects of the aria are intertwined, critics have tended to focus on the musicality of the selection, with one suggesting that the aria showed Somers's ability to "writ[e] brilliantly for the voice" (quoted in Strachan and Nickleson 2018, 87).

18 In 2005, Jeremy Strachan compiled a list, titled "Music Inspired By Aboriginal Sources at the Canadian Music Centre," documenting 200 works by Canadian composers that appropriated Indigenous songs. Numerous collectors and composers, furthermore, openly encouraged composers to appropriate Indigenous songs. The issue of appropriation in the Nisga'a song was also addressed at a symposium around the 2010 restaging of the opera at UBC. In other words, it was no secret in the classical music world that Indigenous song was often appropriated, or that it was an encouraged practice for decades; rather, it was not considered an issue of concern by the majority of those performing the music (see, e.g., Robinson 2020, 159–61).

19 Contributors Sarah Koval and Taryn Dubois use the term Resistance and include a footnote to explain why they have made this choice (2018, 60). The use of the term "rebellion" in other articles was particularly striking to me because, in her presentation for the symposium, Teillet noted that the first act of the "old wolves" (a term coined by Teillet to describe a group of Métis people who began meeting quietly in 1887, collecting firsthand accounts of what happened to Métis post-1885 to set the record straight) was to push back against the term rebellion as applied to the Métis Resistances. She pointed out that this may not seem like a big deal now, but it was to them at that time, having spent so long in hiding.

20 Dr Suzanne Steele holds a BMus, an MLIS, and a PhD. Between 2008 and 2010, she served as a Canadian War Artist in Afghanistan, the first poet to hold this role. Her work, *Afghanistan: Requiem for a Generation* (2012), with composer Jeffrey Ryan, was a result of her time in Afghanistan. In addition to *Li Keur* and other projects, Steele worked with me for more than a year as a postdoctoral researcher, and we have maintained close contact since. As a result, we have had many conversations about *Li Keur*, and about Métis music and dance more broadly. Her work has, in this way, profoundly shaped my thinking over the past two years, certainly well beyond our short formal interview. Nonetheless, all mistakes or misunderstandings remain my own.

21 Steele clarifies that it was "a convent," which (in Canada) does not overtly appear to have the same negative connotations as a residential school, yet, as she states, it was. Steele's point (as I understand it) is that the negative impacts of convent schooling (such as a profound cultural loss and loss of family) need to be acknowledged. She further points to volume three of the TRC Final Report on Métis experiences with residential schooling (Truth and Reconciliation Commission 2015). Métis experiences were somewhat different from the experiences of First Nations and Inuit children, yet often involved similar experiences of abuse and suffering.

22 The translators were Debra Beach Ducharme, Donna Beach (Anishinaabemowin), Lorraine Coutu-Lavallee, Agathe Chartrand, June Bruce, Jules Chartrand (French-Michif), and Verna Demontigny (Heritage Michif).

23 Note that this paragraph and those that follow (until the end of this section) has been written with significant feedback from Dr Suzanne Steele, who read and clarified it, as well as made several suggestions to ensure that it accurately expressed her experience.

POSTLUDE

1 This assertion is based on Steele's experience with the SSHRC grant for *Li Keur*, my own co-application for a SSHRC grant, and ongoing discussions with my graduate students.

2 In using the phrase "live the life their ancestors wanted for them," I am drawing on Steele's conceptualization of resurgence as "living the life we were meant to live" (guest lecture, 27 September 2022).

References

Adams, Gary. 1982. "Art and Archaeology at York Factory." *The Beaver* (Summer): 38–42.

Adaskin, Murray. 1959. *Saskatchewan Legend*. Toronto: Counterpoint Music Library Services.

Adese, Jennifer, and Chris Andersen. 2021. "Introduction: A New Era of Métis Studies Scholarship." In *A People and a Nation: New Directions in Contemporary Métis Studies*, edited by Jennifer Adese and Chris Andersen, 3–17. Vancouver: University of British Columbia.

Agawu, V. Kofi. 1995. "The Invention of African Rhythm." *Journal of the American Musicological Society* 48: 380–95.

– 2003. *Representing African Music*. New York: Routledge.

Ahmed, Sara. 2006. "The Nonperformativity of Antiracism." *Meridians* 7 (1): 104–26.

Amico, Stephen. 2020. "'We Are All Musicologists Now'; or, the End of Ethnomusicology." *Journal of Musicology* 37 (1): 1–32.

Andersen, Chris. 2009. "Critical Indigenous Studies: From Difference to Density." *Cultural Studies Review* 15 (2): 80–100.

– 2014. *"Métis": Race, Recognition, and the Struggle for Indigenous Peoplehood*. Vancouver: UBC Press.

Anderson, Mark Cronlund, and Carmen L. Robertson. 2011. *Seeing Red: A History of Natives in Canadian Newspapers*. Winnipeg: University of Manitoba Press.

Arrell, Douglas. 1999. "The Cosmopolitan, the Cultural Nationalist, and the Egocentric Critic: Harriot Walker, Charles W. Handscomb, and Charles H. Wheeler in Winnipeg, 1898–1906." In *Establishing Our Boundaries: English-Canadian Theatre Criticism*, edited by Anton Wagner, 107–33. Toronto: University of Toronto Press.

Arthur, E., H. Chapman, and H. Massey. 1949. *Moose Factory 1673 to 1947*. Toronto: University of Toronto Press.

Auch, Anne. 1997. "Woodridge." *Steinbach Carillon*. 10 February 1997.

Austin, Jillian. 2009. "Gathering Shows Métis Pride Has No Boundaries." *Brandon Sun*. 30 August 2009.

Avery, Dawn. 2012. "*Tékeni* – Two Worlds, Many Borders: A Look at Classical Native Music through Indigenous Eyes." *Musicultures* 39 (1): 129–68.

Balaton-Chrimes, Samantha, and Victoria Stead. 2017. "Recognition, Power and Coloniality." *Postcolonial Studies* 20 (1): 1–17.

Balfour, Andrew. 2013. *Empire Étrange: The Death of Louis Riel*. Unpublished oratorio.

Ballantyne, Robert Michael. 2007 [1848]. *Hudson Bay*. Project Gutenberg. Accessed 27 February 2024. https://www.gutenberg.org/cache/epub/21758/pg21758-images.html.

Ballantyne, Solomon. 2001. Interview with John Leclair, 3 July, Stanley Mission, SK. Accessed 15 December 2021. https://www.metismuseum.ca/media/document.php/06841.Solomon%20Ballantyne.pdf.

Barkwell, Lawrence. n.d. "Slavey Jargon: A Trade Language of the Metis." Paper for the Louis Riel Institute. Accessed 15 December 2021. https://www.metismuseum.ca/media/document.php/149203.Slavey%20Jargon.pdf.

Bartlett, Cheryl, Murdena Marshall, and Albert Marshall. 2012. "Two-Eyed Seeing and Other Lessons Learned within a Co-Learning Journey of Bringing Together Indigenous and Mainstream Knowledges and Ways of Knowing." *Journal of Environmental Studies and Sciences* 2 (4): 331–40.

Barz, Gregory, and Timothy J. Cooley, eds. 1997. *Shadows in the Field: New Perspectives for Fieldwork in Ethnomusicology*. New York: Oxford University Press.

Beaudry-Loiselle, Lucienne. 2019. *Festival du Voyaguer Hé Ho! A Celebration of Culture and Heritage*. Winnipeg: Vidacom Publications.

Bedard, Mel. 2001. Interview by Herb Lafferty, with Leah Dorion-Paquin. 9 August. Transcription available through the Gabriel Dumont Institute. https://www.metismuseum.ca/media/document.php/06745.Bedard,%20Mel.pdf.

Benham, D.J. 1907. "Sun Dance of the Chippewa Indians." *Manitoba Free Press*. 17 July 1907.

Benjamin, Arthur. c1947. *The Red River Jig* [Orchestral Score]. London: Hawkes and Son.

Blanchard, Jim. 2005. *Winnipeg 1912*. Winnipeg: University of Manitoba.

Bolton, David. 1961. "The Red River Jig." *Manitoba Pageant* 7 (1): https://www.mhs.mb.ca/docs/pageant/07/redriverjig.shtml.

Bone, Robert M. 2002. "Colonialism to Post-Colonialism in Canada's Western Interior: The Case of the Lac La Ronge Indian Band." *Historical Geography* 30: 60–73.

Bouchard, Remi. 1981. *Hommage à Riel Pour Instrumentation Diverse.* St Boniface: L'Editions du Ble.

Boulette, Oliver. 2006. "The 'Red River Jig': A Fiddle Tune and Dance That Defines the Metis." In *Metis Legacy II*, edited by Lawrence Barkwell, Leah M. Dorion, and Audreen Hourie, 162–3. Saskatoon: Gabriel Dumont Institute.

Brandon Sun. 2008. "Metis Honour Stalwarts of Their Community." 5 April 2008.

Braz, Albert. 2003. *The False Traitor: Louis Riel in Canadian Culture.* Toronto: University of Toronto Press.

Brown, Chester. 2003. *Louis Riel: A Comic-Strip Biography.* Montreal: Drawn and Quarterly Publications.

Brown, Danielle. 2020. "An Open Letter on Racism in Music Studies, Especially Ethnomusicology and Music Education." *My People Tell Stories.* Accessed 3 October 2023. https://www.mypeopletellstories.com/blog/open-letter.

Brown, Jennifer S.H., and Elizabeth Vibert. 1996. *Reading Beyond Words: Contexts for Native History.* Peterborough, ON: Broadview Press.

Bulbulian. Maurice. 1987. *Dancing Around the Table.* Canada: National Film Board.

Burnham, Clint. 2010. "No Poems on Stolen Native Land." *West Coast Line* 67: 38–41.

Cajete, Gregory. 1994. *Look to the Mountain: An Ecology of Indigenous Education.* Durango, CO: Kivaki Press.

Campbell, Maria. 1983. "Wehtamatowin Radio Feature on Back to Batoche." Provincial Archives of Alberta. Cassette. PR1993.0633.0043.

– 2010. *Stories of the Road Allowance People.* Saskatoon: Gabriel Dumont Institute.

– 2012. "Foreword: Charting the Way." In *Contours of a People: Metis Family, Mobility, and History*, edited by Nicole St-Onge, Carolyn Podruchny, and Brenda Macdougall, xiii–xxv. Norman: University of Oklahoma Press.

Canadian Charter of Rights and Freedoms, s 27, Part 1 of the *Constitution Act*, 1982, being Schedule B to the *Canada Act 1982* (UK), 1982, c 11.

Cardinal, Harold. 1969. *The Unjust Society.* Edmonton: M.G. Hurtig.

Carillon News. 1953. "Marchand." 10 July 1953.

Cass-Beggs, Barbara. 1967. *Seven Métis Songs of Saskatchewan.* Don Mills, Ontario: BMI Canada.

CBC. 1979. *Riel.* Kleinburg, Ontario: Cinespace Film Studios.

Charette, Guillaume. 1976. *Vanishing Spaces: Memories of Louis Goulet*. Translated by Ray Ellenwood. Winnipeg: Edition Bois-Brûlés.

Chari, Anita. 2004. "Exceeding Recognition." *Sartre Studies International* 10 (2): 110–22.

Chartrand, Yvonne, with Ania Storoszczuk-Smeets. 2000. *Marguerite*. Dance work.

Chartrand, Paul. 2008. "Defining the 'Métis' of Canada: A Principled Approach to Crown-Aboriginal Relations." In *Métis-Crown Relations: Rights, Identity, Jurisdiction, and Governance*, edited by Frederica Wilson and Melanie Mallet, 27–70. Toronto: Irwin Law.

Clark, Caryl, Linda Hutcheon, Sherry Lee, Tegan Niziol, and Carolyne Sumner. 2018. "Editors' Introduction: Hearing Riel." *University of Toronto Quarterly* 87 (4): 1–9.

Clemens, Marion. 1997. "Oakbank/Dugald: Canada Day Celebrations." *Steinbach Carillon*. 30 June 1997.

Commissions of Goods to Servants, 1787–1897. Archival document held at the Hudson's Bay Company Archives, Winnipeg.

Constitution Act, 1982, being Schedule B to the *Canada Act 1982* (UK), 1982, c 11.

Cooley, Timothy. 1997. "Casting Shadows in the Field: An Introduction." In *Shadows in the Field: New Perspectives for Fieldwork in Ethnomusicology*, edited by Gregory F. Barz and Timothy J. Cooley, 1–19. Oxford: Oxford University Press.

Cooper, Michael. 2017. "Canada Turns 150, but a Silent Chorus Isn't Celebrating." *New York Times*. Accessed 27 February 2024. https://www.nytimes.com/2017/04/19/arts/music/canada-turns-150-but-a-silent-chorus-isnt-celebrating.html.

Corntassel, Jeff, and Cheryl Bryce. 2012. "Practicing Sustainable Self-Determination: Indigenous Approaches to Cultural Restoration and Revitalization." *The Brown Journal of World Affairs* XVIII (11): 151–62.

Corntassel, Jeff. 2012. "Re-envisioning Resurgence: Indigenous Pathways to Decolonization and Sustainable Self-Determination." *Decolonization: Indigeneity, Education & Society* 1 (1): 86–101.

Coulter, John. 1962. *Riel: A Play in Two Parts*. Toronto: Ryerson Press.

– 1968a. *The Crime of Louis Riel*. Ottawa: Overon Press.

– 1968b. *The Trial of Louis Riel*. Ottawa: Oberon Press.

Coulthard, Glen. 2006. "Indigenous Peoples and the 'Politics of Recognition.'" *New Socialist*. Republished 23 March 2013. Accessed 21 December 2021. https://newsocialist.org/indigenous-peoples-and-the-politics-of-recognition/.

– 2014. *Red Skin, White Masks: Rejecting the Colonial Politics of Recognition*. Minneapolis: University of Minnesota Press.

Couture, Selena. 2019. "Land Acknowledgements: Speaking Colonial Failure." *Canadian Theatre Review* 177: 27–9.

Coyes, Greg, dir. 2002. *How the Fiddle Flows*. Ottawa: National Film Board of Canada.

Cree, Francis, and Nicholas Vrooman. 2006. "The Fiddle I Give – A Metis Story." In *Metis Legacy II*, edited by Lawrence Barkwell, Leah M. Dorion, Audreen Hourie, 34–9. Saskatoon: Gabriel Dumont Institute.

Daigle, Michelle. 2019. "The Spectacle of Reconciliation: On (the) Unsettling Responsibilities to Indigenous Peoples in the Academy." *Environment and Planning D: Society and Space* 37 (4): 703–21.

Danckert, Paula. 2018. "Louis Riel: History, Theatre, and a National Narrative – An Evolving … Story." *University of Toronto Quarterly* 87 (4): 39–50.

Daniels v. Canada. 2016. S.C.R. 99, 2016 SCC 12.

Dauphin Herald. 1951. "Winnipegosis Agricultural Fair is Successful Two-Day Event." 12 July 1951.

– 1973. "First Metis Festival Rained Out." 5 September 1973.

de Leeuw, Sarah, Margo Greenwood, and Nicole Lindsay. 2013. "Troubling Good Intentions." *Settler Colonialism and Indigenous Alternatives in Global Context* 3 (4): 381–94.

Deloria, Philip. 1999. *Playing Indian*. New Haven: Yale University Press.

– 2004. *Indians in Unexpected Places*. Lawrence: University Press of Kansas.

Derksen, Cris, Jeremy Dutcher, Jessica McMann, Melody McKiver, Sonny-Ray Day Rider, Andrew Balfour, Ian Cusson, Michelle Lafferty, Beverley McKiver, and Corry Payette. 2019. "Appendix E: Statement on Indigenous Musical Sovereignty." In *Re-sounding the Orchestra: Relationships between Canadian Orchestras, Indigenous Peoples, and Peoples of Colour*, edited by Soraya Peerbaye and Parmela Attariwala, 69. N.p.: Orchestras Canada.

Dick, Lyle. 1994. "Historical Writing on 'Seven Oaks': The Assertion of Anglo-Canadian Cultural Dominance in the West." *The Forks and the Battle of Seven Oaks in Manitoba History*, edited by Robert Coutts and Richard Stuart, 65–70. Winnipeg: Manitoba Historical Society.

Dickason, Olive. 1992. *Canada's First Nations: A History of Founding Peoples from Earliest Times*. Toronto: McClelland and Stewart.

Dobbin, Murray. 1981. *The One-And-A-Half Men: The Story of Jim Brady and Malcolm Norris, Metis Patriots of the Twentieth Century*. Regina: Gabriel Dumont Institute.

Doherty, Mike. 2017. "The Real Challenges of Reviving a Louis Riel Opera." *Macleans*. Accessed 10 January 2023. https://www.macleans.ca/culture/arts/the-real-challenges-of-reviving-a-louis-riel-opera/.

Dorge, Claude. 1980. *Le Roitelet*. Saint-Boniface, MB: Editions du blé.

Dorris, Michael. 1979. Native American Literature in an Ethnohistorical Context. *College English* 41 (2): 147–62.

Dowd, Allison. 2008. "Metis Group Honours Work of 54 Community Builders." *Brandon Sun*, 30 March.

Downing, Andrew. 2018. *Red River Fantasy*. Piano quartet commissioned by Ensemble Made in Canada with support from the Toronto Arts Council.

Dreher, Tanja, and Anshuman A. Mondal. 2018. "From Voice to Response: Ethical Responsiveness and the Politics of Difference." In *Ethical Responsiveness and the Politics of Difference*, edited by Tanja Dreher and Anshuman A. Mondal, 1–19. New York: Palgrave Macmillan.

Dueck, Byron. 2007. "Public and Intimate Sociability in First Nations and Métis Fiddling." *Ethnomusicology* 51 (1): 30–63.

– 2013. *Musical Intimacies and Indigenous Imaginaries: Aboriginal Music and Dance in Public Performance*. New York: Oxford University Press.

Dunbar-Ortiz, Roxanne, and Dina Gilio-Whitaker. 2016. *"All the Real Indians Died Off" and 20 Other Myths About Native Americans*. Boston: Beacon Press.

Eber, Dorothy Harley. 1989. *When the Whalers Were Up North: Inuit Memories from the Eastern Arctic*. Montreal: McGill-Queen's University Press.

Edmonton Daily Bulletin. 1911. "Song of the Old Timer." 30 January 1911.

Elliott, Robin. 2018. "The Genesis and First Production of *Louis Riel*." *University of Toronto Quarterly* 87 (4): 10–21.

Erasmus, Peter, with Henry Thompson. 1999. *Buffalo Days and Nights*. Calgary: Fifth House.

Fanon, Franz. 1952. *Black Skin, White Masks*. New York: Grove Press.

Faux, Tom. 2009. "Don Roy, Fiddle Music, and Social Sustenance in Franco New England." *The World of Music* 51 (1): 35–54.

Fernando, Mayanthi. 2019. "Critique As Care." *Critical Times* 2 (1): 13–22.

Forsyth, Malcolm. 1976. *Three Metis Songs of Saskatchewan*. Willowdale, ON: Leeds Music.

Francis, Daniel. 1992. *The Imaginary Indian: The Image of the Indian in Canadian Culture*. Vancouver: Arsenal Pulp Press.

Fraser, Zach. 2016. *Louis Riel: A Comic-Strip Stage Play*. Unpublished play, adapted from Chester Brown's book *Louis Riel: A Comic Strip Biography*.

Gallat-Morin, Elisabeth, and Jean-Pierre Pinson. 2003. *La Vie Musicale en Nouvelle-France*. Sillery, QC: Septentrion.

Gaudet, Cindy. 2019. "Keeoukaywin: The Visiting Way – Fostering an Indigenous Research Methodology." *Aboriginal Policy Studies* 7 (2): 47–64.

– 2023. "Re-matriating Territorial Acknolwedgement: A Métis Women's Perspective." *Pawaatamihk: Journal of Métis Thinkers* 1 (1): 28–36.

Gaudry, Adam. 2011. "Insurgent Research." *Wicazo Sa Review* 26 (1): 113–36.

– 2013. "The Metis-ization of Canada: The Process of Claiming Louis Riel, Metissage, and the Metis People as Canada's Mythical Origin." *Aboriginal Policy Studies* 2 (2): 64–87.

– 2021. "Building the Field of Métis Studies: Toward Transformative and Empowering Métis Scholarship." In *A People and a Nation: New Directions in Contemporary Métis Studies*, edited by Jennifer Adese and Chris Andersen, 213–29.

Gazette. 1906. "Dumont and Riel." 12 July 1906.

– 1924. "Passing of a Pioneer." 25 September 1924.

Gibbons, Roy W. 1980. "La Grande Gigue Simple and the Red River Jig: A Comparative Study of Two Regional Styles of a Traditional Fiddle Tune." *Canadian Folk Music Journal* 8: 40–8.

– 1981. "Folk Fiddling in Canada: A Sampling." Canadian Centre for Folk Culture Studies, Paper No. 35. Ottawa: National Museums of Canada.

– 1982. "As it Comes: Folk Fiddling in Prince George, British Columbia." Canadian Centre for Folk Culture Studies, Mercury Series, Paper No. 43. Ottawa: National Museum of Man.

Gilman, Lisa, and John Fenn. 2019. *Handbook for Folklore and Ethnomusicological Fieldwork*. Bloomington: Indiana University Press.

Giroux, Monique. 2013. "Music, Power, and Relations: Fiddling as a Meeting Place between Re-Settlers and Indigenous Nations in Manitoba." PhD diss., York University. https://yorkspace.library.yorku.ca/items/ba7c2227-ba29-4bb6-8057-56d9b1c7ca22.

– 2015a. "Métis Music and the Settler Imagination." *Canadian Folk Music* 49 (1): 1–8.

– 2015b. "Singing for Frog Plain: Representing Canadian/Metis Relations through Falcon's Songs." *Ethnologies* 37 (1): 43–64.

– 2016. "'Giving Them Back Their Spirit': Multiculturalism and Resurgence at a Metis Cultural Festival." *MUSICultures* 43 (1): 64–88.

– 2018a. "Silencing the Other Within: Metis Music at Manitoba's Old-Time Fiddle Competitions." *Ethnomusicology* 62 (2): 265–90.

– 2018b. "The [Goddamn] Opera is Dead!" *Canadian Notes and Queries*. Accessed 5 January 2023. http://notesandqueries.ca/essays/the-goddamn-opera-is-dead/.

– 2020. "Metis (Style) Fiddling: From Historical Roots to Contemporary Practice." In *Contemporary Musical Expressions in Canada*, edited by Anna

Hoefnagels, Sherry Johnson, and Judith Klassen, 209–41. Montreal: McGill-Queen's University Press.

– 2022. "Ethical Responsiveness at the Intersection of Critical Indigenous Studies and Music Scholarship." In *The Routledge Companion to Ethics and Research in Ethnomusicology,* edited by Jonathon Stock and Beverley Diamond, 34–47. New York: Routledge.

Goertzen, Chris. 2004. "George Cecil McLeod, Mississippi's Fiddling Senator, and the Modern History of American Fiddling." *American Music* 22 (3): 339–79.

Goranson, Faye. 1990. "Preserving Metis Culture." *Stonewall Argus and Teulon Times*. 25 July 1990.

– 1994. "Metis Days Features Popluar [sic] Event: Peguis 'Boggers' Excel in St. Laurent." *The Interlake Spectator*. 8 August 1994.

Government of Canada. 1969. *Statement of the Government of Canada on Indian Policy*. Ottawa: Indian Affairs and Northern Development.

Greenhill, Pauline. 1999. "Backyard World/Canadian Culture: Looking at Festival Agendas." *Canadian University Music Review* 19 (2): 37–46.

Greer, Allan. 1997. *The People of New France*. Toronto: University of Toronto Press.

Guest, Bill. 1985. "'Down East' Fiddling." *Canadian Folk Music Bulletin* 19 (3): 11–12.

Hage, Ghassan. 2000. *White Nation: Fantasies of White Supremacy in a Multicultural Society*. New York: Routledge.

Haig-Brown, Celia, and David A. Nock. 2006. *With Good Intentions: Euro-Canadian and Aboriginal Relations in Colonial Canada*. Vancouver: UBC Press.

Handscomb, C.W. 1903. "Winnipeg Warmly Welcomes Chicago's Peerless Orchestra." *Manitoba Free Press*. 16 November 1903.

– 1906. "Grand Opera Festival Brilliantly Opened with Loeengrin – La Boheme this Afternoon and Rigoletto To-Night." *Manitoba Free Press*. 6 March 1906.

Hargrave, Joseph James. 1871. *Red River*. Montreal: John Lovell.

Healy, W.J. 1923. *Women of Red River: Being a Book Written from the Recollections of Women Surviving from the Red River Era*. Winnipeg: The Women's Canadian Club.

Hemetek, Ursula. 2006. "Applied Ethnomusicology in the Process of the Political Recognition of a Minority: A Case Study of the Austrian Roma." *Yearbook for Traditional Music* 38: 35–57.

Hill, Kanonhsyonne Janice C. 2019. "Rethinking the Practice and Performance of Indigenous Land Acknowledgement." *Canadian Theatre Review* 177: 22–4.

Hiscott, Jim. 1991. *Spirit Reel*. CD. CD-BOR 0191.

Hogan, Dorothy, and Homer Hogan. 1977. "Canadian Fiddle Culture." *Canadian Studies* 3: 72–101.

Hogue, Michel. 2015. *Metis and the Medicine Line.* Regina: University of Regina Press.

Hornby, James John. 1985. A Survey of Fiddling on Prince Edward Island. *Canadian Folk Music Bulletin* 19 (3): 7–10.

Howe, Craig. 2002. "Keep Your Thoughts Above the Trees: Ideas on Developing and Presenting Tribal Histories." In *Clearing a Path: Theorizing the Past in Native American Studies*, edited by Nancy Shoemaker, 161–79. New York: Routledge.

Hutcheon, Linda, and Michael Hutcheon. 2016. "Identity Crisis." *Louis Riel at 50.* Accessed 3 November 2023. http://uoftmusicicm.ca/wp-content/uploads/2017/04/Riel-OC-5742017-Hutcheons.pdf.

Indian Act, RSC 1985. https://canlii.ca/t/5439p.

Innes, Robert Alexander. 2013. *Elder Brother and the Law of the People: Contemporary Kinship and Cowessess First Nation.* Winnipeg: University of Manitoba.

Iseke, Judy, and Bmjk Brennus. 2011. "Learning Life Lessons from Indigenous Storytelling with Tom McCallum." In *Indigenous Philosophies and Critical Education,* edited by George J. Sefa Dei, 245–61. New York: Peter Lang.

Iseke, Judy. 2013. "Indigenous Storytelling as Research." *International Review of Qualitative Research* 6 (4): 559–77.

Jackman, Kate. 2007. "Hunter Volunteer of the Year." *Neepawa Banner.* 19 February 2007.

Johnson, Sherry, editor/producer. 2006. "Negotiating Tradition in Ontario Fiddle Contests." PhD diss., York University.

– 2012. *Bellows and Bows: Historic Recordings of Traditional Fiddle and Accordion Music from Across Canada.* St John's, NL: Research Centre for the Study of Music, Media, and Place.

Jones, Mike. 2002. "Volunteers Needed to Help Stage 2003 Games." *Brandon Sun.* 15 December 2002.

Joseph, Bob. 2018. *21 Things You May Not Know About the Indian Act.* Port Coquitlam, BC: Indigenous Relations Press.

Kallman, Helmut. 1981. "Fiddling." In *Encyclopedia of Music in Canada*, edited by Helmut Kallman, Gilles Potvin, and Kenneth Winters, 325–26. Toronto: University of Toronto Press.

Kaminsky, David. 2014. "'Just Exotic Enough': Swedish Chamber Klezmer as Postnational World Music and Mid-East Proxy." *Ethnomusicology* 58 (2): 254–77.

Kermoal, Nathalie, and Chris Andersen. 2021. "Introduction." In *Daniels vs.*

Canada: In and Beyond the Courts, edited by Nathalie Kermoal and Chris Andersen, 1–13. Winnipeg: University of Manitoba Press.

Kilvert, Francis, edited and introduced by William Plomer. 1964. *Kilvert's Diary*. London: Jonathan Cape.

Knight, Lindsay. 2015. "Rhyming Out the Future: Reclaiming Identity through Indigenous Hip Hop." *Decolonization: Indigeneity, Education & Society*. Accessed 3 November 2023. https://decolonization.wordpress.com/2015/03/31/rhyming-out-the-future-reclaiming-identity-through-indigenous-hip-hop/.

Kovach, Margaret. 2009. *Indigenous Methodologies: Characteristics, Conversations, and Contexts*. Toronto: University of Toronto Press.

Koval, Sarah, and Taryn Dubois. 2018. "Can Opera Listen? Canada's (Sesqui) Centennial Opera, *Louis Riel*." *University of Toronto Quarterly* 87 (4): 59–72.

Lachnit, Rachel. 2006. "Woodridge: Heritage Day." *Steinbach Carillon*. 5 July 2006.

LaRocque, Emma. 2010. *When the Other is Me: Native Resistance Discourse, 1850–1990*. Winnipeg: University of Manitoba Press.

Laut, Agnes Christina. 1900. *Lords of the North*. New York: J.F. Taylor & Company.

Laxer, Daniel. 2015. "Listening to the Fur Trade: Sound, Music, and Dance in Northern North America 1760–1840." PhD diss., University of Toronto. https://hdl.handle.net/1807/77710.

– 2022. *Listening to the Fur Trade: Soundways and Music in the British North American Fur Trade, 1760–1840*. Montreal: McGill-Queen's University Press.

Le Camp, Lorraine. 2005. "Racial Considerations of Minstrel Shows and Related Images in Canada." PhD diss., University of Toronto.

Leary, James. 2015. *Folksongs of Another America: Field Recordings from the Upper Midwest, 1937–1946*. Madison: University of Wisconsin Press.

Lecker, Barbara. 1965. "Fiddlin' Away from Mersey Beat." *Winnipeg Free Press*. 17 July 1965.

Lederman, Anne. 1986. Old Native and Métis Fiddling in Two Manitoba Communities: Camperville and Ebb and Flow. MA thesis, York University.

– 1988. "Old Indian and Métis Fiddling in Manitoba: Origins, Structure and Question of Syncretism." *The Canadian Journal of Native Studies* VIII (2): 205–30.

– 2009. "Métis Fiddling: Found or Lost?" In *Histoires et identités: homage á Gabriel Dumont/Métis Histories and Identities: A Tribute to Gabriel Dumont*, edited by Denis Gagnon, Denis Combet, and Lise Gaboury-Diallo, 365–75. Winnipeg, MB: Press Universitaires de Saint-Boniface.

– 2013. "Aboriginal Fiddling: The Scottish Connection." In *Irish and Scottish Encounters with Indigenous Peoples: Canada, the United States, New Zealand, and*

Australia, edited by Graeme Morton and David A. Wilson, 323–40. Kingston: McGill-Queen's University Press.

– n.d. *Spirit of the Narrows*. Unpublished theatrical work.

Lederman, Anne, and Christina Smith. 2014. "Fiddling." In *The Canadian Encyclopedia*. Accessed 27 December 2022. www.thecanadianencyclopedia.ca/en/article/fiddling-emc.

Lee, Sherry. 2018. "Radical Modernism, Operatic Failure, and *Louis Riel*'s Challenge to Reconciliation." *University of Toronto Quarterly* 87 (4): 22–8.

Lemieux, Ron. 2005. "Report from the Legislature." *Winnipeg Free Press*. 31 March 2005.

Leroux, Darryl. 2019. *Distorted Descent: White Claims to Indigenous Identity*. Winnipeg: University of Manitoba Press.

Lidov, David. 1970. *The Vision of Louis Riel*. Unpublished score.

Lizotte, Brianna. 2022. "Power of a Fiddle: Healing through Music." *Indigenous 150+*. Podcast. 20 September 2022. Accessed 27 September 2022. https://indigenous150plus.libsyn.com/power-of-a-fiddle-healing-through-music?fbclid=IwAR24qCooV2WoQEqY6PbZqGhmvxVkSQNwjSucmauSG6BfogGd-yrU-csIlcI.

Loukinen, Michael. 1991. *Medicine Fiddle*. Marquette, MI: Up North Films.

Luong, Michael. 2022. "Dreaming of Indigenous Futures." *Yes!* Accessed 20 September 2023. https://www.yesmagazine.org/social-justice/2022/11/24/dreams-indigenous-heritage.

Mackey, Eva. 2002. *The House of Difference: Cultural Politics and National Identity in Canada*. Toronto: University of Toronto Press.

Mackintosh, Joe. 2010. *Andy Dejarlis: The Life and Music of an Old-Time Fiddler*. Winnipeg: Great Plains Publications.

Manitoba Act, 1870, SC, c3, reprinted in RSC 1985, App II, No. 8. Manitoba Act, 1870, SC – PrimaryDocuments.ca

Manitoba Daily Free Press. 1887. "City and Province." 31 January 1887.

Manitoba Free Press. 1908. "A Wedding in the Far North." 22 December 1908.

– 1911. "Brilliant Affair Held by Old Timers." 15 December 1911.

– 1912. "Old Timers' Annual Ball Decided Success." 19 December 1912.

– 1924. "The Clock Swings Back: Winnipeg Is Fort Garry as Old Timers do Jigs." 11 December 1924.

– 1927. "CKY for Next Week." 16 July 1927.

– 1930a. "Dancing and Social." 5 July 1930.

– 1930b. "The Folk Song-Folk Dance Festival!" 28 March 1930.

– 1930c. "Victor Company Records Pioneer's Red River Jig." 1 November 1930.

Manitoba Leader. 1948. "Andy Dejarlis Is New Fiddle Champion." 7 October 1948.

– 1949. "Portage Musician Wins Mayfair Trophy for the Second Time." 6 October 1949.

– 1950. "Poplar Point Man Crowned King of Manitoba Old-Time Fiddlers, 2,400 Persons Crowd Drill Hall." 2 November 1950.

– 1951. "Entertainers are Lined Up for May 24th." 17 May 1951.

– 1952a. "Provincial Fiddlers' Contest to be Held in Arena Rink This Year." 4 September 1952.

– 1952b. "Des Jarlis Top Fiddler in Province." 2 October 1952.

– 1956a. "Curlers Hold Lively Semi-Annual Meeting." 22 November 1956.

– 1956b. "Manitou Fiddler Wins Championship." 27 September 1956.

– 1957. "Lacroix Wins Fiddling Title." 11 July 1957.

Manitoba Morning Free Press. 1899. "The Red River Cart: 'The Race has Almost Perished.'" 22 April 1899.

– 1902. "Paying Treaty to Dusky Allies." 2 August 1902.

Maraldo, Jaclyn. 2023. "From Francophone Frontier to Melting Pot Metropolis: Discovering Expressions of French-Canadian and Métis Identity in the Detroit River Region." PhD diss., Tulane University.

Marley, David. 2008. *Wars of the Americas: A Chronology of Armed Conflict in the Western Hemisphere*, 2nd edition. Denver: ABC Clio.

Marquis, Greg. 2022. "The Folk Fight Back: Protesting the Cancellation of *Don Messer's Jubilee* in 1969." *Canadian Historical Review* 103 (2): 228–51.

Martineau, Jarrett. 2015. "Creative Combat: Indigenous Art, Resurgence, and Decolonization." PhD diss., University of Victoria. http://hdl.handle.net/1828/6702.

McCauley. n.d. *Louis Riel Overture*. Unpublished score.

McIlroy, Randal. 1982. "Concerts, Workshops Fill Days." *Winnipeg Free Press*. 3 July 1982.

McLeod, Alexander D. 1924. "A Daughter of the Ranch: A Story of Romance and Adventure of Western Pioneer Days." *Stonewall Argus*. 4 June 1924.

Mindess, Mary. 1966. "Spring, Bagpipe Music, A Fiddler, And the Red River Jig Was Born." *Winnipeg Free Press*, 25 June 1966.

Mishler, Craig, recorder and editor. 1974. *Music of the Alaskan Kutchin Indians*. Featuring Charlie Peter. Folkways Records FE 4070.

– 1993. *The Crooked Stovepipe: Athapaskan Fiddle Music and Square Dancing in Northeast Alaska and Northwest Canada*. Urbana: University of Illinois Press.

Moore, Mavor, Jacques Languirand, and Harry Somers. 1967. *Louis Riel: A Musical Drama*. Unpublished score, printed by CMC.

Nash, Rachel. 2001. "Legalizing Multiculturalism: Changes in Discourse, Changes in Attitude." *Textual Studies in Canada* 13/14: 113–30.

National Inquiry into Missing and Murdered Women and Girls. 2019. *Reclaiming Power and Place: The Final Report of the National Inquiry into Missing and Murdered Indigenous Women and Girls.* https://www.mmiwg-ffada.ca/wp-content/uploads/2019/06/Final_Report_Vol_1a-1.pdf.

Nettl, Bruno. 2010. *Nettl's Elephant: On the History of Ethnomusicology*. Chicago: University of Illinois.

Newhouse, David. 2005. *Telling Our Story.* In *Walking a Tightrope: Aboriginal People and Their Representations,* edited by Ute Lischke and David T. McNab, 45–52. Waterloo, ON: Wilfrid Laurier University Press.

Oster, Bailey. 2021. "Introduction." In *Stories of Métis Women: Tales My Kookum Told Me*, edited by Bailey Oster and Marilyn Lizee, 4–7. Calgary: Durvile & UpRoute Books.

Oster, Bailey, and Marilyn Lizee, eds. 2021. *Stories of Métis Women: Tales My Kookum Told Me.* Calgary: Durvile & UpRoute Books.

Ostick, Stephen. 1990. "Metis, Native Groups Enrich Festival." *Winnipeg Free Press.* 12 February 1990.

Ouvrard, Jessica, with William Benoit and Janet La France. 2016. *Hiding in Plain Sight: The Métis Nation*. Podcast. Accessed 22 September 2023. https://library-archives.canada.ca/eng/collection/engage-learn/podcast/Pages/metis-nation.aspx.

Payment, Diane. 1990. *"The Free People – Otipemisiwak": Batoche, Saskatchewan 1870–1930.* Ottawa: National Historic Parks and Sites, Parks, Service, Environment Canada.

Pelletier, Jeanne, and Clementine Longworth. 2004. Interview with Maria Campbell, Qu'Appelle Valley, SK. Accessed 15 December 2021. https://www.metismuseum.ca/media/document.php/07384.Pelletier,%20Longworth%20(Tape%202).pdf.

Perea, Jessica Bissett. 2021. *Sound Relations: Native Ways of Doing Music History in Alaska.* New York: Oxford University Press.

Podruchny, Carolyn. 2006. *Making the Voyageur World: Travelers and Traders in the North American Fur Trade.* Toronto: University of Toronto Press.

Pole, Christopher, ed. 2005. *Fieldwork, Volume 1: Sage Benchmarks in Social Research Methods.* Thousand Oaks: Sage Publications.

Polgar, Tibor. 1967. *The Last Words of Louis Riel.* Unpublished score.

Porter, Michelle. 2020. *Approaching Fire.* St John's: Breakwater.

Povinelli, Elizabeth. 2002. *The Cunning of Recognition*. Durham, NC: Duke.

Pratt, Yvonne Poitras. 2020. *Educating With Digital Storytelling: A Decolonizing Journey for an Indigenous Community*. Philadelphia: Routledge.

Proctor, George A. 1985. "Fiddle Music as a Manifestation of Canadian Regionalism." In *Explorations in Canadian Folklore*, edited by Edith Fowke and Carole Carpenter, 225–36. Toronto: McClelland & Stewart.

Purser, Richard. 1967. "The First Great Canadian Opera." *Winnipeg Free Press*. 4 November 1967.

Quick, Sarah. 2008. "The Social Poetics of the Red River Jig in Alberta and Beyond: Meaningful Heritage and Emerging Performance." *Ethnologies* 301 (1): 77–101.

– 2009. "Performing Heritage: Metis Music, Dance, and Identity in a Multicultural State." PhD diss., Indiana University.

– 2010. "Two Models in the World of Métis Fiddling: John Arcand and Andy DeJarlis." In *Crossing Over: Fiddle and Dance Studies from Around the North Atlantic 3*, edited by Ian Russell and Anna Kearney Guigné, 114–29. Aberdeen: Elphinstone Institute.

– Forthcoming. "Hungry Narratives Turned on Their Head (or Danced on Their Toes?): Towards Decolonial Listening in Ethnohistorical Practice." In *Great Plains Ethnohistories*, edited by Rani-Henrik Andersson, Logan Sutton, and Thierry Veyrie. Lincoln: University of Nebraska.

Reaney, James. 1975. "III Le Tombeau de Pierre Falcon." In *Selected Longer Poems*, edited by Germaine Warkentin, 32–3. Don Mills, ON: Musson Book Company.

Redbird, Duke. 1980. *We Are Metis: A Metis View of the Development of a Native Canadian Peoples*. Willowdale: Ontario Metis and non-Status Indian Association.

Regan, Paulette. 2010. *Unsettling the Settler Within: Indian Residential Schools, Truth Telling, and Reconciliation in Canada*. Vancouver: University of British Columbia Press.

Reid, Jennifer. 2012. *Louis Riel and the Creation of Modern Canada: Mythic Discourse and the Postcolonial State*. Winnipeg: University of Manitoba Press.

Renihan, Coleen. 2018. "Haunting Riel." *University of Toronto Quarterly* 87 (4): 51–8.

Rice, Tim. 2007. "Reflections on Music and Identity in Ethnomusicology." *Muzikologijia* 7: 17–38.

Richard, Lucie. 1994. "Richer: Raspberry Festival." *Steinbach Carillon*. 17 August 1994.

Rickaby, Franz. 1926. *Ballads and Songs of the Shanty-Boy*. London: Oxford University Press.

Robbins, Heather. 2009. "Manitoba Metis Dance Group to Perform at Olympics." *Selkirk Journal*. 23 December 2009.

Robinson, Dylan. 2012a. "Listening to the Politics of Aesthetics: Contemporary Encounters between First Nations/Inuit and Early Music Traditions." In *Aboriginal Music in Contemporary Canada*, edited by Anna Hoefnagels and Beverley Diamond, 222–48. Montreal: McGill-Queen's University Press.

– 2012b. "'A Spoonful of Sugar': The Medicinal Redress of The Dakota Music Tour." *MUSICultures* 39 (1): 111–28.

– 2016. "Intergenerational Sense, Intergenerational Responsibility." In *Arts of Engagement: Taking Aesthetic Action in and Beyond the Truth and Reconciliation Commission of Canada*, edited by Dylan Robinson and Keavy Martin, 43–65. Waterloo, ON: Wilfrid Laurier Press.

– 2019. "Rethinking the Practice and Performance of Indigenous Land Acknowledgement." *Canadian Theatre Review* 177: 20–22.

– 2020. *Hungry Listening: Resonant Theory for Indigenous Sound Studies*. Minneapolis, MN: University of Minnesota Press.

Robinson, Henry Martin. 1879. *The Great Fur Land or Sketches of Life in the Hudson's Bay Territory*. New York: G.P. Putnam's Sons.

Rosenberg, Neil. 1994. "Don Messer's Modern Canadian Fiddle Canon." *Canadian Folk Music Journal* 22: 23–35.

Roux, Jean-Louis. 1967. *Bois-Brûlés*. Montreal: Editions du Jour.

R. v. Powley. 2003. 2 S.C.R. 207, 2003 SCC 43.

Sarath, Ed. 2018. *Black Music Matters: Jazz and the Transformation of Music Studies*. Lanham, Maryland: Rowman & Littlefield.

Saul, John Ralston. 2008. *A Fair Country: Telling Truths About Canada*. Toronto: Viking Canada.

Scott-Maxwell, Aline. 2013. "Creating Indonesia in Australia: Bridges, Communities and Identities through Music." *Musicology Australia* 35 (1): 3–19.

Sellick, Lester B. 1969. *Canada's Don Messer*. Kentville, NS: Kentville Publishing.

Senungetuk, Heidi Aklaseaq. 2019. "*Pagmapak*: In Modern Times." In *Music and Modernity Among First Peoples of North America*, edited by Victoria Lindsay Levine and Dylan Robinson, xiii–xviii. Middleton, CT: Wesleyan University Press.

Shore, Fred. 1991. "The Canadians and the Métis: The Re-Creation of Manitoba, 1858–1872." PhD diss., University of Manitoba.

– 2001. "The Emergence of the Metis Nation in Manitoba." In *Metis Legacy*, edited by Lawrence J. Barkwell, Leah Dorion, and Darren R. Préfontaine, 71–8. Winnipeg: Pemmican Publications.

Simeonov, Jenna. 2003. "A New Wave of Indigenous Opera Arrives in Canada." *Globe and Mail*, 28 September 2023. Accessed 27 February 2024. https://www.theglobeandmail.com/arts/theatre-and-performance/article-a-new-wave-of-indigenous-opera-arrives-in-canada/.

Simoens, Joanna. 2023. "*Dans cette maison, on parle français*": Performing Franco-Manitoban Pluralism at Winnipeg's Festival du Voyageur." MA major research paper, Memorial University of Newfoundland.

Simonot-Maiello, Colette. 2018. "'Decolonizing' Riel." *University of Toronto Quarterly* 87 (4): 73–82.

Simpson, Audra. 2014. *Mohawk Interruptus: Political Life Across the Borders of Settler States.* Durham: Duke University.

Simpson, Leanne. 2008. *Lighting the Eighth Fire: The Liberation, Resurgence, and Protection of Indigenous Nations.* Winnipeg: Arbeiter Ring Publishing.

– 2011. *Dancing on Our Turtle's Back: Stories of Nishnaabeg Re-Creation, Resurgence and a New Emergence.* Winnipeg: Arbeiter Ring Publishing.

Sium, Aman, and Eric Ritskes. 2013. "Speaking Truth to Power: Indigenous Storytelling as an Act of Resistance." *Decolonization: Indigeneity, Education & Society* 2 (1): i–x.

Slater, Lisa. 2018. "The Anti-Festival: Kimberley Aboriginal Cultural Politics and the Artful Business of Creating Spaces for Kardiya to Hear and Feel Across Difference." In *Ethical Responsiveness and the Politics of Difference*, edited by Tanja Dreher and Anshuman A. Mondal, 169–86. New York: Palgrave Macmillan.

Small, Christopher. 1998. *Musicking: The Meanings of Performance and Listening.* Middletown, CT: Wesleyan University Press.

Snelgrove, Corey, Rita Kaur Dharmoon, and Jeff Corntassel. 2014. "Unsettling Settler Colonialism: The Discourse and Politics of Settlers, and Solidarity with Indigenous Nations." *Decolonization: Indigeneity, Education & Society* 3 (2): 1–32.

Sobo, Elisa, Michael Lambert, and Valerie Lambert. 2021. "Land Acknowledgements Meant to Honor Indigenous People Too Often Do the Opposite – Erasing American Indians and Sanitizing History Instead." *The Conversation*, 7 October 2021. Accessed 27 February 2024. https://theconversation.com/land-acknowledgments-meant-to-honor-indigenous-people-too-often-do-the-opposite-erasing-american-indians-and-sanitizing-history-instead-163787.

Springfield Leader. 1954. "Manitoba's Oldest Resident Celebrated 107th Birthday." 20 April 1954.

– 1955. "Birds Hill Sponsors Fiddling Contest." 1 November 1955.

Steele, Suzanne. 2020a. "Li Keur Podcast: Episode One with Dr. Suzanne M. Steele." With Hannah Connelly and Bryna Link. Accessed 10 January 2023. https://omeka.cmu.ca/s/Riel-Heart-of-the-North/item/608.

– 2020b. "Li Keur Podcast: Episode Six with Conversation Led by Dr. Suzanne Steele with Student Assistants Bryna Link and Hannah Connelly." Accessed 10 January 2023. https://omeka.cmu.ca/s/Riel-Heart-of-the-North/item/683.

– 2020c. "Introductory Essay: Li Keur Aesthetic Translation of Indigenous Languages Database." Unpublished article.

– 2023. Guest lecture for class titled "Indigenous Musics," University of Lethbridge.

– librettist. 2024. *Li Keur: Riel's Heart of the North.* Unpublished opera, with music by Alex Kusturok and Neil Weisensel. Premiered Winnipeg, November 2024.

Steele, Suzanne, and Jeffrey Ryan. 2012. *Requiem for a Generation.* Toronto: Canadian Music Centre.

Steinbach Carillon. 1958. "St. Boniface Jubilee Advertisement." 6 June 1958.

– 2005. "Metis Welcomed at Ste. Anne Assembly." 3 March 2005.

Stevenson, Winona. 2000. "Decolonizing Tribal Histories." PhD diss., University of California, Berkeley.

Stonewall Argus and Teulon Times. 1950. "Argyle Legion Picnic A Success." 19 July 1950.

– 1953. "Fine Weather Favors Brant-Argyle Legion Old-Timers' Picnic." 22 July 1953.

– 1990. "Metis Days: A Celebration of Heritage." 8 August 1990.

– 2005. "Red River Metis Days Advertisement." 12 August 2005.

Stonewall Argus. 1930. "Argyle Notes." 12 March 1930.

– 1936. "Teulon." 5 February 1936.

– 1955. "4H Club Doings: Poplar Heights Swine Club Wins Provincial Trophy." 30 March 1955.

St-Onge, Nicole, Carolyn Podruchny, and Brenda Macdougall, eds. 2012. *Contours of a People: Metis Family, Mobility, and History.* Norman, OK: University of Oklahoma Press.

Stonyk, Nicole. 2023. "The Embodiment and 'Refusal' of the White Possessive in Opera: A Comparative Analysis of *Louis Riel* and *Li Keur*." MA thesis, University of Manitoba.

Strachan, Jeremy. 2005. *Music Inspired by Aboriginal Sources at the Canadian Music Centre.* Toronto: Canadian Music Centre.

Strachan, Jeremy, and Patrick Nickleson. 2018. "Doing Long Work: Critical Perspectives on Indigenous-Settler Collaboration in Canadian Art Music." *University of Toronto Quarterly* 87 (4): 83–101.

Studewell, William. 1997. *The Americana Song Reader*. New York: Haworth Press.

Sunabacka, Karen. 2015. *Mama's Painting: Louis Riel's Dream*. Toronto: Canadian Music Centre.

Supernant, Kisha. 2021. "From Hybridity to Relationality: Shifting Perspectives on the Archaeology of Métis Emergence." In *Routledge Handbook of the Archaeology of Indigenous-Colonial Interaction in the Americas*, edited by Lee M. Panich and Sara L. Gonzalez, 357–73. London: Routledge.

Swan Valley Star and Times. 1930. "Palace Theatre Movies Ad." 27 February 1930.

– 1973. "Camperville to Host Metis Days." 23 August 1973.

Taylor, Charles. 1992. "The Politics of Recognition." In *Multiculturalism: Examining the Politics of Recognition*, edited by A. Gutmann, 25–73. Princeton: Princeton University Press.

Taylor, Drew Hayden, director. 2018. *Searching for Winnetou*. Toronto: Paul Kemp Productions.

Teillet, Jean. 2012. "The Métis and Thirty Years of Section 35: How Constitutional Protection for Métis Rights has Led to the Loss of the Rule of Law." *The Supreme Court Law Review: Osgoode's Annual Constitutional Cases Conference* 58: 333–49.

– 2017. "The Old Wolves." Lecture for *Hearing Riel Symposium*. 21 April 2017. University of Toronto, Toronto, Ontario. https://www.youtube.com/live/lrCP1bm2TPQ?si=BsJzfvRpjPHdU-gE.

– 2018. "The Sermon from the Mount: The Messages in the Canadian Opera Company's Remount of the *Riel* Opera." *University of Toronto Quarterly* 87 (4): 29–36.

Thistle, Jesse. 2016. "The Puzzle of the Morrissette-Arcand Clan: A History of Metis Historic and Intergenerational Trauma." MA thesis, University of Waterloo. https://uwspace.uwaterloo.ca/handle/10012/10872

Thobani, Sunera. 2007. *Exalted Subjects: Studies in the Making of Race and Nation in Canada*. Toronto: University of Toronto Press.

Thompson, Brian Christopher. 2015. *Anthems and Minstrel Shows: The Life and Times of Calixa Lavallée, 1842–1891*. Montreal: McGill-Queen's University Press.

Thompson, Cheryl. 2021. "*Black* Minstrelsy on Canadian Stages: Nostalgia for Plantation Slavery in the Nineteenth and Twentieth Centuries." *Journal of the Canadian Historical Association* 31 (1): 67–94.

Thompson, Debra. 1986. "Tribal Days Celebration." *Brandon Sun*. 3 February 1986.

Thwaites, Reuben Gold, ed. 1898. *The Jesuit Relations and Allied Documents: Travels and Explorations of the Jesuit Missionaries in New France, 1610–1791*. Cleveland: Burrows.

Titley, E. Brian. 1986. *A Narrow Vision: Duncan Campbell Scott and the Administration of Indian Affairs in Canada*. Vancouver: UBC Press.

Titus, Joan. 2011. "*Waila* as Transnational Practice." In *Transnational Encounters: Music and Performance at the U.S.-Mexico Border*, edited by Alejandro Madrid, 149–67. Oxford: Oxford University Press.

Trew, Johanne. 2000. "Music, Place and Community: Culture and Irish Heritage in Ottawa Valley." PhD diss., University of Limerick.

– 2002. "Conflicting Visions: Don Messer, Liberal Nationalism and the Canadian Unity Debate." *International Journal of Canadian Studies* 26: 41–58.

– 2009. *Place, Culture and Community: The Irish Heritage of the Ottawa Valley*. New Castle upon Tyne: Cambridge Scholars.

Truth and Reconciliation Commission of Canada. 2015a. *Canada's Residential Schools: The Métis Experience,* volume 3. Montreal: McGill-Queen's University Press. https://caid.ca/TRCFinVol32015.pdf.

– 2015b. *Honouring the Truth, Reconciling for the Future: Summary of the Final Report of the Truth and Reconciliation Commission of Canada*. Ottawa: Truth and Reconciliation Commission. https://irsi.ubc.ca/sites/default/files/inline-files/Executive_Summary_English_Web.pdf.

Tuck, Eve, and K. Wayne Yang. 2012. "Decolonization Is Not a Metaphor." *Decolonization, Indigeneity, Education & Society* 1 (1): 1–40.

Urion, Carl. 2022. "Some Precepts Taught by Two Cree Elders and Their Implications for Talking About Music." In *The Routledge Companion to Ethics and Research in Ethnomusicology*, edited by Jonathan P.J. Stock and Beverley Diamond, 21–33. New York: Routledge.

Verney, Jack. 1991. *The Good Regiment: The Carignan-Salières Regiment in Canada 1665–1668*. Kingston, ON: McGill-Queen's University Press.

Villeneuve, Joanne. 2006a. "Focus on Awesome Entertainment." *Brandon Sun*. 29 January 2006.

– 2006b. "Culture of 'Métisville' Adds Spice to Boissevain's Homegrown Reunion." *Brandon Sun*. 23 July 2006.

– 2008. "Celebrating Métis Heritage in Boissevain." *Brandon Sun*. 24 July 2008.

Vivian, Shelley. 2002. "Students Experience Native Culture." *Brandon Sun*. 9 May 2002.

Vizina, Yvonne. 2008. "Métis Culture." In *kā-kī-pē-isi-nakatamā Our Legacy: Essays*, edited by Cheryl Avery and Darlene Fichter, 169–82. Saskatoon: University of Saskatchewan.

Vowel, Chelsea. 2016. *Indigenous Writes: A Guide to First Nations, Métis and Inuit Issues in Canada*. Winnipeg: Highwater Press.

Vrooman, Nicholas, producer. 1984. *Turtle Mountain Music*. Folkways Records FES 4140. LP.

– 2012. *"The Whole Country Was … 'One Robe'": The Little Shell Tribe's America*. Helena, MT: Drumlummon Institute.

Walker, Morley. 1998. "Blistering Hot Bows: Forty Fiddling Fanatics Ready to Scorch Violin Strings." *Winnipeg Free Press*. 12 February 1998.

Wallace, Russell. 2012. "Intercultural Collaboration." In *Aboriginal Music in Contemporary Canada: Echoes and Exchanges*, edited by Anna Hoefnagels and Beverley Diamond, 218–21. Kingston: McGill-Queen's University Press.

Waller, Lisa. 2018. "Indigenous Research Methodologies and Listening the Dadirri Way." In *Ethical Responsiveness and the Politics of Difference*, edited by Tanja Dreher and Anshuman A. Mondal, 227–42. New York: Palgrave Macmillan.

Watson, Franceene. 2002. *Andy De Jarlis: Master of Métis Melodies*. Victoria: Self-Published.

Wente, Jesse. 2021. Interview in *Land Governance: Current Crisis and Rise of Land Back*. DavidSuzukiFDN. https://davidsuzuki.org/what-you-can-do/what-is-land-back/.

Whidden, Lynn. 1993. *Métis Songs: Visiting was the Métis Way*. Regina: Gabriel Dumont Institute.

– 1995. *A Metis Suite*. Brandon, MB: All Media Musics. VHS.

Whiteway, Doug. 1985. "It's Folklorama Time: Festival of Nations Provides a Look at Various Cultures." *Winnipeg Free Press*. 10 August 1985.

Wiebe, Ruby. 1977. *The Scorched-Wood People*. Toronto: McClelland and Stewart.

Wilkins, Frances. 2010. "The Fiddlers of James Bay: Transatlantic Flows and Musical Indigenization among the James Bay Cree." *MUSICultures* 40 (1): 57–99.

Wilson, Shawn. 2008. *Research is Ceremony: Indigenous Research Methods*. Winnipeg: Fernwood.

Winick, Stephen, and Peter Bartis. 2016. *Folklife and Fieldwork: An Introduction to Cultural Documentation*. 4th ed. Washington, DC: American Folklife Centre, Library of Congress.

Winnipeg Daily Tribune. 1893. "The Treaty Payment." 10 July 1893.

– 1894. "A Dance in the West." 7 April 1894.

– 1903. "New Year's in Fort Garry Days." 30 December 1903.

Winnipeg Evening Tribune. 1917. "Ad [In ye olden days]." 31 March 1917.
– 1925. "Late Participants in Radio Dance Parties should not Wait for Official Entries." 9 December 1925.
– 1934. "800 Present at Celebration by Native Sons." 12 December 1934.
– 1935. "Dancing and Social." 12 November 1935.
Winnipeg Free Press. 1932. "An Old-Time and Modern Dance." 26 November 1932.
– 1933. "Radio Flashes." 18 November 1933.
– 1934a. "Scottish Sports to Have New Events on Labor Day." 26 June 1934.
– 1934b. "To Address Pioneers." 24 February 1934.
– 1935. "Dancing Instructors." 22 August 1935.
– 1937. "Genthon's Grainbelters." 11 September 1937.
– 1938a. "Epic Story: La Verendrye Fete has Colorful Start." 5 September 1938.
– 1938b. "Police Ball Gives Promise of Outdoing Predecessors of Last Thirteen Years." 12 February 1938.
– 1939. "Radio Programmes." 7 January 1939.
– 1941. "Pioneer Winnipeg Days Recalled by Old-timers at Happy Reunion." 18 February 1941.
– 1942a. "Ad." 22 January 1942.
– 1942b. "Old-Timers of Norwood Hold Reunion." 14 February 1942.
– 1943. "Leonard Moen Wins Prize." 4 May 1943.
– 1944. "Dancers Crowd 3 Ballrooms for Annual Policemen's Ball." 17 February 1944.
– 1946. "Fiddling and Jigging Revive Old Times at Annual Picnic." 22 July 1946.
– 1948. "Kin of Pioneers Planning Reunion." 22 January 1948.
– 1949a. "Colorful Scenes Enliven Rupert's Land Pageant." 6 October 1949.
– 1949b. "Old Timer Roots for a Jig as Winnipeg Gears for Fete." 18 January 1949.
– 1950a. "'Bang Up' Plans for Pioneer Picnic Sunday." 14 July 1950.
– 1950b. "First Symphony Ball Merges Old and New in Joyous Harmony." 13 January 1950.
– 1951. "Old Timers Will Vie for Jig Honors." 3 August 1951.
– 1952. "Winnipeg's Andy Sweeps to Fanciest Fiddler Title." 25 September 1952.
– 1953. "Radio Highlights." 14 March 1953.
– 1955. "Red River Families Celebrate at Site of Riel's Old Home." 21 June 1955.
– 1969. "Operatic Work Tells Saga of Louis Riel on Television." 1 November 1969.
– 1975. "Events." 6 September 1975.
– 1997. "Canada Day Advertisement." 29 June 1997.
– 2000. "Festivals and Fairs: Destination Manitoba." 13 May 2000.
– 2001a. "Destination Saskatchewan." 19 May 2001.

– 2001b. "Artistes/Performers." 3 February 2001.

– 2002. "Festival du Voyageur." 2 February 2002.

Winnipeg Tribune. 1906. "Ten Years Hence." 3 November 1906.

– 1911. "The Old-Timers' Ball: A Glimpse into the Good Old Times of Yore." 21 April 1911.

Wuttunee, Winston. 1983. "Wehtamatowin Radio Feature on Back to Batoche." Provincial Archives of Alberta. Cassette. PR1993.0633.0043.

INTERVIEWS

Alvis, Cole. 2017. Interview with author. Telephone, 18 May.

Anonymous. 2009a. Interview with author. Miami, MB, 13 October.

Anonymous. 2009b. Interview with author. Brandon, MB, 18 October.

Anonymous. 2009c. Interview with author. Winnipeg, MB, 24 October.

Anonymous. 2009d. Interview with author. Portage la Prairie, MB, 25 October.

Anonymous. 2009e. Interview with author. Winnipeg, MB, 7 November.

Anonymous. 2009f. Interview with author. Winnipeg, MB, 14 November.

Anonymous. 2009g. Interview with author. Brandon, MB, 15 November.

Anonymous. 2009h. Interview with author. Winnipeg, MB, 17 November.

Anonymous. 2009i. Interview with author. Portage la Prairie, MB, 30 November.

Anonymous. 2012. Interview with author. Winnipeg, MB, 25 June.

Anonymous. 2013. Interview with author. Winnipeg, MB, 16 May.

Anonymous. 2016. Interview with author. Lorette, MB, 9 March.

Anonymous. 2017a. Interview with author. Winnipeg, MB, 26 June.

Anonymous. 2017b. Interview with author. Winnipeg, MB, 24 June.

Anonymous. 2017c. Interview with author. Telephone, 17 May.

Aubicon, Riel. 2018. Interview with author. Back to Batoche Festival Site, SK, 20 July.

Blais, Simone. 2015. Interview with author. Midland, Ontario, 22 August.

Carlson, Jeanne. 2012. Interview with author, 30 May.

Charette, Jigs. 2018. Interview with author. Choteau, Montana, 9 June.

Diotte, Auriele. 2016. Interview with author. Oshawa, Ontario, 25 June.

Goodon, Dan. 2012. Interview with author. Telephone, 30 August.

Hince, Henri. 2012. Interview with author, 22 May.

Kusturok, Alex. 2021. Interview with author. Zoom, 15 September.

LaPlante, Leah. 2010. Interview with author. Telephone. 25 November.

Larouche, Marcel. 2017. Interview with author. Telephone, 19 May.

Lizotte, Brianna. 2018. Interview with author. Back to Batoche Festival Site, Saskatchewan, 20 July.

McLennan, Larry. 2009. Interview with author, 30 November.

Mitchell, Lynn. 2008. Interview with author, July 15.

MNO Youth workers. 2016. Interview with author. Oshawa, Ontario, 25 June.

Moran, Kathy. 2019. Interview with author. Choteau, Montana, 14 June.

Pelletier, Jeanne. 2021. Interview with author. Telephone, 13 July.

Pilon, Robert. 2017. Interview with author. Telephone, 30 April.

Snider, Jean. 2012. Interview with author. Portage la Prairie, 4 June.

St Goddard, Melissa. 2018. Interview with author. Back to Batoche Festival Site, Saskatchewan, 20 July.

Steele, Suzanne. 2021. Interview with author. Zoom, 11 February.

Wagar, Cecile. 2016. Interview with author. Oshawa, Ontario, 7 July.

Weisensel, Neil. 2021. Interview with author. Zoom, 29 September.

Index

accompaniment, 22, 28, 116, 121, 122 table 5.3, 125–6, 149, 181
affect, 117, 166–7
Ahmed, Sara, 131
Alberta, 8, 28, 187
Alloway, C.V., 3
Alvis, Cole, 176–7, 182–3
ancestors, xii–xvi, 9, 28, 75, 94; and Back to Batoche, 135, 137–9, 147; and Choteau cemetery, 152, 154; and resurgence, 20–1, 187, 206; and Steele, 189–92
Andersen, Chris, 15–16, 18, 22, 81
Anderson, Mark Conlund, 60–1, 84
animal nations, 54
Anishinaabemowin, 191, 193
Anishinaabe peoples, xi, xii, xv, 6, 42, 44
anticolonialism, 22–3, 196
Appleyard, Jason, 159
appropriation: of Métis fiddling, 3, 18; of Métis identity, 5, 12, 128–32; and opera, 33, 170–1, 177–8, 180–4, 206
Arcand, John, 125, 189
archival research, 28, 35, 60–1
Archives of Manitoba, 28
Arnold, Ian, 198
arts sector institutions, 25, 170–1, 176, 180, 183, 196, 202
Asham, Arnold, 50
Ashdown, James, 3
assimilation, 17–18, 22, 86–7, 107, 204–5, 215n4; policies of, 8–10, 13, 31, 101, 131
Assiniboine peoples, 6
A Tribute to Manitoba's Golden Boy (Messer), 96
Aubicon, Riel, 146
audiences, 90; and Métis festivals, 137, 144, 163, 167, 205; and Métis fiddling, 77–8, 90, 92–3, 107, 112, 124; non-Indigenous, 61, 64, 122, 127; and opera, 173–6, 178, 182–3, 186, 191–2, 199; and storytelling, 47
Austria, 16–17
authenticity, 17, 23, 130, 186; and Indigeneity, 127, 171, 178, 184; and Métis fiddling, 31–2, 98, 104, 109, 124, 126; and old-time fiddling, 91, 100, 123

Back to Batoche Days, 12–13, 18, 23, 32, 83, 135–48, 151, 167, 205
Baffin Bay, 43
bagpipes, 50–1
Ballantyne, Robert, 37, 40–1
Ballantyne, Solomon, 37
balls, 7, 40–1, 67, 74–7, 132, 205
barbarity, xiv, 67, 69
Barbeau, Marius, 177
Barkwell, Lawrence, 43
Batoche National Historic Site, 13, 136, 145, 147
Battle of Batoche, 8, 142
Baylee, Charles, 37

Beach, Donna, 193
Beach Ducharme, Debra, 193
Beaudry, Linda, 149
Bedard, Mel, 96–7, 107–8; *Métis Fiddler*, 113
Bedson, Sam, 76
Benham, D.J., 67
Bennett, Carolyn, 144
Bercier, Josue, 155
big band music, 93
"Big John McNeil," 125
Bijou Opera House, Winnipeg, 66
Blackface minstrelsy, 89–90
Blackfoot confederacy, xi
Blais, Simone, 163
Blanchard, Jim, 3, 74
Blue Danube waltz, 65
Bolton, David, 80
Bouvette, Reg, 82, 113
Brandon, Manitoba, 114, 191
Brandon Winter Fair, 111, 119 table 5.2
Braybrooke, Lord, 94
Braz, Albert, 175
British Columbia, 79
Brooklin Community Centre, Whitby, 157
Brown, Chester, *Riel: A Comic-Strip Biography*, 172
Brown, Jennifer, 34, 58–9
buffalo hunting, 6, 42, 155, 164, 177, 180–1, 194
Burnham, Clint, xi
Burt, Joanna, 170, 172, 177

Cajete, Gregory, 46
Calgary Folk Festival, 73
Campbell, Maria, 48, 56, 137, 199
Camperville, Manitoba, 81
Canada 150 New Chapter Award, 187
Canada First Party, 174
Canadian Broadcasting Corporation (CBC), 98–9
Canadian identity, 60, 73, 110, 128–9, 133, 175, 223n15; and fiddling, 18, 26, 95–101, 129; and multiculturalism, 10, 13, 83, 131; and opera, 171, 175
Canadian Mennonite University, 192, 196–7
Canadian Opera Company (COC), 171, 175–7, 182, 184–5, 201
Cape Breton fiddling, 99, 102, 106
Cardinal, Harold, *The Unjust Society*, 10
care, practice of, 107–8
Carignan-Salières Regiment, xiv
Carlson, Jeanne, 88, 94
Catholicism, xiv
celebrations, 27, 37, 40–1, 48, 52, 55, 71, 81, 143, 205
Celtic fiddling, 83
cemeteries, 139, 141 fig. 6.4, 147, 152, 154–5
Chabdikouechich, Agnes, 36
Charette, Fred "Jiggs," 148–51, 154–7
Charter of Rights and Freedoms, 10
Chartier, Clément, 144, 172
Chartrand, Brendan, 159
Chartrand, Yvonne, 159; *Marguerite*, 173
Cherny, Al, 103
Chez Isidore, 92
Chicago symphony, 65
Chrétien, Jean, 9
Christian celebrations, 37, 40–1, 48, 52, 71, 147
civilization, 12, 31, 63–4, 67–71, 84, 110, 215n4
Clark, Caryl, 172
Clarkson, Adrienne, 172
classical music, 3–4, 64–6, 127, 196. *See also* opera
classism, 28, 35
Clements, Marie, 172
clogging, 105, 116, 121, 126, 133–4, 222n9
Clouston, Lenore, 173
collaboration, 30, 33, 193, 196, 199, 201
Commission from Canadians, 10
Commission on Bilingualism and Biculturalism (1963), 10
Confederation of Canada, 7, 62, 184
Connelly, Hannah, 195, 197
Constitution Act, 10–11, 15, 151
Corntassel, Jeff, 19–20
Coulter, John, 172, 185
Coulthard, Glen, 14–16, 18, 22
country music, 90, 134, 158

court cases, 10–11, 215n2
COVID-19 pandemic, 145, 193, 203
Cree, Frances, 54–6
Cree peoples, xi, 37, 94
critique, 28–30
cross-cultural encounters, xv, 5, 26–9, 45, 161, 196; and appropriation, 130; and fiddle contests, 116–19, 123; and fur trade balls, 41; normalization of, 110–11
cultural heritage, 10, 16–17, 80, 83, 131–2
Cusson, Ian, 180

Dakota peoples, xi
dance halls, 92–4, 98, 205
Danckert, Paula, 176
Daniels, Harry, 11
Daniels v. Canada, 11
Dauphin, Manitoba, 92
Dauphin Herald, 81
DeBaillon, Catherine, xv
decolonization, 20–3, 46, 145, 206, 213
Dejarlis, Andy, 31, 50–1, 79–80, 88–90, 92–8, 100, 104, 107, 113–14, 125
Delorme, Bill, 95–6
Delorme, Minnie, 96
Desjarlais, Dolly, 93
Desjarlais, Ed, 82
Desrochers, Larry, 198–9
Devine, Heather, 189
Dick, Lyle, 75
difference: management of, 13–16, 18, 22, 131; and Métis fiddling, 24–5, 104–5, 127–8, 133, 204; and multiculturalism, 101–2; and musical encounters, 117–19, 125
Diotte, Auriele, 159, 163
discrimination, 10, 18, 62, 142, 154, 211n4
distancing, 31, 42, 46, 63–6, 69–72, 77, 80, 111, 129, 204–5
Dixieland music, 93
Don Messer's Jubilee, 92, 95, 98–9
Dorris, Michael, 46
Dreher, Tanja, 24, 169
Drewry brothers, 3
drums, Indigenous, 40, 49–50
Ducharme, Catherine, xv
Duck Dance, 53–4
Duck Lake, 138–9, 139 fig. 6.1, 140 fig. 6.2, 141 fig. 6.3
Dumas, Rene, xiv

Eagle's Nest Ranch, Alberta, 106
East Kildonan, Winnipeg, 77
Eber, Dorothy Harley, 43
economic capital, 8
Elders, Indigenous, 126, 135, 137–8, 143–4, 147–9, 164, 170, 195, 198–9
Elliot, Robin, 185
English settlers, 6, 38, 62
equality, 10, 147, 230
equity, 14, 28
Erasmus, Peter, *Buffalo Days and Nights*, 48, 51, 154
erasure, 204; and archives, 28, 61; of Métis music, 31, 72–80, 84–5, 105, 118, 133, 205; and opera, 33, 170, 172, 176, 186, 201, 206; and settler colonialism, xi, 4, 8
ethnicity, 10, 16, 41, 82, 101–2, 157, 216n15, 216n18
ethnography, 66–7, 167
ethnomusicology, 27, 30, 44, 47, 129
European fiddling, 34, 46, 58
exchange, cultural, 116–23; and fiddling, 31, 35, 45, 58, 86–7, 108, 111, 123
extermination, 8–10

Falcon, Pierre, 94, 129, 180–1
Fanon, Franz, *Black Skin, White Masks*, 14
Faux, Tom, 17–18
feasting, 49, 71, 81, 158
Fernando, Mayanthi, 29
Festival du Voyageur, 4, 82–3, 111, 114, 117, 120, 128
fictional distancing, 31, 42, 62, 69, 71–2, 80, 129, 204
fiddle, history of, 36–9, 58
fiddle classes, 106
fiddle tunes: from Blackface minstrelsy, 90; Dejarlis', 93–4; at fiddle competitions, 112,

121–3, 125–6; genealogies of, 44–6, 58–9, 204; on Gwich'in territory, 43; "Irish Washerwoman," 68; jigs, 39, 50–2; Messer's, 95–6, 99; Métis, 104–5, 194; at Métis festivals, 134, 146–7, 154, 161; and mythical origins, 50, 53, 56, 58; "Red River Jig," 3, 12, 44, 49–51; reels, 39–41, 49–50, 75, 99, 112, 125, 222n9, 226n8; schottisches, 75, 112
fiddling style, 88; compartmentalization of, 102–3, 204; Messer's, 99–100; Métis, 32, 114–32; Red River, 104–11
field research, 27–30, 104, 111, 116; interviews, 138, 150, 157–60, 163–7, 178–9, 187–8, 190–5, 198–9; notes, 136, 139–40, 143–4, 148–9, 186
les filles du rois, xv–xvi
Fingers, Justin Many, 177
Finley, Les, 93
First Nations peoples, 110, 152, 165, 186, 189; and fiddle dance, 30, 38, 42; and settler colonialism, 4, 7, 9, 62
First Nations women, 39–40
Fish Creek, 139, 142
Fitzgerald, Ella, 93
Fleury, Norman, 143, 170
folk music, 16, 18, 104–5, 170
Folkorama, 82
Fonseca, W.G., 71
footwork, 105, 116, 121, 126, 133–4, 222n9
The Forks, Winnipeg, 4, 38, 50, 82
Fort Alexandria, 41
Fort Des Prairie, 41
Fort Edmonton, 48
Fort Garry, Manitoba, 7, 77
Fort Gibraltar, Manitoba, 4
Fort Totten, 67
Forty Fiddling Fanatics, 83
Fort Yukon, 43
Franco-American fiddling, 17
French Canadians, xiii, 43–4, 51, 69; Métis referred to as, 69–70, 72–3, 79, 133, 189; tunes of, 83
French identity, 6–8
French Métis, 49
Froese, Vic, 197
funding, 81, 101, 137, 144–5, 159, 165, 187, 197, 203
fur trade, 6, 8, 30, 48, 50; and fiddling, 34, 37–42, 58, 88, 154
future generations, 20, 35, 47, 127, 193–6
futurity, 33, 55, 203, 206–7; Métis exclusion from, 71–2; and Métis music, xvii, 155–6

Gabriel Dumont Virtual Museum, 47
Gaudry, Adam, 116, 123, 172, 182, 185–6
Gaudry, Louis, 188
Gaudry Brothers, 159
geneological approaches, 30, 44, 46, 59, 204
genocide, 8, 19
Genthon, Del, 90, 92, 94
Genthon, Frédéric, 74–5, 78, 80
Georgian Bay, 157
Gervais, Daniel, 106
Gibbons, Roy, 44, 104
Gillespie, Rufus, 181
Goodon, Dan, 134
Goulet, Elzéar, 94
Goulet, Louis, 49–51, 92
Goulet, Maxime, 94
Goulet, Robert Léon "Bob," 79, 90, 94, 107–8
government: federal, 11, 13, 62, 145, 167; funding, 81, 101, 137, 144–5, 165, 167, 187; and recognition, 135, 151
Gowler, Jimmy, 90, 92, 94
grandmothers, 54–6, 94, 137, 152, 155, 173, 189, 220n12, 915
Gravel Road Fiddlers, 159
groupness, 7, 15
Gwich'in peoples, 42–3

Hage, Ghassan, 131
Handscomb, Charles W., 3–4, 64–6, 206
Hargrave, Joseph James, 39
Harmon, Daniel, 41
Haudenosaunee peoples, xi–xiv
Healy, William James, *Women of Red River,* 42
Hearing Riel symposium, 172, 176
Hemetek, Ursula, 16, 157
The Hills Are Alive Camp, 106

Hince, Henri, 93
Hinton, Peter, 171–2, 176, 182, 184–5
Hogan, Dorothy and Homer Hogan, 103
Holiday, Billie, 93
Houle, Antoine, 43
Houle, Laurence "Teddy Boy," 159
Howard, Joseph Kinsey, *Strange Empire*, 173
Hudson's Bay Company (HBC), 7, 37–41, 43, 94
hunting rights, 11
Hutcheon, Linda, 172
Hutcheon, Linda and Michael Hutcheon, 175

immigration, 4, 8, 88–9, 98, 101, 130
inclusion, 11, 28, 82, 101, 131, 176–7, 182, 224n17, 227n13; and music, 117–18, 121–2
Indian Act, 8–10
Indian Affairs, 8–10
Indian Friendship Centre, Winnipeg, 81
Indian problem, 9–10, 13, 85, 212n14, 215n4
Indian Tribes, 9
Indigeneity, 130, 132; and Métis fiddling, 36, 103–4, 107; and Métis identity, 6, 9, 129; and opera, 181–2; and resurgence, 18–23
Indigenization, 41, 127
Indigenous activism, 19–21, 172, 201
Indigenous ceremony, xiii, 21, 23, 40, 66–8, 132, 184, 203, 216n7
Indigenous creatives, 22, 171, 177, 196, 198, 200–2, 206
Indigenous fiddlers, 41, 103–4, 118, 133, 188, 213n2
Indigenous hip hop, 127
Indigenous law, 22
Indigenous Performing Arts Alliance, 176
Indigenous rights, 10–11, 14–16, 132, 169
Indigenous studies, 19, 26
Innes, Robert, 6
innovation, 23, 105–6, 194, 197
Institute for Music in Canada, 172
instrumentalization, 31, 61, 72, 84–5, 133
intercultural encounter, 5, 117, 200–1
International Peace Garden, 166
intersubjectivity, 14
Inuit peoples, 9, 43
Irish fiddling, 44, 102
Iroquois peoples, 41
Isaac, Tom, 143
Isbister, William, 76

Jackson, Taryn, 171
James Bay, 37
jam sessions, 26, 125, 135, 149–50, 161, 162 fig. 6.8
Jesuit Relations, 37
Jesus, 52, 57, 155
Jewish communities, 130
jigging, 126, 135, 138, 144, 159, 180; early, 28, 52, 60, 72, 78, 81–2
jigs, 39, 50–2
John Arcand Fiddle Festival, 114
Johnson, Sherry, 99, 113
Johnson, Sylvia, 137
judges, 113, 119–22, 125, 128, 131, 222n8–222n9, 223n13

Kahnawà:ke, 19
Kallman, Helmut, 103
Kaminsky, David, 110, 130, 132
Kingston, Ontario, xi, 26
kinship, 6–8, 73; and cultural gatherings, 27, 81–5, 135–7, 145–57, 167–8; and Métis music, 36, 58, 107–9, 111; and opera, 171, 188–92, 196, 199, 201. *See also* relationships
klezmer, 130
Klinck, Jean, 181
Knight, Lindsay, 127
knowledge, xiii, 25, 35–6, 46, 58
Kovach, Margaret, 47
Koval, Sarah, 171
Kusturok, Alex, 33, 106, 108–9, 169, 193–4, 197

"La beau sha shoo," 55–8
"La Chanson de la Gournouillère" (Pierre Falcon), 94
Lac Ste Anne, 49
Lafferty, Herb, 96
LaFrenière, Jellicoe, 78, 80
"La grande gigue simple," 44, 50

Lamb, Grant, 103
Lamoureux, Joel, 113
land: acknowledgments, xi–xiii; and fiddle dance, 37, 58–9; land back, 13, 18, 145, 206, 212n16; and opera, 171, 187–8, 190, 196, 201; relations to, 22, 46, 48, 136–43, 152, 154, 167, 204; rights to, 7–8, 11, 14–16; and settler colonialism, 4, 142
languages: English, 62; French, 17–18, 28; Métis, 7, 23, 134, 143, 149, 155, 184, 189; official, 10; in opera, 170–1, 175, 177–8, 182, 190–3, 197; in press coverage, 70
Languirand, Jacques, 33, 170, 175, 181
LaPier, Rosalyn, 152
LaPlante, Leah, 114, 118–20
La Rance, Marguerite, 154
LaRocque, Emma, 127
Larouche, Marcel, 178–9
Latour, Bruno, 29
Laut, Agnes, *Lords of the North*, 181
Lauzon, Jani, 170, 177, 182
Lavalee, Darren, 158
Lavalee, JJ, 159
La Vérendrye, 38
Laxer, Daniel, 37, 89
learning, 46, 54, 58, 182, 199; language, 43, 192–3, 197; to listen, 25, 30, 59, 104; at Métis festivals, 160–4, 167; musical, 56–7, 76, 89, 93–6, 99–100, 106–8, 122–5, 130, 222n11
Lederman, Anne, 3, 5, 44, 100, 104–5, 129, 206
Lee, Sherry D., 172, 174
Lelong, Marie, xiv–xv
Lepine, Garry, 106, 109, 113
Lepine, Jason, 113
Leroux, Darryl, *Distorted Descent*, 5, 15
Lethbridge, Alberta, 27
Lewistown, Montana, 149
liberalism, 14, 19, 46
Li Keur: Riel's Heart of the North (opera), 33, 117, 169–71, 186–201, 206–7
l'Incarnation, Mother Marie de, xiv, 36
Link, Bryna, 195, 197
listening, 30; and Métis women, 56, 200; to relationships, 106, 108–9; and responsiveness, 25, 183–4, 202; and storytelling, 35, 47
Little Black Reserve, 96
Little Shell Tribe of Chippewa Indians, 9, 152
Lizotte, Brianna, 23, 145
Lord Selkirk Association of Rupert's Land, 78
Lorette, Manitoba, 114, 119
Louis Riel (opera), 33, 170–86, 200–2, 206
Louis Riel Day, 5
Louis XIV of France, xiv–xv
Lowe, Helen, 93
lumber camps, 88–9

Macdonald, Sir John A., 173–4
Mackey, Eva, 100, 102, 131–2
MacKinnon, Catherine, 99
Mackintosh, Joe, 89, 92–3
MacLean, Allison, 97, 99
MacLeod, Margaret Arnett, *Songs of Old Manitoba*, 181
Mahmood, Saba, 29
Maine, US, 17
Manitoba, 117, 187; and Don Messer, 95, 100; early history in, 62–80; and fiddle competitions, 112–16; and Métis identity, 128–32; recent history in, 81–5; and Red River fiddling style, 87
Manitoba Act (1870), 7, 62
Manitoba Fiddle Association (MFA), 114
Manitoba Free Press, 65, 73–4
Manitoba Leader, 78
Manitoba Legislature, 7
Manitoba Métis Federation (MMF), 81, 114, 118–23
Manitoba Museum of Man and Nature, 81
Manitoba Open Old Time Fiddle Championships, 114, 115 table 5.1, 118–19, 121–2, 128, 130
Manitoba Opera Company, 169, 198–9
"Manitoba Waltz" (Dejarlis), 96
marginalization, 17, 25, 101, 131
Marquis, Greg, 98
Marshall, Albert, 30, 36
Martineau, Jarrett, 19, 22–3, 196

material culture, 152, 153 fig. 6.6, 154, 163–4, 178
McBeth, Jack, 76
McCallum, Glen, 147
McLachlin, Beverly, 172
McLennan, Larry, 114
McLeod, Alexander D., 69–71
McLeod, Archibald, 41
McTavish, Jack, 76
meaning, 26, 34, 174; of Métis fiddle dance music, 32, 35, 45–6, 88
Memoranda of Understanding (MOUs), 144
mental health, 173, 179–80
Messer, Don, 31, 87, 94–100, 107
methodology of book, 27–30
Métis communities, xiii, 11, 15, 29–30; and cultural gatherings, 27, 81–5, 135, 137, 145–8, 158–61, 205; and fiddle competition styles, 122–3; history of, 4–10, 62, 150–2, 153 fig. 6.6, 154–5, 164; and opera, 175–7, 181–2, 189–90, 193–4, 196–9, 201–2, 206
Metis Days, 81
Métis festivals, 26–8, 50–1, 205; Back to Batoche Days, 12–13, 18, 23, 83, 136–48; Metisfest, 134, 167, 219n31, 224n1–224n2; Métis Heritage Celebration, 157–66; Métis Music and Art Festival, 148–57; and resurgence, 23–4, 32–3, 81–2, 124–8, 134–6, 166–8
Métis fiddle dance music, 30, 44, 99, 204; and Dejarlis, 92–3; history of, 36–45, 88–9; and multiculturalism, 24, 31, 83, 87, 98–107, 109, 111, 127–8, 133; as recognized style, 87, 104–5, 107–11, 205; and social dances, 39–43, 48–54, 154; storytelling about, 45–58; and Two-Eyed Seeing, 58–9
Métis Heritage Celebration, 27, 157–66, 168
Métis Homeland, xi, 6, 45, 50, 59, 74, 134–5, 142, 157–8, 167, 175, 187–8
Métis identity, xiii, 6–8; appropriation of, 3, 5, 12, 128–32, 204; and fiddling, 73, 79–80, 83, 94, 105, 113, 115, 133; Métis-ness, xiii, 15, 32, 75, 157, 167, 179, 205, 218n25; and multiculturalism, 31, 176; and recognition, 13–19; visible, 81–2, 84, 135–6, 150–2
Métis music: and fictional distancing, 69–80; and spatial distancing, 80–5; and temporal distancing, 62–72. *See also* Métis fiddle dance music; opera
Métis Music and Art Festival, 32, 135, 148–58, 167
Métis music studies, 25
Métis Nation, xi, 32, 81, 94, 120, 134–7, 176–7, 205–6, 211n10; Alberta, 218n27, 225n6; British Columbia, 225n6; National Council, 144, 172; Ontario, 157, 160–1, 225n6; Saskatchewan, 13, 143–5, 147, 218n7, 225n6
Métis-ness, xiii, 5, 12, 15, 32, 75, 105, 128–32, 157, 167, 179, 205, 218n25
Métis Society of Saskatchewan, 137
Métis women, 39–41, 56, 171, 187, 189, 195–6, 200
Miami Fun and Fiddle Festival, 113–14, 121
Michel, Jacquette, xiv–xv
Michel "Kiki" Bohémier Memorial Fiddle Contest, 114
Michif, 7, 134, 143, 149, 155, 184, 189
Michif Heritage Keepers, 156
Michigan, xv, 89
Michigan, Lake, 42
Middleton, General, 142
Mignier, André, xiv
Mi'kmaq peoples, 37
military, xiv, 7, 94
Mindess, Mary, 50–1
Mishler, Craig, *The Crooked Stovepipe*, 42–3
Missouri River, 50, 188
Mitchell, Lynn, 95, 112
Mitchif Heritage Keepers, 135
mixed-ness, 5–6, 30, 34, 38, 46, 55, 59, 212n10, 214n13, 224n3
modernity, 98, 169
Moggie, Brad, 159
Mohawk people, 19
Mondal, Anshuman A., 24, 169
Monet dit Belhumeur, Marguerite, 173, 178
Montana, 8, 27, 149, 152, 187–8; Choteau, 32, 135, 148, 151, 154–6
Montreal, Quebec, 92, 175

Moore, Mavor, 33, 170, 173, 175, 181, 185
Moose Factory, 37
Moran, Julie, 149, 155
Moran, Kathy, 148–9, 155
Morrison, Everett, 170
Mouse River, 41
multiculturalism, 10, 13, 46, 61, 80, 131, 175, 204; and containment, 24, 31, 83, 87, 98–107, 109, 111, 127–8, 133; and festivals, 26, 32, 82, 84–5, 137, 144, 167; and Métis identity, 31, 176, 204
mythical stories, 51–4

Nash, Rachel, 80
nationalism, xii, xiv, 7, 10, 16, 33, 99, 102, 131, 176, 226n8, 227n10; and opera, 170, 174, 184, 187
nation-to-nation relationships, 11, 117, 135
Neef, Alexander, 176
Nehiyaw peoples, 6
Nelson, George, 42
neocolonialism, 18
New Brunswick, 94
New France, xiii–xvi, 36–7
Newhouse, David, 34, 45, 59
Nisga'a nation, 170–1, 177–8, 180–1
Nixon, Billy, 93
Niziol, Tegal, 172
Noble, Sierra, 113
Norman Chief Memorial Dancers, 167
Norman Hall, 92
Norquay, John, 76
North Dakota, 8, 28, 54, 188; Bismarck, 189
North Dakota State Archives, 189
North West Company (NWC), 37, 41
Northwest Resistance, 8–9, 139, 142
Norwegian fiddling, 44
Nova Scotia, 96, 99, 102, 106

October Crisis, 175
Off, Carol, *Halfbreed,* 199
Oji-Cree peoples, xi
Old North Trail, 154
old-time festivals, 28
old-time fiddle competitions, 26, 221n2; category changes, 110–13; and Dejarlis, 80, 92; in early press coverage, 70, 77–8; and Métis style categories, 32, 82, 113–16, 118–33; structure of, 117–18
old-time fiddling, 28, 31–2, 83, 90–1; and compartmentalization, 98–106; as exchange, 88–97, 116–17; and Red River style, 26, 87, 107–9, 125–6, 131
old-timers, 48, 73–80, 91, 132
Olivine Bousquet Métis Dancers, 159
Ontario: English immigrants from, 74–7, 210n1, 210n3; and Métis festivals, 135; Oshawa, 27, 32, 157–8; Ottawa, 171, 178
Ontario Power Generation (OPG), 165
opening ceremonies, 4, 12–13, 143–7, 166
opera, 25, 90, 194–5, 206; *Li Keur: Riel's Heart of the North,* 33, 117, 169–71, 186–201, 207; *Louis Riel,* 33, 171–86; Wagner, 3–4, 65, 169
oral histories, 46–7, 58, 152, 204
Orangemen, 173–4, 185
Orcadian settlers, 6, 38, 40, 43
Oshawa and Durham Region Métis Council (ODRMC), 157–9
Oshawa Métis Heritage Festival, 32, 135
Ostick, Stephen, 82
otherness, 25, 71, 127, 130

Pantages Theatre, Winnipeg, 66
Paquin, Louis, 82
Parks Canada, 38
Payment, Diane, 136
Peguis First Nation, 69
Pelletier, Jeanne, 51–2
pemmican, 72, 134–6, 167, 217n19
Pemmican Trail, 134–6, 167
Perea, Jessica Bissett, 21–3
personal stories, 48–51
Pilon, Robert, 158–9
Pilot Mound, Manitoba, 95
"Pilot Mound Waltz" (Delorme), 96
pioneers, 28, 68–9, 72–3, 75, 78, 80, 98, 132
place: and fiddling style, 103; and Métis festivals, 136; and Métis history, 152; responsibility to, xi

Podruchny, Carolyn, 34–5, 41
politicians, 9, 74, 98, 137, 144–5, 157, 166–7, 173–4
politics, 22, 32, 175; of Métis festivals, 135–7, 144–6, 205; of recognition, 10–19, 24, 30–1, 61, 151–2, 204–5
Portage la Prairie, Manitoba, 114
Porter, Michelle, 28, 72–3, 79, 107–8
positionalities, 109
poverty, 8, 155, 188
power, 29; of music, 5, 55–6, 116–17, 206; political, 7, 14, 18, 25, 31, 84–5, 101–2; and storytelling, 34, 46, 59
Powley Case (2003), 11
powwow, 132, 134, 152
Prairie du Chien, 56
Prairie Schooner, 90
Pratt, Yvonne Poitras, 45
preservation, 10, 20, 81, 111
press coverage, 13, 28, 205; and distancing Métis, 62–72, 204; and early Métis music, 31; of early Winnipeg, 3–4, 39; and euphemizing Métis, 72–80; and Métis recognition, 80–5; of opera, 169, 171, 173, 182, 195, 197, 200
pride, xvi, 81–2, 84, 133, 158, 195
prizes, 112, 114, 115 table 5.1, 119 table 5.2, 121, 222n10
processions, 144, 147, 148 fig. 6.5
Proctor, George, 103
progress, colonial, 4, 63, 65–6, 173
Protestants, 7, 62, 174
Purser, Richard, 171, 173

quadrilles, 67–8, 75
Québec, 10, 37; fiddling, 34, 50, 99, 102, 106, 125; Québec City, 171; separatism, 175
Quick, Sarah, 30, 147
Quiet Revolution, 175

Rabbit Dance, 52–3
racialization, 6, 9, 98
racism, 9–10, 28, 35, 40–2, 89–90, 176, 181, 196
radio, 31, 78, 90–2, 95–6, 98, 100, 107, 137
Rae, Ramsey, 159
Raisin, Marguerite, xv
recognition, Indigenous: and cultural practice, 16–19, 23; and Indigenous rights, 9, 111; and Métis festivals, 32–3, 135–6, 145–7, 156–8, 164–8, 205–6; and Métis music, 30–1, 81–5, 111, 128; and opera, 33, 169–70, 178, 181; politics of, 10–19, 24, 30–1, 61, 151–2, 204–5
reconciliation, 117, 144, 196, 199–200
recordings, 100, 123; early fiddle, 78–9, 90–2
Redbird, Duke, 137
Red River carts, 48, 63–4, 149, 161, 164, 216n6
"Red River Jig," 3, 12, 44, 49–50, 60–1, 129; in early press coverage, 3–4, 65–8, 72–80, 90; at fiddle competitions, 125; at Métis festivals, 143, 149
Red River Resistance, 7–8, 94, 136–8, 147, 184
Red River Settlement, 41, 48, 51, 56, 94, 188; cultural practices of, 71, 74–5; histories of, 7–9, 26, 38–9
Reed, Trevor, 22
reels, 39–41, 49–50, 75, 99, 112, 125, 222n9, 226n8
Reid, Jennifer, 110, 116, 128–9
relationality, xiii, 22, 32, 47, 49, 58, 87–8, 106–7
relationships, xiii, xvi, 27, 204; imagining, 5, 29; and Métis music, xvii, 107–9, 111, 116, 133, 204; and musical encounters, 117–18, 123; and opera, 33, 183, 191, 193–9, 201–2, 206; and press coverage, 62, 69–70; and "Red River Jig," 50; and storytelling, 35. *See also* kinship
Renihan, Coleen, 185
representation: by non-Métis, 23–4, 26, 35; and opera, 33, 170, 172, 175–80, 206. *See also* press coverage
residential schools, 9, 189
resistance, Indigenous, 10, 19, 35, 131
responsiveness, ethical, 24–6, 30, 33, 169–70
resurgence, Indigenous, 12, 14, 204; and artistic practice, 19–24, 170, 192–3, 196–7; and Métis festivals, 23–4, 32–3, 81–2, 135–6, 166–7, 205–6; post-TRC, 169
Reynolds, Ken, 97, 99

Rickaby, Franz, 88
Riel, Louis, 5, 7, 74, 110, 129, 147, 188; and Canada, 172–3, 175, 184; in opera, 178–9, 186–90, 206–7
Ritskes, Eric, 45–6
Robertson, Carmen L., 60–1, 84
Robideau, Baptiste, 189
Robinson, Dylan, xi–xii, 109–10, 117–18, 123, 130, 133, 177, 203
Robinson, Henry Martin, 39, 42
rock music, 93, 98, 134, 159
Rocky Mountains, 152, 154
Rodgers, Frankie, 103
Romani music, 16–17, 157
Ronald, Darlene, 198
Rosenberg, Neil, 95
Royal Alexandra Hotel, Winnipeg, 74, 76, 91
Royal Manitoba Winter Fair Contest, 114, 119
rules, 117, 120–2, 122 table 5.3, 125, 222n9

Saint-Antoine-de-Padoue Parish, Saskatchewan, 142
Sainte-Claire, Sister Anne de, 36
Saint-François Xavier, Manitoba, 142
Saint-Joseph, Mother Marie de, 36
Sarath, Ed, 24, 102–3
Saskatchewan, xvi, 8, 28, 66, 83, 114, 187; Back to Batoche Days, 12–13, 18, 23, 32, 83, 135–48, 151, 167, 205; Batoche National Historic Site, 13, 136, 145, 147
Saskatchewan Health Authority, 144
Saskatchewan School Boards Association, 144
Saul, John Ralston, 172, 186; *A Fair Country*, 5–6, 110, 116, 128–9
schottisches, 75, 112
Schultz, John Christian, 3, 174
Scofield, Gregory, 172
Scotch reels, 40
Scott, Duncan Campbell, 8–9
Scott, Thomas, 174
Scottish Amateur Athletic association, 78
Scottish fiddling, 44, 102
Scottish settlers, 6–7, 38, 51
scrip, 7, 9
self-determination, xv, 14, 22, 33, 144, 147, 212n16
Selkirk, Manitoba, 67, 77
Selkirk settlers, 75
Sellick, Lester, 99
Senungetuk, Heidi, 127
settler colonialism, xii–xvi; and fiddle competitions, 32, 112; histories of, 4–10, 142; and Métis erasure, 74–80, 84–5, 154, 204; and Métis festivals, 33, 82, 135–7, 144, 147, 167, 205; and Métis-ness, 5, 12, 128–32; and opera, 171, 174, 176, 181–3, 196, 201–2; and recognition, 14–16, 31, 151–2; and resurgence, 19–20, 46; and temporal distancing of Métis, 62–72
sexism, 28, 35, 40–1, 196
sheet music, 89, 92, 220n8
Shelburne, Ontario, 113
Shook, Estelle, 170, 172, 182
Shore, Fred, 7
silencing, 30, 33, 36, 170, 177
Simonot-Maiello, Colette, 180, 185
Simpson, Audra, 13, 15, 18–19
Simpson, Leanne, 19–20; *Dancing on Our Turtle's Back*, xv
Sitting Bull, 188
situatedness, 27, 32, 45–6, 51, 54
Sium, Aman, 45–6
Snider, Jean, 113
social capital, 8
sociality, 49, 58
social justice, 25, 112, 202
Somers, Harry, 33, 170, 180–1, 185
songs, 50, 172; Michif, 149, 155; Nisga'a, 170–1, 177–8, 180–1
soundscapes, 12, 36, 42, 87, 89–90, 107, 191
sovereignty, xv, 13–15, 21, 117
spatial distancing, 31, 46, 62, 66, 69, 80, 204
spirit, xi, 4, 58, 105, 128, 132, 135, 138, 154, 189
spirituality, 7, 21, 23, 56, 106, 127, 147, 228n16
spirit world, 58
sponsorship, 114, 118, 221n4, 123
square dance troupes, 134
"St Anne's Reel," 125

St Boniface, Manitoba, 4
Steele, Suzanne, 30, 33, 59, 206–7; *Li Keur: Riel's Heart of the North*, 117, 169, 172, 186–97
Stevenson, Winona, 47
St Goddard, Melissa, 146–7
St Laurent shrine, 138–9
Stonewall, Manitoba, 89
Stonyk, Nicole, 198, 200
storytelling, 23, 27, 34, 204; author's, xiii–xvi; Métis, 30, 35–6, 152; and Métis fiddle dance music, 45–59; and opera, 170, 183, 191, 196, 199
St Peter's Reserve, Manitoba, 67–9
Strathroy, Ontario, 98
Summer Youth Cultural Group, 161
Sumner, Carolyne, 172
Sunabacka, Karen, *Mama's Painting: Louis Riel's Dream*, 173
Swain, Marie, 155
Swan Valley Star and Times, 81
Swedish klezmer, 130
swing music, 93
syncretic traditions, 44

Taylor, Charles, "The Politics of Recognition," 13, 15
Teillet, Jean, 172, 175, 182–6
television, 91–2, 95, 98–9
temporal distancing, 31, 62–6, 69, 77, 80, 129, 204
Thobani, Sunera, 131
Thomas, Theodore, 65
Toronto, Ontario, xi, 171, 176, 200
Toronto Harbourfront Centre, 200
Tourand, Josephte, 142
Tourand's Coulee, 139, 142
tours, 92, 95
traditionality, 125–6, 132–3
transformation, 19–23, 44–5, 86, 117, 124
translation, 170, 181, 188, 190–3, 195, 229n22
travel writing, 34–5, 39–40, 42, 48, 60
treaty days, 67–8
Trew, Johanne, 95, 100
Trudeau, Pierre, 9
Truth and Reconciliation Commission (TRC), 9, 111, 169, 176
Turtle Mountain Michif, 9, 155
Two-Eyed Seeing, 30, 36, 58–9

Ukrainian fiddling, 44, 92, 102
United States, 9, 88–9, 151
University of British Columbia, 196
University of Toronto, 171–2, 186
University of Toronto Quarterly, 172, 180, 182–3
Urion, Carl, 31, 86, 106, 108
Ursulines, xiv, 36

Vancouver, BC, 182, 187
Vandal, Dan, 13, 145
vaudeville shows, 89–90
Verney, Jack, xiv
veterans, 143–4, 147, 166
Vibert, Elizabeth, 34, 58–9
Victor Company recordings, 78
violence, colonial, xv, xxi, 7–9, 62, 142, 183, 192–3, 213n4
viols, 36–7
voice, 36; and fiddle competitions, 111, 118, 122, 133; limits of, 24–5, 169–71
Volksgruppe, 16–17
voyageurs, 28, 41, 44, 72, 82, 224n17
Vrooman, Nicholas, 38, 54–6, 104, 152, 156, 188

Wade, George, 94
Wagar, Cecile, 159, 164–6
Wagner, Richard, 3–4, 65, 169
Walters, Vic, 98
waltzes, 65, 70, 74, 89, 95–6, 112
ways of being, 21–3, 82, 108, 127
Weisensel, Neil, 33, 169, 187, 190, 192–3, 195, 197
Westminster Act, 78
whalers, 43
Wheeler family, 97, 109
"Whiskey before Breakfast," 125

white legacy institutions, 33, 171, 201, 206
whiteness, 42, 62, 129, 131, 181
White Paper, 9–10, 14, 19
Whiz Bang Review, 89
Wilkins, Frances, 43
Williams, Hank, 149
Wilson, Shawn, *Research Is Ceremony*, xiii, 203
Winnipeg, Manitoba, xi, 66, 95, 191; and early Métis music, 71–6; *Li Keur* in, 197–8; settler colonialism in, 3–4, 69; shows and dances in, 91–3
Winnipeg Daily Tribune, 71
Winnipeg Folk Festival, 82
Winnipeg Free Press, 82–3, 173
Winnipeg Friendship Centre, 79
Winnipeg Symphony, 196
Winnipeg Tribune, 75
Wiseman, Al, 149–50, 152, 153 fig. 6.6, 154, 156
Woodridge, Manitoba, 91
worldviews, 7, 59, 196
Wuttunee, Winston, 137–8, 147
Wynette, Tammy, 149

XY company, 41

York Factory, 37–8, 89
York University, 26
youth, 3, 77; and fiddling, 112–13, 119 table 5.2; at Métis festivals, 155, 161, 162 fig. 6.7, 166
youth workers, 160–1, 163